Joseph W. Shaw II, ACSA, CISSP, EnCE, is principal and owner of Shaw Digital Forensics Services. He has more than 17 years of experience in the management of the entire lifecycle of information security threats, with specific focus on detection, response, and postmortem investigations.

About the Technical Reviewers

Joseph W. Shaw II, ACSA, CISSP, EnCE, is principal and owner of Shaw Digital Forensics Services. He has more than 17 years of experience in the management of the entire lifecycle of information security threats, with specific focus on detection, response, and postmortem investigations.

Suzanne Widup holds a B.S. in Computer Information Systems and an M.S. in Information Assurance. She is the president and founder of the Digital Forensics Association and the author of "The Leaking Vault" data breach report series. She is currently pursuing a Ph.D. in Information Systems with a concentration in Information Security from Nova Southeastern University.

Computer Forensics
InfoSec Pro Guide

David Cowen

Mc
Graw
Hill
Education

New York   Chicago   San Francisco
Lisbon   London   Madrid   Mexico City
Milan   New Delhi   San Juan
Seoul   Singapore   Sydney   Toronto

Cataloging-in-Publication Data is on file with the Library of Congress

McGraw-Hill books are available at special quantity discounts to use as premiums and sales promotions, or for use in corporate training programs. To contact a representative, please e-mail us at bulksales@mcgraw-hill.com.

Computer Forensics: InfoSec Pro Guide

1 2 3 4 5 6 7 8 9 0   DOC DOC   1 0 9 8 7 6 5 4 3

ISBN   978-0-07-174245-0
MHID   0-07-174245-X

Sponsoring Editor   Amy Eden Jollymore

Editorial Supervisor   Janet Walden

Project Editor   LeeAnn Pickrell

Acquisitions Coordinators   Ryan Willard, Amanda Russell

Technical Editors   Joseph Shaw, Suzanne Widup

Copy Editor   Lisa Theobald

Proofreader   Susie Elkind

Indexer   Karin Arrigoni

Production Supervisor   George Anderson

Composition   Cenveo© Publisher Services

Illustration   Cenveo Publisher Services

Art Director, Cover   Jeff Weeks

Cover Designer   Jeff Weeks

*To my wife, Mireya, for her support and patience while
I wrote another book, and to my children, Vivian and Bear,
for falling asleep early enough for me to be able to write most nights.*

Contents at a Glance

Contents

PART IV   Defending Your Work

Acknowledgments

You may not know this, but writing a book is a time-consuming undertaking. Most authors don't make it rich by writing books. We write these books simply to help others who are new in the field learn from our mistakes and experiences. (We also write them so you'll buy us a beer if you see us!)

I'd also like to thank those people in my life who made it possible for me to write this book. I'd like to thank my wife, Mireya, for motivating me, supporting me, and giving me time away from our lives together to work on the book. I'd also like to thank my kids for (usually) going to sleep at a decent hour so I could write a couple hours at night.

It always takes longer than one thinks it will to write a book! I need to thank Amy Jollymore, my editor, and her colleagues for their patience with me in the process. I'll admit, this book wasn't written on its original schedule, and it doesn't contain what I originally imagined it would, but I can say that, thanks to Amy and her colleagues, it was completed—and the finished book contains everything I wish someone told me when I started my first forensic investigation.

I'd like to thank my coworkers at G-C: David Dym, Ralph Gorgal, and Rudi Peck, who all stepped up to help get chapters done and flesh out those details and lessons we've shared over the years. Lastly I'd like to thank Joseph Shaw, who not only made time to be my technical editor but also stepped up when I needed him by contributing a chapter.

—David Cowen, 2013

Introduction

This book was written to help those of you already working in IT to cross over to a career in computer forensics without failing horribly. This book contains the lessons learned from 14 years of experience performing computer forensics and running a private computer forensics lab.

Who Should Read This Book

This book is meant for those already in the IT field who have a working technical knowledge of computers, including how they work and how to repair them. I expect you to know what a hard drive is, how to remove a hard drive, what a serial number is, and the basics of modern operating systems.

What This Book Covers

This book will walk you through the following:

- Investigating a career in computer forensics
- Getting trained and keeping current in computer forensics
- Starting a forensic lab

- Preserving evidence

- How to approach investigations

- How to investigate the most common kinds of cases

- Documenting your findings and presenting them

How to Use This Book

This book is meant to be read from start to finish, as the lessons and knowledge builds with each chapter. To supplement the book and keep it current, I created a web site, www .learndfir.com, where you can access the documents and tools discussed in this book. In addition, I am making video tutorials and example images for each of the investigation chapters for you to download and try at home. This book is meant to be used in conjunction with these online resources so the information won't get stale.

How Is This Book Organized?

This book is organized into the following parts.

Part I: Getting Started   Part I of the book tells you what you need to know before you try to do any evidence preservation and analysis. Starting with an introduction of what computer forensics is and how to get started, this part continues with how to go about learning computer forensic techniques and how to build your first forensic lab.

Part II: Your First Investigation   Part II covers evidence preservation, forensic procedures, tool testing, and the other fundamental parts of computer forensics that you should understand before you start your first examination.

Part III: Case Examples: How to Work a Case   Part III discusses the five most common forensic investigations encountered by most first-time examiners. It lays out how to work through the investigation and what artifacts to look for, and it provides practical advice in understanding what happened. It also helps you figure out how to determine what kind of investigation you're facing.

Part IV: Defending Your Work   Part IV ends the book with two chapters covering how to document and present your findings. You'll learn how to write reports for your employer and what details should be included, with templates showing how to provide those items. The last chapter offers a quick primer of how you, as an examiner, fit into the legal system and important report requirements.

About the Series

I worked with the publisher to develop several special editorial elements for this series, which I hope you'll find helpful while navigating the book—and furthering your career.

Lingo

The Lingo boxes are designed to help you familiarize yourself with common security terminology so that you're never held back by an unfamiliar word or expression.

IMHO

When you come across IMHO (In My Humble Opinion), you'll be reading my frank, personal opinions based on my experiences in the security industry.

Budget Note

The Budget Notes are designed to help increase your ease while discussing security budget needs within your organization. They also provide tips and ideas for initiating successful, informed conversations about budgets.

In Actual Practice

Theory might teach us smart tactics for business, but there are in-the-trenches exceptions to every rule. The In Actual Practice feature highlights how things actually get done in the real world at times—exceptions to the rule—and why.

Your Plan

The Your Plan feature offers strategic ideas that can be helpful to review as you get into planning mode, as you refine a plan outline, and you embark on a final course of action.

Into Action

The Into Action lists are "get-going" tips to support you in taking action on the job. These lists contain steps, tips, and ideas to help you plan, prioritize, and work as effectively as possible.

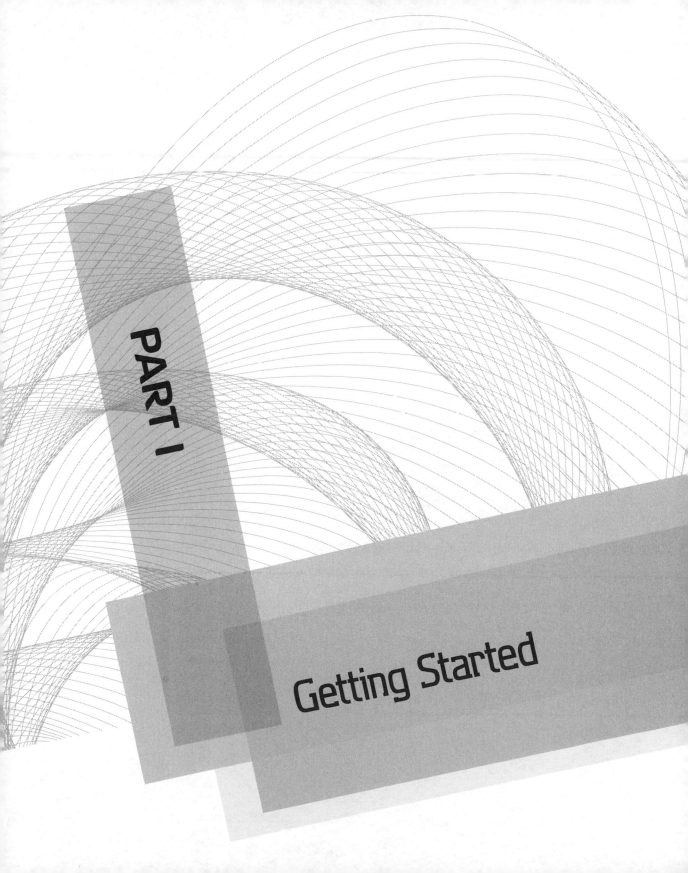

PART I

Getting Started

CHAPTER 1

What Is Computer Forensics?

We'll Cover

- What you can do with computer forensics

- How to get involved with computer forensics

- The difference between incident response and traditional computer forensics

- How computer forensic tools work

- Professional licensing requirements

When I meet people in social situations, the usual first question after names are exchanged is, "What do *you* do?" When I answer, "computer forensics," I typically get a very puzzled look. Most folks assume I do something involving fingerprints or blood, which I guess is an easier concept to grasp than computer security, which can also lead some people to think that I physically guard computers. So to help you in similar awkward situations, this is my reliable answer: I tell people that I find the bad things that people did using their computers.

When I'm asked the question in a more official capacity, such as while testifying in court, my answer is this:

> Computer forensics is the practice of determining the past actions that have taken place on a computer system using computer forensic techniques and understanding artifacts.

LINGO
An **artifact** is a reproducible file, setting, or system change that occurs every time an application or the operating system performs a specific action. For instance, you can detect the first time a user logs into a Windows system by inspecting the creation time of the user's home directory. The creation time does not change no matter how many times the user logs into the system, and the action can be repeated on multiple systems to verify its reliability.

What You Can Do with Computer Forensics

Any professional looking to specialize in a new field such as computer forensics may be wondering, Why is this something I would want to learn? Computer forensic techniques can tell us many things about what has occurred on electronic storage media.

Following are some examples of how forensics can help:

- Recover deleted files.
- Find out what external devices have been attached.
- Determine what programs have been run.
- Recover what web pages users have viewed.
- Recover the webmail that users have read.
- Determine what file servers users have used.
- Discover the hidden history of documents.
- Recover deleted private chat conversations between users.
- Determine what users have been accessing from external devices.
- Recover call records and Short Message Service (SMS) messages from mobile devices.
- Recover what a user did within a virtual host.
- Find out who is reading another user's e-mail.
- Find out if malware is installed and determine what has been captured.
- Find out who is not working and instead embezzling millions!

Computer forensics is a science, and the techniques that you learn and, in the future, possibly discover must be documented, tested, and verified if you expect them to hold up to scrutiny. This book will illustrate how to learn, test, and execute these techniques and will point you to resources where you'll find more information and advanced techniques as your confidence and capabilities grow as a forensic examiner.

How People Get Involved in Computer Forensics

Most people enter the computer forensics industry via four tracks: law enforcement, military, university programs, and IT and/or computer security. Each of these professionals imparts certain strengths as forensic examiners, and one track is no better than another. If you are looking to see where you can get started as a forensic examiner or to understand where other examiners came from, I've compiled my experiences in the following sections.

The following illustration may help you more clearly understand the overlap of the various disciplines with regard to computer forensics. All four areas touch computer

you've shown five

forensics, but that does not mean forensics makes up the individual's entire job. This book will help you make the transition into that middle circle.

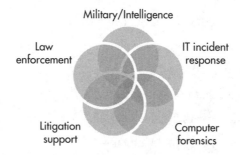

Law Enforcement

This track includes former and current local, state, and federal law enforcement officers/ agents who received forensics training as part of their duties. The large majority of law enforcement's current computer forensics case load deals with child pornography, an unfortunate statistic. That is not to say that law enforcement has no other exposure to computer forensic cases. Computers are a daily part in almost everyone's life, from desktops and laptops, to cell phones, and criminal do some crimes, or at least research them, on these devices. This means that law enforcement officials have to review everything they seize for computer forensic evidence, in cases from fraud to murder. Because of this, law enforcement officials have a good exposure to standard computer forensic techniques for examining systems. They also have good exposure to testimony and solid, documented chain-of-custody practices due to the nature of their work.

Military

Former military who were trained for either analysis or first responder duties in gathering evidence from hostile sources in the battlefield make excellent forensic examiners. Military forensic examiners are divided into two camps. The first camp includes those who are testing, identifying, and gathering evidence in the field. These professionals receive good training on how to image and identify multiple sources of electronic evidence. The other camp analyzes this evidence for rapid intelligence gathering and responding to incidents of security breaches, which exposes them to forensic techniques in server and desktop systems. Most military forensic examiners do not gain testifying experience, however.

In Actual Practice

The exception to the military track is the military investigation units, such as the Army Criminal Investigation Command (CID), who investigate crimes that occur within the military community. These investigators get more exposure to standard forensic techniques as would law enforcement personnel and are frequently asked to testify in military trials.

University Programs

This is a relatively new track for entrance into the computer forensics industry. Universities around the world are now offering bachelor's and master's degrees in computer forensics. University programs often focus on incident response techniques, because this is a well-funded research area and there are multiple free sources of test images to practice on. Some universities also have traditional forensic classes that focus on law enforcement forensic techniques in finding illicit images. University programs do not, however, provide exposure to testimony experience, but they are a great way to get the qualifications you need to enter the field in an entry-level position without any prior work experience. Community colleges are also getting into the mix, partnering with four-year universities to offer complete associate's to bachelor's degree programs in computer forensics. This is great news, because it opens the door for a lot of working professionals who find community college schedules more flexible and tuition more affordable.

IT or Computer Security Professionals

This is how I got started doing forensics. During the normal course of your work as an IT or computer security professional, people come to you asking for help determining how someone broke into a system. Many people in this track start by doing strictly incident response and move into more mainstream computer forensics as they learn more about it. As an IT professional, you are already exposed to system setup, configuration, and maintenance, and this forms a solid base from which your forensic knowledge can grow. You can learn about computer forensic techniques from taking training courses and self study. It may take many years before your work either as an in-house examiner or an external consultant is trusted enough that a lawyer will feel comfortable using you to testify.

IMHO

I got into computer forensics while working in information security in 1999. I had a client who needed someone to determine what a rogue executive was doing with keyloggers on the company's network. After writing a report the size of a small book on his nefarious activities, I was hooked, and I spent four more years working in the field before a lawyer felt comfortable enough with me to testify.

In Actual Practice

However you arrive at computer forensics does not determine whether or not you will be a good examiner. That distinction is up to you. The most important trait of a good examiner is never relying on facts that can't be tested or verified. If you can't explain how something came to exist and can't illustrate any examples of why the lack of something existing is proof of something in itself (as often used in cases of wiping), then there is a good likelihood that you shouldn't be relying on it. When you get involved with nontechnical parties in your examination process, they may press you to agree to certain facts or conclusions that are not supported by the evidence. In those circumstances, you must remember that it is your reputation and credibility that are on the line and not theirs; stick to the evidence and you won't have to worry.

To prepare yourself for testifying, you can take classes, read books, study prior testimony, and watch other experts give testimony (if their testimony is not covered under some kind of protective order). However, none of the preparation you do will get you on the stand. Becoming a testifying witness is a choice made by the attorney representing your client, company, customer, agency, or other entity. Until an attorney feels confident that your testimony will not fall apart on the stand, he or she will not allow you to testify.

I refer to this to friends as a "catch-22 of the testifying witness." Attorneys want you to testify, but they want you to have already testified for someone else first.

Incident Response vs. Computer Forensics

Many people from outside the industry get confused distinguishing incident response (IR) from computer forensics. They are, in fact, two very different fields of work. The most common computer forensic techniques focus on *post-mortem analysis*; this means that we are examining a forensic image of a computer system after something bad has occurred. Incident response is usually focused on the examination of a live running system.

Incident response is a different topic altogether from computer forensics and is covered at length in other books. However, there is nothing wrong with bringing standard computer forensic procedures and preservation methods into an IR scenario if you have time to do the work involved. It will always be up to the responder to decide what time and necessity will allow for, since most IR cases will never reach litigation.

The line between forensics and IR can often be crossed by either side, with IR people utilizing standard forensic techniques during a live analysis, or forensic examiners utilizing incident response techniques to capture the contents of RAM of a live system or making a forensic image of a running system. Most often than not, though, that line separates the two disciplines and the focus of their analysis techniques and tools.

LINGO

When laypeople refer to "images," they're talking about pictures of things, such as vacation scenes or friends. When IT people refer to "images," they are talking about system images captured from programs such as Norton Ghost, VMware, or Windows Virtual PC. When a forensic examiner refers to an "image," he or she is talking about a **forensic image**—a complete bit-for-bit copy of a piece of electronic media. The major difference between the IT and forensic definition is that a bit-for-bit copy includes all of the unallocated or free space of the electronic media, while a standard Norton Ghost image captures only the allocated space by default. Many tools can capture a forensic image—Norton Ghost can, for example, do so—but tools made particularly for image capture also produce digital fingerprints in varying hash standards (MD5, SHA-1, etc...) that allows an examiner to show that the contents of a forensic image have not been changed.

IMHO

Another major difference between incident response and computer forensics, in my experience, is how the project ends. In an IR case, if you are dealing with an outside attacker breaching the security of your system, the attacker is quite often a) outside of your country's legal jurisdiction, b) lacking in assets that could be used to pay back the cost of the breach, or c) not worth the time for law enforcement to pursue. These factors lead to most IR projects ending with the identification of the breach, the impact to any data stored within the system, and either the system being secured or reinstalled, with the possibility that those individuals affected will be notified if their information was breached.

This is in contrast to a civil computer forensic investigation, which is usually started in the pursuit of termination of an employee and/or litigation against an employee or third parties. One examiner can and will often perform both the roles of a forensic examiner and an incident responder, but while working in the current role, it's important that the examiner understand the results he or she is being asked to provide.

I am generalizing this example with regard to IT professionals and civil litigation, but you could make similar comparisons to IR versus criminal or military intelligence–focused computer forensics as well. Under my definition of computer forensics, it's the end goal of the project or case that you are undertaking that defines its place.

How Computer Forensic Tools Work

The standard computer forensic tool suites work by parsing the entire forensic image that you created. This means that the tool has its own file system parser that rebuilds both active and deleted files. Using forensic tools, you can recover deleted files, identify artifacts, view all files even if they are being hidden by some kind of rootkit, and perform analysis to determine what occurred on a system.

Types of Computer Forensic Tools

Computer forensic tools come in two major categories: *forensic suites* that attempt to provide an overall forensic workbench for an examiner to begin an investigation and *specialized tools* that are designed to pull out artifacts related to a single application. Each type of tool is available from *commercial* sources (fee-based) or *open source* (free software available to the general public with full source code included).

Suites

Multiple tool suites are available with varying capabilities, costs, and difficulty. You'll find commercial tools as well as open source tools that are available for free. You'll learn how to select the best one for your lab in Chapter 3.

Commercial Tools   The majority of commercial tools are written for Windows, because the majority of examiners and examinations deal with Windows systems. The one exception is SMART Forensics, which is a Linux-based tool suite.

IMHO

I find commercial tools to be friendlier than open source, because they come with manuals that explain their usage and the meaning of artifacts, and they offer support forums where you can ask questions. Open source tools tend to be more terse in their documentation for usage but are accompanied by large amounts of research with regard to the type of data they recover or parse. This is typically because the tool is released in conjunction with some type of research and was written as a proof of concept. The Linux kernel is an example of an extremely popular open source project.

Open Source Tools   Tools such as The Sleuth Kit, SANS SIFT, and Volatility are all open source tools. Most are written for Linux, but now work on other platforms, and initially have an incident response focus, although many such as SIFT are expanding into a full computer forensic suite comparable to commercial packages.

Specialized Tools

Specialized tools generally start off as one-offs in your collection and grow into a library of tools that you learn to use to deal with artifacts and programs not directly supported by your forensic suite. These include specialized file carvers, web history parsers for newer or nonstandard browsers, and decryption or steganography tools.

LINGO
Steganography is the science of hiding data in plain sight, the most popular method being hiding data within pictures. It's not limited to pictures though; researchers have found ways to hide data in everything from music to the deleted space on a disk.

LINGO
File carving commonly refers to techniques involving recovering full or partial remnants of files from the unallocated space of the disk or within large files. It's called carving because you remove pieces of data from a large set and put the data aside, much like you would carve a turkey, taking the meat but leaving the bones.

Commercial Tools Popular tools such as NetAnalysis are almost specialized suites, because they support so many different types of web browser history parsing formats. They still fit in this category, however, because they focus on only one type of application.

Open Source Tools Open source tools such as Scalpel allow specialized and advanced carving beyond what most forensics suites are capable of.

Professional Licensing Requirements

Today, many states in the United States require a private investigator's license for an external consultant who wants to perform computer forensics work for a client. Law enforcement, military, and internal corporate examiners are normally exempt from these laws. People who are performing only electronic discovery are also sometimes exempted from the licensing requirement. These folks gather evidence to provide to a legal team that reviews it; they do not analyze the information or provide an opinion about it as an expert witness.

It's important that you research your state's, province's, or country's laws with regard to computer forensic examinations to make sure that you are in compliance. In the United States, you can check the following site to determine whether your state requires some kind of professional license: www.investigation.com/surveymap/surveymap.html. If you do not comply with these laws, penalties can range from disqualification and your client losing their ability to present the evidence you gathered, to fines and your business being shut down until you come into compliance with licensing.

IMHO

I am currently a licensed private investigator in the state of Texas. I am licensed because the state required that I do so in order to operate a business that performs computer investigations for clients. Many people in our profession view the licensing requirements as a barrier to entry into the market; they think that existing private investigators wanted to find a way to keep competition from taking their work and commoditizing the practice. The real pain comes when you work in more than one state, in which case you have to determine whether the state you plan to work in also requires licensing and what you have to do to meet those needs.

I am not opposed to licensing, but I do agree with those who say that we are not private investigators and that the tests and regulations that document the work of private investigators do not include our work—other than we create evidence and present it in court. If at some point the state of Texas creates a computer forensic licensing board, I would be happy to accept it.

We've Covered

You've made it through the first chapter—congratulations! We won't get into how to analyze a forensic image until much later into the book and there is a reason for that. You need to know a lot before you can even begin to analyze a system and the majority of this book is here to help you understand those things so you will find success at the end of your first investigation instead of embarrassment. In the next chapter, we'll cover where and how to get training and continue on from there.

What you can do with computer forensics

- Retrieve hidden data and deleted information.
- Recover access information.
- Determine what tools have been used by an attacker.
- Compile evidence to help build a case.

How to get involved with computer forensics

- Paths include law enforcement, military, university programs, or IT and/or computer security.
- What makes a good examiner?
- Prepare for testifying.

The difference between incident response and computer forensics

- Computer forensics focuses on post-mortem analysis.
- Incident response focuses on a live running system.

LINGO
Electronic discovery, or **e-discovery**, is a legal term that distinguishes the collection, processing, and review of paper documents from electronic documents. Electronic discovery professionals collect data in the form of forensic images, backup tapes, document collections, archives, and other sources of data that can be reviewed by a legal team if they think it might contain information pertinent to a legal matter. Electronic discovery is a separate field from computer forensics, though at times they borrow tools from one another the end result is different. Electronic discovery begins with the collection of evidence and ends with the review and production of specific documents from that collection being produced in a legal matter.

How computer forensic tools work

- Computer forensic tools can be divided into two types:
  - Suites
  - Specialized tools

Professional licensing requirements

- Some states require licenses.
- Know and follow requirements and laws or suffer the consequences.

CHAPTER 2

Learning Computer Forensics

We'll Cover

- Where and how to get training

- Where and how to get certified

- How to stay current

Chapter 1 defined computer forensics—what it is, who does it, and the traditional ways people enter the field. This chapter offers information about how you can learn more about computer forensics. Although this book will give you a strong foundation that will get you started on your career as a computer forensics professional, it does not contain everything you'll ever need to know. I hope that the resources in this chapter will help you find additional information as you get the experience you need to take on more complicated cases.

Where and How to Get Training

One of the first things you should be looking to do—beyond buying this book, of course— is getting hands-on training. Hands-on training will help you get comfortable with the tools and procedures detailed in this book.

Although this chapter focuses on industry training and certification, there is another option. Many traditional two- and four-year undergraduate programs, along with graduate programs, from accredited colleges have added digital forensics as a degree option. I don't cover this option in detail in this chapter, because I assume you are already a working professional and not looking for a years-long ramp-up period before you get started in a new niche.

In Actual Practice

I have a degree in computer science, and most law enforcement computer forensic examiners have degrees in criminal justice. What degree you have does not determine your level of success in the field of computer forensics, however. A computer forensics degree will certainly provide you with a breadth of information from a formal training program that can only help you succeed, but don't think that you must obtain a degree in computer forensics before pursuing a career in it.

If you are interested in an academic program in computer forensics, it can only help you in the long run. Go to www.digitalforensicsassociation.org/formal-education/ for a current list of available programs out there.

IMHO

I highly suggest that you do not attempt any investigations for another person or any organization without first getting adequate training. Not only might you mess up the evidence, but you might miss the "smoking gun" in the evidence as well! Computer forensics is not just about creating a forensic image of a piece of electronic media; it's also about knowing how to interpret artifacts found in the forensic image and how to recover more of them. Without the appropriate training, you will not know how to locate and interpret every nuanced or subtle sign, or you may be unable to explain to someone else what it all means.

For example, I participated in one case in which the opposing expert had no prior computer forensic experience. He was wrong in all of his conclusions, and his client's case was dismissed. It was certainly not a good day for him or his client. Don't be that guy. Get training and practice in performing a computer forensic examination before offering to perform one for someone else.

If, even after my advice, you do not receive training, before you perform your first computer forensic investigation for someone other than yourself (and you are free to mess up your own evidence for testing), you must explain that you've received no formal training, because that person needs to understand that you might mess up the evidence and prevent them from entering a court of law with the evidence. And then you should at least make sure that you have thoroughly tested and documented your procedures in case someone presses you on your results.

Law Enforcement Training

Law enforcement, depending on the level (federal, state, or local), usually provides officers with free training from multiple sources. These free courses are typically restricted to law enforcement only (and, yes, you actually have to provide identification to register, so no sneaking in for free). Since this book is not intended for those pursuing careers in criminal investigation, I won't delve further into this topic.

Corporate Training

Corporate training is computer forensic training for the rest of us—those of us who are not law enforcement and have no special programs we can join to get training. Corporate employees and the general public can access training from a large variety of organizations and vendors. Some of the most popular training courses lead to some sort of certification, which is something else I would recommend you do. Computer forensic certifications are detailed in the following section; however, the list that follows does not include information on training courses whose only end goal is certification. These computer forensic training courses do not end in certification—there are surprisingly few.

Mobile Forensics

viaForensics   https://viaforensics.com/

The folks at viaForensics offer great courses for Android and iPhone analysis techniques. These go beyond the typical phone backups and get into physical inspection of deleted artifacts.

Teel Technologies   http://teeltech.com/tt3/class-list.asp

In partnership with Wild PCS, Teel Technologies offers advanced classes in mobile forensics that involves learning how to physically remove NAND (flash) memory from devices for physical inspection.

BK Forensics   http://www.bkforensics.com/training.html

BK Forensics provides free training on mobile devices both online and in person—you can't beat that!

Vendor Training

X-Ways Forensics   http://www.x-ways.net/training/index.html

X-Ways Forensics provides training on its forensic products without a certification involved. X-Ways makes the computer forensic tools X-Ways Forensics, X-Ways Investigator, and WinHex. Although the training focuses on how to use X-Ways' tools to perform computer forensics, the knowledge you gain can be applied to any tool.

IMHO

I've always heard great things from people who took these classes, and many of them have converted to the X-Ways methods of performing computer forensics.

Where and How to Get Certified

Certification is a great way to show others that you've mastered a certain part of the computer forensics skill set. There are two types of certifications available, vendor and vendor-neutral. Choosing which certification is right for you and your career can be difficult, but hopefully, after reading this chapter, you'll come away understanding what's best for you.

In Actual Practice

If you have no prior computer forensics experience, certification goes a long way toward getting a job in the field. Certification shows that you've met the requirements to pass the test and have a sufficient mastery of the information. Although certification does not mean that you are an expert, it certainly does comfort those who need to trust that you will perform a diligent investigation and not mess up the evidence.

Tip

Keep a record of your trainings, as you normally would for your resume. Listing your training and experience is something you'll have to do when you provide any type of report, statement, or testimony to the courts.

Vendor Certifications

Most established computer forensic software vendors have created certifications to establish that a person has taken their classes and/or exams and passed them. This shows to your employer, prospective employer, or opposing parties that you have been properly trained to use the tools you have chosen to employ. A wide variety of certifications are available in this category, and choosing the one that's right for you is more of a "which product do you use" question than a "which is better" question.

EnCase Certified Examiner

http://www.guidancesoftware.com/computer-forensics-training-ence-certification.htm

Guidance Software, makers of EnCase, created the EnCase Certified Examiner (EnCE) certification. It requires that you as an examiner can demonstrate either 12 months of on-the-job experience or 64 hours' worth of its training from Guidance, a government agency, or an accredited institution. Once you've proved you have the required experience, you can sit for the exam, which is half multiple-choice question and half practical examination with a full report write up. If you or your company has chosen EnCase as your primary forensic suite, this is a good certification to strive for.

Paraben Certified Mobile Examiner

http://www.paraben-training.com/pcme.html

Paraben, makers of forensic software and hardware, have been one of the longer standing contenders in the mobile device forensic space. If you or your company has chosen Paraben Device Seizure as your primary mobile forensic tool, this is a good certification to strive for.

SMART Certified Examiners

http://www.asrdata.com/forensic-training/overview/

ASR Data, makers of SMART forensic products, is the only forensic suite made to run natively in Linux. If you or your company has chosen SMART as your primary forensic tool, or if you want more exposure to forensics using Linux-based systems, this is a good certification to strive for.

AccessData Certified Examiner

http://accessdata.com/training/certifications#ace

AccessData, makers of the Forensic Toolkit, provides the AccessData Certified Examiner (ACE) certification at no cost to those who can pass the examination. If you or your company has chosen the Forensic Toolkit as your forensic suite of choice, this is a good and free certification to strive for. There are no perquisites for education or experience; just know the tools and how to use them during your analysis.

[

IMHO

I'm not recommending one vendor certification over another. Instead, I am stating that you should get the vendor certification that corresponds to the tool you are using. Having a certification that shows the mastery of a tool that you don't use in your investigations isn't helpful. You would be better served by getting a vendor-neutral certification, listed in the next section. Having said that, if a vendor certification is offered for a tool that you are actually using, I would recommend getting it to show your proficiency with the tool.

]

Vendor-Neutral Certifications

Vendor certifications certify your knowledge of how to use their tools to perform a computer forensic examination, but they do not attest to your overall general forensic knowledge. The vendor-neutral certifications listed in this section allow you to show others that you have mastered the body of knowledge that they cover. These certifications typically go beyond a vendor certification, because they cover areas of forensic analysis outside those the vendor may support. In an ideal world, you would have both a vendor certification for the tool you use and a vendor-neutral certification to show your mastery of the forensic process.

The International Society of Forensic Computer Examiners
http://www.isfce.com

ISFCE maintains the Certified Computer Examiner certification, which has grown to be one of the most recognized vendor-neutral computer forensic certifications. After 18 months of documented experience, attending their training camps, or documented original research, you can sit for the certification test. You must take a written test and examine and report on a test forensic image to obtain the certification.

High Tech Crime Network
http://www.htcn.org

HTCN offers multiple levels of certification depending on your experience and practical work experience. Once you have been working as an examiner for three years, you might want to check out HTCN and get certified.

SANS
http://www.giac.org/certifications/forensics/

SANS focuses on a series of Global Information Assurance Certification (GIAC) specialties and specifically offers a computer forensics track. SANS has a history of focusing mainly on incident response, with an emphasis on system administrator IR certifications, but its course content has expanded to traditional computer forensic techniques as well.

International Association of Computer Investigative Specialists
http://www.iacis.com/

IACIS provides the Certified Forensic Computer Examiner (CFCE) certification, which was previously open to law enforcement personnel only but is now open to the general public. For the many years it existed, IACIS was a de facto law enforcement officer certification resource; the organization has a good reputation.

Budget Note

Some certificate programs are free, some require a training class, and some require fees for the testing. The biggest return on your investment right now would be to choose among the ENCE, ACE, and CCE certifications. These are three most recognizable certificates out there, and when recruiters and human resources folks are reviewing resumes, keyword filters will be looking for these certifications.

- The ENCE program requires 64 hours of computer forensic training if you don't have 12 months of experience. The test costs $200 and requires that you go to a testing center or conference to take it. The cost of Guidance Software's ENCE training class is $2500 at the time of this writing.

- The ACE test is free, it's online, and ACE offers study materials on its web site. However, the ACE does require that you already own a licensed copy of AccessData's tools, which at the time of this writing can cost around $2000.

- The CCE is the least expensive of the bunch. Go to its web site to get the latest standards. You can sit for the test having no other experience or training classes. The test costs only $395, and you can use any tool you like.

IMHO

I am currently in the process of becoming a CCE. I've held off on any certification since they were either vendor-specific or still building credibility. In the end, as someone who runs a computer forensics lab and testifies as an expert witness, I felt that the CCE had the most to offer with their relationship with the Laboratory Accreditation Board of the American Society of Crime Laboratory Directors (ASCLD/LAB). ASCLD/LAB is, in my opinion, the Next Big Thing in our field. More labs will be getting their procedures certified by ASCLD/LAB and this certification may become a requirement in the future.

Staying Current

New information and research is always coming out as applications, operating systems, and technologies change. After you are certified, you should look for new sources of information to keep you up-to-date on what's happening so you can stay current.

In addition, you'll need to stay current to fulfill your continuing education requirements, which are required for most of the new certifications you receive. In this section, I list the many ways you can stay current with the latest computer forensic advances; whether you choose to do just one or all of them is up to you (and your budget).

You should expect that you will regularly attend, listen to, or read at least one of the items listed in each category. Computer forensics is a young field, and each version of a popular application or operating system creates new challenges and opportunities for an examiner. If you do not keep up with the ever-changing field, or at least have the resources to find new information when you need it, you will miss critical evidence in your cases.

Conferences

Although you'll find many computer forensic–focused conferences throughout the world today, each has a specific focus. Some focus on research, others on specific technologies, and others on the impact of the law on forensics. In this section, I detail the conferences that provide the best information for someone looking to keep up-to-date on general computer forensic techniques.

HTCIA International

http://www.htciaconference.org/

Once a year, the High Technology Crime Investigation Association International Conference is held at a different location. The conference is open to members and nonmembers alike and offers tracks for all skill levels. Although many of the attendees are law enforcement, very few of the labs are off limits to those not in the law enforcement field.

CEIC

http://www.ceicconference.com/

Guidance software puts on CEIC on a yearly basis; the conference is alternately held in Las Vegas, Nevada, and Orlando, Florida. The conference sometimes offers tracks devoted to the use of EnCase, but it also contains good sessions on vendor-neutral topics. (I spoke at CEIC 2011 and CEIC 2012, and maybe I will see you at CEIC 2013!)

Techno Forensics

http://www.techno-forensics.com/

Once a year, the TECHNO Forensics Conference provides a non-vendor–driven conference. There is no specific focus on law enforcement, so any type of computer forensic examiner is welcome. This conference is typically held in Myrtle Beach, South Carolina.

Black Hat

http://www.blackhat.com

Black Hat is primarily a computer and network security conference, but in recent years it has also began accepting computer forensic presentations as well. Held yearly at Caesars Palace in Las Vegas, Nevada, Black Hat is the best general computer security conference for networking and learning about new topics.

IMHO

I attend Black Hat every year, and I've found it to be one of the best overall conferences around. However, I was very impressed with CEIC in 2012 and plan to return in subsequent years, even if I'm not speaking there (but hopefully I will be!). I spoke at HTCIA International in 2010 and noticed that overall attendance has dropped greatly since I first started attending in 2000. If you have to make a choice between the two, I'd suggest you attend CEIC rather than HTCIA International for the time being.

SANS

http://computer-forensics.sans.org/events/

SANS produces a range of conferences and events through the year. Some events specialize in forensics, and they usually offer the SANS forensic classes for your GIAC certification needs. In addition to these conferences, SANS also provides several summits that take place around the country.

Blogs

Blogs are great resources for computer forensics information. In years past, most computer forensics techniques and procedures were considered secrets, and most people hesitated to detail them outside of private members-only forums. However, with the rapid expansion of our industry and the large availability of books such as this one, the cat is out of the bag, so to speak. Blogs have been sprouting up in earnest with various specialties providing new research and tools to the general public. Here is a list of the blogs that I follow to keep current.

IMHO

Blogs are what I follow the most on a day-to-day basis to stay current. I've subscribed all of these blogs to a Google reader account and I read them when I have free time during the day either on my PC or smartphone.

Hacking Exposed Computer Forensics Blog by David Cowen

http://hackingexposedcomputerforensicsblog.blogspot.com

This is my blog, and I read it often! All kidding aside, this blog is for computer forensic topics too advanced to be included in this book or for those that supplement the information in McGraw-Hill's *Hacking Exposed Computer Forensics* series. I update the blog weekly and typically have some kind of multiple-part series going all the time.

SANS: Computer Forensics and Incident Response with Rob Lee

http://computer-forensics.sans.org/blog

Rob Lee and his team at SANS produce a great blog that is constantly updated with new techniques and free tools that they either promote or develop themselves. Two of the largest projects they've contributed to open source computer forensics is the SIFT workstation and log2timeline, both of which are covered in this book. If you need an open source library of tools for your arsenal, this is blog is a must.

Windows Incident Response by Harlan Carvey

http://windowsir.blogspot.com/

Harlan Carvey has written many books on forensics and incident response. In his blog, he keeps his readers up-to-date on new tools, techniques, and topics he is researching. Harlan also developed the free and open source Perl program RegRipper and Forensic Scanner. (Don't worry; he distributes it as a Windows executable as well.)

Forensics from the Sausage Factory by Richard Drinkwater

http://forensicsfromthesausagefactory.blogspot.com/

This blog whose name is almost as long as mine, brought to you by Richard Drinkwater, who goes by the name DC1743, reflects a great deal of quality and unique information. Richard provides forensic information that I have not found elsewhere. From details on the forensics of GPS devices to new operating system forensic techniques, this blog delivers new and relevant information.

Forensic Focus Blog by Jamie Morris

http://forensicfocus.blogspot.com/

Forensic Focus is one of the best publicly accessible computer forensics forums around right now. Jamie Morris writes the blog and keeps it updated with new content from columnists, interviews, and new events. Following this blog is often easier than trying to keep up with the forums, which are very active.

Forums

Forensic Focus

http://www.forensicfocus.com

Forensic Focus is the most active public computer forensic forum that I am aware of. With daily topics spanning a range of international questions, from law, to ethics, to technology, there is always something new to learn at the Forensic Focus forums.

Vendor Forums

Beyond the general forum described so far, each of the major vendors operates a forum for its users to discuss its product, troubleshooting problems, and new techniques. Whatever forensic suite you end up deciding to use, find out what forums are available and get involved. Typically, a vendor forum will require that you have a validated licensed version of the software to gain access.

Podcasts

Podcasts can be a nice change from your daily routine. Listening to a podcast while driving, working out, or working in the lab can be a very effective way to keep up with the latest news. This section covers the three most popular podcasts, but there are more every day as our field keeps growing.

Forensic 4cast

http://www.forensic4cast.com/

Forensic 4cast is one of the most popular podcasts around today and focuses exclusively on computer forensics. The web site offers a mixture of episodes and articles that make for good reading and listening. One of the other fun things that Forensic 4cast does is run a yearly contest, with awards for the best blogs, tools, web sites, and so on, in the field. This is a must listen.

CyberSpeak

http://www.cyberspeak.libsyn.com/

CyberSpeak offers a mix of computer forensics and computer security information. If you are looking for good computer forensic information along with information security topics, this is a good choice.

Inside the Core

http://insidethecore.com/

Inside the Core, the 2010 Forensic 4cast Award winning podcast, is unique in that it focuses only on Macintosh forensics. All Apple products are included here, and the information covered is very much needed. Mac forensics is not as well researched as Microsoft forensics and is a field that we must keep up with, as Apple devices have skyrocketed in popularity.

Associations

Networking can also be a great way to stay current. The contacts you make in the industry at conferences or association meetings can often be of great help when you find yourself in new territory.

High Tech Crime Investigators Association International

http://www.htcia.org

HTCIA is one of the oldest computer forensic organizations around. With chapters around the world, HTCIA provides local training and networking to criminal and civil forensic examiners. To join the HTCIA, one of your primary job duties must include computer forensic examinations and/or the development of security technologies. (Note that you'll have to undergo a criminal background check when you apply for membership.) You should attend a meeting first, however, because they also ask for other members to sign your application.

The major restriction that HTCIA places on its members is that they are not allowed to do forensic examinations for criminal defense cases.

Association of Certified Fraud Examiners

http://www.acfe.com/

Although not strictly a computer forensic organization, many people must be familiar with fraud and computer forensics in their work. If your investigations take you into the realm of fraud, this organization offers a good way to meet peers and learn what trends are forming. It also offers a certification that you can achieve remotely.

We've Covered

In this chapter, I've given you my opinions on the best places for training, keeping up with forensic research, and getting certified. Other people you meet will have different opinions; some may even say how wrong I am, and that's OK! As you attend conferences, listen to podcasts, read blogs, and go to trainings, you'll form your own opinions and find what works for you. In the next chapter, I talk about how to build your forensic lab, so things are about to get interesting!

Where and how to get training

- Get training while working in law enforcement.
- Get training from corporations.
- Focus on specialties within training.

Where and how to get certified

- Sign up for the most popular vendor and vendor-neutral certifications.
- Determine which type of certification you qualify for.

How to stay current

- Attend conferences.
- Read blogs.
- Visit forums.
- Listen to podcasts.
- Join associations.

CHAPTER 3

Creating a Lab

We'll Cover

- Choosing where to put your lab
- Gathering the tools of the trade
- Choosing forensic software
- Storing evidence

In the last chapter, we talked about where to get training and certifications for your budding computer forensics career. Now you've made it to the part of the book where you start to get down to the business of actually performing computer forensics. Before we can perform our first examination, however, we need to have a few things in place, including the following:

- A space for your lab
- Hardware tools
- Software tools
- A place to store evidence

Creating your first lab can be a bit overwhelming if you don't have the experience to know exactly what you need and don't need. Many newcomers turn to documentation provided by federal law enforcement agencies for lab creation and storage, mainly because they offer documentation free on the Internet for state and local agencies to follow. But, truth is, you can't perform criminal investigations—only law enforcement and those they contract with can do so. After all, you have to take reasonable steps to protect your evidence, but you don't need to build an air gap network with radio frequency shielding around it just to find out if someone was playing games at work! Your lab can perform forensic investigations for your employer or for customers who you represent in civil court. You could assist law enforcement if you hand a case over that they agree to take on, but law enforcement typically will re-create your work and present it themselves in court. You could also help criminal defendants in their cases, but that's beyond the scope of this book.

Choosing Where to Put Your Lab

A forensic lab can be located inside any building if it can provide the proper controls and resources. The most important factors when choosing where to place your lab are access controls (both physical and network), electrical power, air conditioning, and privacy.

Access Controls

Any lab needs to have stringent physical and network access controls in place. Controlling who can access your equipment, evidence, and forensic images is important, because you'll need documented proof that you've properly maintained custody of evidence you've taken into your possession.

Documenting Chain of Custody

A chain of custody document simply states who has had possession of something—no matter what the thing is—and where it has been stored. The document can be as simple as a piece of paper stored with the object, to as complicated as a radio frequency ID (RFID) tag attached to the object, tracking its every movement. Regardless of how complicated you make it, to establish chain of custody with regard to a piece of evidence, you need to document the following:

LINGO
The process of proving who had access and control of something is called its **chain of custody**. A lot of people think of the chain of custody as some complicated mechanism that is fragile and difficult. In reality, however, the concept of the chain of custody has been in existence way before computers and before all the technical controls people put in place even existed. The chain of custody is just a document listing who has had possession of an item.

- Where you received the evidence
- Who you received evidence from
- When you received evidence
- What you did with the evidence
- Where you stored evidence

Figure 3-1 shows a sample chain of custody document.

MEDIA TRACKING AND CHAIN OF CUSTODY FORM

CASE # ______________________ DATE: ________________
EVIDENCE # ________________

TYPE EQUIPMENT (Circle)
HARD DISK / DESKTOP / LAPTOP / SERVER / CD | DVD / OTHER ___________

SOURCE:

MANUFACTURER	MODEL	SERIAL NUMBER

TO:

MANUFACTURER	MODEL	SERIAL NUMBER

RECEIVED FROM: ________________ ORGANIZATION: ________________

HISTORY/CHAIN OF CUSTODY

DATE	INITIALS	ACTION

NOTES:

Custodian Name:
Bios Time:
Actual Time:
Timezone:

Figure 3-1 Chain of custody document

To maintain the chain of custody of a forensic image, three things must be captured and preserved:

- **Information about the physical system where the evidence came from** This could be a desktop, laptop, DVD, thumb drive, or an external hard drive, for example. You must include information that identifies the physical system, such as the make, model, and serial number, which can be verified later if necessary.

- **Information about where the forensic image is stored**   You must include the make, model, and serial number of the drive or the server/network attached storage (NAS) on which the forensic image is being stored.

- **The forensic image itself**   If you follow the proper procedures as laid out in this book, the forensic image will contain a hash value either embedded within it or in a separate file. The hash value allows you and others to know that the contents of the image have not changed since they were captured originally.

LINGO
Hash or **hashing** refers to a mathematical algorithm that takes data of any length and converts it to a fixed set of hexadecimal characters that represent that data. Showing that a hash value is the same from the time evidence was gathered to the time it is provided to the court proves to others that the data has not been changed.

In Actual Practice

The two most popular hash systems used in computer forensics, Message-Digest algorithm 5 (MD5) and Secure Hash Algorithm-1 (SHA-1), both create a unique summation of your data, but SHA-1 uses more bits (160, while MD5 uses 128) to represent the data, allowing for less chance of any two documents having the same hash value. So, for instance, if you made a forensic image of a 1 TB drive and made a SHA-1 hash of its contents, you would get a 160-bit value that represents its content. You can't go from the 160-bit hash back to the 1 TB of data, so it's safe to share the hash value with others, and the hash value is repeatable.

As long as the contents of the forensic image do not change, the hash value will always remain the same. No matter the length of data you hash—be it a megabyte, a gigabyte, or a terabyte—if you change even 1 bit of information within the data, the hash value will change. This unique summation of data combined with the fact that you cannot determine the data hashed from the hash itself (which makes this a *one-way hash*) make hashes the standard for evidence authentication.

Physical Access Controls

Physical access controls can be a human guard, a lock with a key, a combination door lock, a padlock, or a proximity card sensor. Whatever it is, a physical access control is used to keep out people who should not have access to your evidence, and to ensure that only people who should have access to your lab can be there. You do not want the cleaning crew or facilities people to have access to your forensic lab. If you have a choice in the matter, your physical access control should include some form of logging to keep track of who has gone in and out of your lab. If your budget, location, or company restricts such a device, you should demand that no master keys be in the possession of anyone but those performing the investigative work. The goal here is to prevent someone from trying to discredit your evidence by claiming that an unauthorized person easily gained access to your lab and tampered with the evidence.

Network Access Controls

Just as you need to protect physical access to your lab, you must protect network access. The images you create and your analysis of those images will be performed on workstations in your lab, and you need to be able to protect the network from claims of tampering. To accomplish this, some people create a network for their forensic workstations that is separate from the company network and bring new software over via external storage.

Your Plan

To determine whether you need to keep your forensic workstation off the company network, answer the following questions. If you answer "no" to any of them, you may need to keep evidence on a separate network.

❑ Do you have super user control of your workstation?

❑ Can you keep other IT personnel from having access to your workstation?

❑ Can your workstation have its own domain or workgroup?

❑ Can you install a firewall on your workstation that prevents outside connections?

❑ Can you control whether or not domain policies are pushed to your workstation?

❑ Are you allowed to install and control your own security and antivirus software?

If you've made it this far with only "yes" answers, you can successfully use logical access controls to keep your forensic workstation on the company network. You will want to make sure that you know who has the ability to access your forensic network and keep a log of who has accessed it.

If you answered "no" to any of these questions, you should think about removing your forensic workstation from the company network. Although this may not be convenient, it will prevent possibly sensitive information in your investigations from being leaked out by a curious IT administrator.

In either case, appropriate network access controls will allow you to state that no one else but you or other authorized personnel could physically or virtually access the images stored on the workstation. This is what will allow you to defend your evidence from crazy conspiracy theories made by guilty parties who watch too many movies.

Electrical Power

This may seem obvious, but as your lab grows, you will need to make sure you can provide enough dedicated power to all the equipment that will find its way into your lab. The more cases you work, the more storage you'll need, and the more storage and images you have, the more processing power your system will need. It's a cycle that gets going pretty rapidly as you prove your capabilities to others and your workload increases. As people find out what you are capable of, you'll find new uses for your skills that you may not have thought of before.

Make sure you have at least one dedicated circuit available as you grow the lab. Make sure you use uninterruptible power supplies to connect to that dedicated circuit. A UPS ensures that you won't lose your work in the event of a power outage.

> **LINGO**
> An **uninterruptible power supply (UPS)** is a battery powered device that serves two purposes: It provides battery power in case the circuit loses power, preventing your workstation from powering off while doing something important, such as capturing a forensic image. It also ensures that the power that reaches your equipment is *conditioned*, meaning that the UPS will eliminate any variances in voltage that could potentially damage your equipment.

Some companies may have UPSs integrated into the outlets—congratulations if you are this lucky. Otherwise, you'll have to determine how much load your workstation and those accessories that can't be turned off, such as a USB hub that your external storage is plugged into, draw to see how long a particular UPS will last. Some of the newer consumer UPS models will display the current power draw and the estimated amount of time that the battery will last; this is useful if you don't have the experience to determine your power draw otherwise.

Air Conditioning

When you have enough steady power flowing into your workstation and accessories, you'll quickly find out that what they take in for power, they expel out in heat! Your hardworking equipment will produce a lot of heat as it keeps those fans spinning to keep up with the heavy load imposed on your systems by your forensic analyses. The more systems in your lab, the more heat is generated.

Budget Note

You might find that installing a portable air conditioner can be expensive. You can buy an inexpensive small temperature probe to record the high temperatures in the lab and keep track of whether they show a potential for equipment damage. You might find that, even without air conditioning, the room may stay cool enough to accommodate the full system without any problems.

More and more buildings are no longer providing air conditioning 24 hours day. This means that at night, while your equipment is running (and you are hopefully sleeping), the heat generated will be trapped in your lab with nowhere to go. If enough heat builds up, it can lead to system failure and loss of data, neither of which helps you make your deadlines, or cases. This is especially true if your lab is in an area with hot summer months, especially if no air conditioning is provided over the weekends.

The answer to this problem is air conditioning and ventilation; typically, a portable air conditioner (amazon.com and newegg.com both sell them) will suffice in a small lab.

In Actual Practice

Because you are obviously a scientist, or a soon-to-be computer scientist (put on your lab coats!), you realize that to cool the air, heat must be removed. This means that your handy lab air conditioner or ventilation system needs to have somewhere to put all that heat. The other byproduct of the process is water vapor, and most of today's consumer units can expel that vapor with the hot air exhaust.

You might be able to place the exhaust of your portable air conditioner into the register of the building's existing air conditioning system. Otherwise, you may be able to route the unit's exhaust into the ceiling, but make sure you check with your building management before doing this.

(continued)

If your lab space is small and you are drawing in the air from the same space, you may encounter a condition called "negative pressure": this means that the air conditioner is constantly recycling the air in the room into and out of the unit. This can cause the system to become inefficient, and in long-term use it could lower the unit's lifespan. You can cure this problem with a dual-hose portable air conditioner, but it means you now have to run two lines—one for air into your unit from another space and one to run out the hot air.

Privacy

Privacy may be the most practical requirement for your lab. As you undergo your investigations, you will be viewing materials that can be sensitive or incredibly offensive even to the most hardened Internet veteran. What you don't want is that nice new employee who is unscarred by the Web's horrors to get his or her first glimpse of its ugly underbelly while walking by your cube. Nor do you want delicate personnel matters to be visible to people walking by. This means that, above all, you and your lab need privacy. You should not work with your lab door open, and you should never perform your examinations in a cubicle surrounded by other employees' cubicles.

If you work in a corporate environment where only employees of a certain level are granted an office with a door, you should explain that you also need an office with a door that closes. Let them know that it's better and less expensive to bruise the ego of a manager who must now work in the cube with the fake door than to endure the hostile workplace lawsuit filed by the sensitive worker who claims to have been scarred by the "sexual tendencies of fellow employees on display on your examination workstation."

IMHO

Although no lawsuits may be filed, there is no reason to subject coworkers to some of the strange things you will see as you work investigations. At a minimum, you can expect some complaints to human resources and some coworkers who can no longer look you in the eye. If you work in this field long enough, at some point, nothing will shock you anymore. My latest discovery on a suspect's system was quicksand erotica; I don't think I can ever unsee that.

In Actual Practice

Here are two choice stories from other examiners who had to have their lab in an open-cube environment:

I was once forced to conduct an investigation in my cubicle, and there was a significant amount of disturbing pornography on the system being examined. Some of the offensive materials were seen by a large portion of the IT staff, as my cubicle was at a well-traveled intersection and the short cubicle walls provided no real privacy. While no lawsuits were filed, there were a couple of complaints to HR. And many of them could no longer look at two popular superheroes the same way again.

I had an open-cube setting at a prior company, and a member of the InfoSec Engineering team sat next to me. He was fond of holding conferences in his cube space (usually with project managers and customers for the various projects he was consulting on), and I had to refrain from conducting certain investigations at work during that time for just this reason. I did get a privacy filter for my monitors, but since they were directional filters, if the visitors moved to the right angle, they'd still get an eyeful.

Gathering the Tools of the Trade

After you've secured the physical space to start your lab, you'll need to fill that space with all the hardware and software you'll need for your investigations. The available range of tools can fill a room pretty quickly, so let's talk about what you actually need to get started.

Write Blockers

A *write blocker* …well, it blocks writes. As simple as that sounds, a write blocker is one of the most fundamental tools in your lab. Every time you are working from a piece of original evidence, you need to prevent writing to it, unless it's impossible to do so. There will be times when what you are forensically imaging does not have a write blocker available, and you are using enterprise forensic software that runs as an agent on the suspect's computer, or lawyers agree not to write block so the server can keep running while you make the forensic image; barring that and any other situation you find yourself in, don't write to original evidence. If you do, make sure that you document your actions so you can exclude them from your investigation later.

Budget Note

Write blockers used to be considered expensive, at around $1000. However, at the time of this writing, you can purchase a Serial Advanced Technology Attachment (SATA) write blocker from Digital Intelligence on the Web for less than $400. If that's out of your price range, you might want to reconsider doing this work, because all the blank drives you'll need to store the forensic images you create will quickly outpace that.

Your ability to protect the state of the original evidence during its preservation will help you avoid challenges to the evidence you create. Write blockers are key in this regard, because they physically connect between your workstation and the original evidence to prevent any writes from occurring. They simply return a successful write to the operating system, without passing the data on to the device it is protecting.

Write blockers come in many varieties, as shown in Figure 3-2: you'll find USB write blockers (A), FireWire write blockers (B), SATA write blockers (C), and more. To decide which write blocker to choose, look at your environment to see what type of equipment is in use. If you are doing computer forensics within a corporate environment, you may have standard hardware configurations, and this makes it much simpler to know what write blockers you need to purchase. If you are planning on offering computer forensics as a service to third parties, you'll need to be prepared for anything, which means getting all the different write blockers you can afford, or at least the most popular such as SATA, Parallel ATA (PATA), and USB.

Not all write blocking has to be done using physical hardware. You can also write block using software, which provides a much more flexible option to protect original evidence. Software write blocking can occur at the interface level. Windows supports USB

LINGO
Original evidence refers to the source of your evidence. For instance, if you were asked to investigate an employee's desktop, the desktop and its hard drive would be considered the original evidence. The forensic image you make from that hard drive is not original evidence; it is a copy of it. The same concept applies to CDs, DVDs, thumb drives, cell phones, tablets, and any other source of electronic data you are asked to investigate.

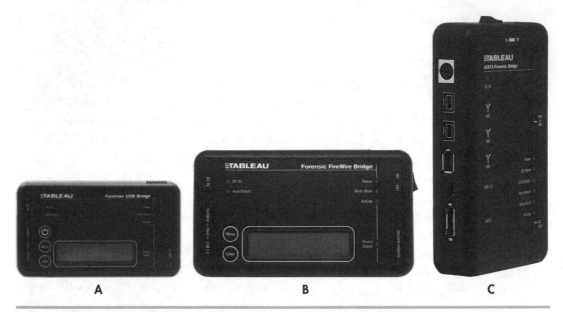

Figure 3-2 (A) USB write blocker, (B) FireWire write blocker, and (C) SATA write blocker

write blocking via registry tweaks or from the operating system level. Windows Server Standard FE and Linux/BSD both can be configured not to write to drives that are attached without being instructed to do so. (See Chapter 5 for more information.)

In Actual Practice

Many examiners just starting out feel uncomfortable with the idea that they may accidently write to a piece of original evidence. This is legitimate fear, because forensic imaging is a procedure that, although simple, can make the biggest impact if you make a mistake, which may even mean you lose a case. This can lead many to use portable imaging devices that have built-in write blocking and can offer some serious speed in its acquisition of data. There is nothing wrong with using these devices, but they can be expensive, and their exclusive use can cause issues in scaling out your imaging to meet the demand of imaging many machines at once.

Note

Many people say that if a disk gets written to while imaging, it will automatically end a case. That is not exactly true, however. If you document what went wrong and contain the impact to the disk and explain the issue, you will likely be able to get the evidence admitted in civil court.

Drive Kits

If you choose to use a software write blocker, drive kits will become your best friends. These typically USB-based adaptors, such as the one shown in Figure 3-3, provide an easy and compact connection for an internal hard drive to your workstation.

Figure 3-3 shows a drive kit that connects a USB 3.0 port on my workstation directly to a SATA laptop drive. You can see that the power plugs into the drive kit directly, which provides a very portable adaptor for attaching drives to a workstation or laptop. When I go onsite, I'm usually armed with my laptop, a write blocker, these drive kits, and software write blocking.

Figure 3-3 A drive kit

In Actual Practice

Make sure you test your equipment before you go onsite. Especially when dealing with drive kits which are fairly cheap, you need to test them: If they even work, you may get a bad one from time to time that you have to return. In addition, their speed can vary. Almost all of the drive kits are sourced from no-name manufacturers, so two boxes could have two different chip sets. The same advice goes to any equipment you plan to bring with you out of the lab environment. You need to make sure you are prepared and have everything you need, and that everything is working as it should, so you don't waste time.

If you are looking for a more permanent solution to place in your lab, look into purchasing an external drive dock (see Figure 3-4). They allow you to place the empty dock on a stable service in your lab and keep the power and cables attached. Just place the drive in the dock and power it on with your favorite software write blocker turned on.

Figure 3-4   External drive dock

This can also be handy when you don't want to use external drives to store images, because it can be a pain to keep up with all the different AC adaptors they come with.

External Storage

The key to successful external storage usage is getting the highest transfer rate available to you. USB 3 is pretty great, external SATA (eSATA) is becoming the standard on more systems, and the new Intel/Apple Thunderbolt interface standard is starting to get traction. You also need to make sure your external storage has good heat dissipation. Nothing can ruin your day faster than an external drive overheating and crashing after being three-quarters of the way done imaging a 2-terabyte hard drive.

IMHO

When I was first working cases, I lived off of external storage. I would dedicate one external drive to each case and place both the forensic image and the case data on it. Now that the scale of my work demands large servers and storage systems, I still use external storage when I'm creating forensic images.

Screwdriver Kits

Most electronic stores sell these kits; you'll want a kit with what is commonly called a "jewelers" set of screwdrivers. You can use these smaller screwdrivers to unscrew all of the tiny screws you'll find in many laptops. Other good things to look for in screwdriver kits are Torx head and star heads for those vendors who don't want to make it easy to remove a hard drive from their device. If you get a Torx head kit, make sure to get the ones that fit the security bits as well, because they can be used on regular and secure Torx head screws. The only real problem with screwdriver kits is that if you have to travel to do your work, Transportation Security Administration (TSA) agents may take them away at the airport.

Antistatic Bags

You'll find that many people buy official bags that say "EVIDENCE" on them, but that's really unnecessary, because you already know that it's evidence and anyone who does not know that shouldn't be handling them. Any, preferably resealable, antistatic bag is as good as another. Antistatic bags prevent static shock from damaging the components that allow your original evidence to work and are always a good idea to have around. These bags are cheap and recommended for your kit, because a drive dying due to static shock equals a bad day.

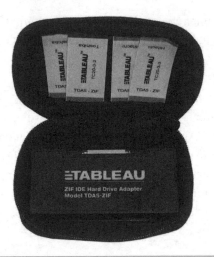

Figure 3-5 ZIF interface adaptor

Adaptors

As you open up more and more computers, especially ultra-portable laptops, you'll find new hard drive interfaces you didn't even know existed! When this happens, you'll need an adaptor to bridge from that new interface (such as a ZIF [Zero Insertion Force] interface, shown in Figure 3-5) to something you can handle with your current equipment, such as SATA.

In Actual Practice

You'll never know what type of adaptor you'll need until you actually need it. The best way to prepare is to find out from your IT staff what standard equipment they deploy and what interfaces to the hard drives need to be covered 90 percent of the time. This is a broad statement, however, because new laptops and devices (such as tablets) always introduce new drive standards. If you are in a corporate environment where such hardware is controlled and defined, adaptors will be less of an issue for you.

Forensic Workstation

Any good desktop PC can be used as a forensic workstation. Although many companies out there want to sell you a purpose-built forensic workstation, you don't have to buy one to perform an examination. What you do need is all of the processing power, memory, and storage space you can afford to get to handle the complicated tasks ahead of you. As your lab grows larger, you may find yourself migrating these tasks to dedicated servers with even more power to handle the growing demands of ever larger cases.

IMHO

Many people start their first examinations using their work-issued laptop. There is nothing wrong with this, but you'll quickly find that having to leave your laptop running overnight processing evidence becomes a hindrance when you need to get other work done. Even if an available desktop is slightly less powerful than your laptop, it might be dedicated to the long-term tasks you assign to it, and desktops are usually better than laptops at handling the heat that builds up from long-term operation.

Choosing Forensic Software

You have your space, you have your hardware, and now you need to figure out what software you are going to use for your analyses. For most computer forensic professionals, the choice of whether to use open source and free tools or commercial tools comes down to budget. This book covers three popular forensic suites used for analysis: SANS Investigate Forensics Toolkit (SIFT), Guidance Software's EnCase Forensic, and AccessData's FTK Digital Forensics Software.

In Actual Practice

There are many other options on the market as well. Although this book focuses on SIFT, EnCase Forensic, and FTK, this does not imply that you could not or should not choose another application that you find more suitable. You'll find the need for many specialty computer forensic software packages as your career progresses. You might need software to acquire data from certain types of smartphones, to recover certain types of data, to parse certain types of data, and more! You won't know you need it until you need it, so make sure to keep Google handy when someone asks you, "Can you do *X* with that?"

Open Source Software

You might hear a lot of legal conjecture arguments for and against open source software. One camp likes to say that open source is better, because you can easily defend and explain to the smallest detail what your program is doing because you have access to the source code. The other camp says that a closed source vendor's software is better because they will testify regarding the validity of their tool.

IMHO

For civil work, I have found the neither camp's argument holds any weight. If you can represent that your analysis can be confirmed using multiple tools when questioned, then there is rarely an issue. For criminal work, where guilt beyond a reasonable doubt must be proven, I can see this being a bigger issue, but we in the civil world don't have these concerns. Choose your tools because of your comfort and experience with them, not because of what someone tells you is bulletproof in court.

SIFT

Lots of open source tools and bootable environments are available today, but the one I like the most and spotlight in this book is SIFT. Although most open source tools are packaged in bootable environments, SIFT is made to run as a static virtual environment that you can optionally install to a drive, making it a great tool for both Linux users and Windows users who want to learn more about it without leaving behind their current environment.

You can download a virtual image of SIFT from http://computer-forensics.sans.org/community/downloads/.

Budget Note

Many people start off with open source software because of budget issues. You may have to successfully analyze an image and solve a case before a business is willing to get behind you and support your efforts with funding. All commercial tools support raw images, and you can easily move cases between the two, so don't think that because you start with open source that you can't transition between it and commercial tools. Many forensics professionals use both commercial and open source.

Commercial Software

If you are not familiar with Linux and are more comfortable in Windows, it might be best to stick with a commercial forensic suite. The end product of any tool you choose should be the same, in that your analysis should reach the same artifact no matter which tool you use that supports the file system or application you are analyzing. There are open source Windows tools, but none of them have been combined into a single package equal to SIFT, which is also well supported. Until that fact changes, that is the line we draw.

LINGO

A **raw image**, also called a "dd image" (for the dataset definition command, dd), is a computer forensic image of a system in which the data from the storage device is stored as a single file or multiple files, but without any type of container that stores checksums or hashes. For example, EnCase's image format E01 contains the same data as a raw image but adds on cyclic redundancy checks (CRCs) and information about the image (such as what version of EnCase was used to make it, who made it, and its hash values).

IMHO

Every investigator should learn two things: Linux and programming. If you stick to just Windows and never learn how to program, you will be limiting your growth as an investigator. No single computer forensic tool provides every feature you want, and no operating system (OS) can provide all the functionality you need; you eventually will use every tool and OS you can get your hands on.

EnCase

EnCase Forensic version 7, the current version at the time of writing, has been dramatically updated to keep up with competitors, including support for distributed processing and better e-mail functionality. I've found EnCase to be not particularly user-friendly to a new user and new examiner, so I recommend you get training on the product if you plan to use it. A lot of the product's extended functionality comes in the form of programs called EnScripts that can run within the tool and manipulate data in the images.

FTK

AccessData's Forensic Toolkit (FTK) version 4 is the current version. FTK has become the tool to beat in my opinion. FTK is very user-friendly and provides base training materials and certification for free on the company web site. FTK supports distributed processing, offers fantastic e-mail support, is good support for encryption products, and offers one of the best imaging tools around: FTK Imager.

IMHO

Other commercial tools are on the market, such as ProDiscover, SMART Forensics, X-Ways, and more. On a daily basis, the one I use the most is FTK. It gives me the information I want to see in the best form for my workflow. After 14 years on the job, this is my favorite tool. What works best for you will be something you discover as you try more tools and analyze more data. Having said that, I own licenses for every major forensic suite except for ProDiscover, which some people love and some hate.

Storing Evidence

Evidence storage might be the most worrisome part of building a forensic lab. Many people involved in discussions that focus on computer forensics have never been to court and have never offered evidence to the court. As such, they have no practical experience as to what the court requires for evidence storage and tend to cite criminal best practices from the Secret Service or FBI. But evidence storage involves much more. Evidence storage requires that you keep physical access controls in place for the evidence, but does not dictate in what form that must be; read on to learn how to store evidence for civil cases.

Securing Your Evidence

When I first started working forensic cases, my original "evidence locker" was a locking file cabinet. From there, I moved up to a fireproof safe, and now I have a bona fide evidence room. All of these options are acceptable if you can prove chain of custody and show who had access to the storage system and the evidence stored within it. The question to ask is, who has access?

If your file cabinets have generic master keys, you should not use file cabinets to store evidence, unless you place some kind of secondary lock on them with a secure code that only you and the people who should have access know. This can be a padlock, but make sure it's a top-notch padlock.

In Actual Practice

Even if your company's management say that nobody has a master key, locking file cabinets are pretty terrible for evidence storage. They are easily forced open and their locks are very easy to open with something as easy as a paperclip.

If you can't put your evidence in a separate physical space, a safe is a great option. Multiple safe options include fireproof types with electronic locks that let you use individual codes to access the contents.

Tip
Safes can be heavy. Make sure the floor can support the weight of the safe.

If your collection of evidence is quickly filling up your safe (or safes), you should consider creating an evidence room. This can be as simple as a closet, or as large as a closed-door office space. You should make sure of the following:

- The walls go to the ceiling all around the room; this means that even in a drop-down ceiling environment people can't just crawl over.

- There is controlled access to the room, preferably with a digital lock just like the lab itself.

- There is no unsupervised access to a cleaning crew or other unauthorized personnel.

- Any fire suppression system is "dry pipe," which means you might have a chance to save your drives and systems from water damage. Remember, water/chemicals and electricity do not mix.

Organizing Your Evidence

Just as important as securing your evidence from alteration is being able to find it. Some people go as far as RFID tracking, but in a small lab you don't need such a sophisticated system. You do need to create standards for how to label your evidence and track which drive it is located on, and where that drive is physically located.

Labeling

The more cases you work, the more organized you need to be. You can start with a spreadsheet if you are working alone, but as soon as you move beyond just you, then you need to provide something multiple people can access and modify. A hosted Google docs, SharePoint, or other type of multi-user document sharing site would work well for this. Make one row for each case listing the prefix, who the contact is for the person requesting the work, and how to get a hold of them.

For each case, you'll need to create a standard label to keep track of all the evidence. If you are providing investigations inside a company, then you can adapt this naming scheme as well. You could prefix it with the initials of the person making the request, like *JD-1-1* for John Doe's first case and first evidence number. What you use for a prefix does not matter; you could use the state the case is in, for example. What does matter is that you are consistent with your naming and you keep track of it.

Tracking

On the same spreadsheet you're using to keep track of cases, you should add a tab for each case listing the chain of custody basics, such as make, model, serial number of the drive you have copied the image on, or the original if you still have it, as well as the location of the drive. Don't just use "the lab" as the location; you need to be specific about where, exactly, you are storing the evidence: a file cabinet, safe, room with shelves, and so on. And label the different shelves and areas with a letter-number combination to make it easy to identify where in that stack of drives the one you want is located.

Disposing of Old Evidence

When a case is over, never assume you can destroy the evidence. Ask your client or employer before you destroy anything. Then make sure you keep the e-mail or other document that says you are clear to destroy the evidence. Just because a case has been inactive for a year does not mean that some kind of litigation is still involved with the case. The more cases you work, the more drives you'll need to store on indefinite hold. If you begin running out of space, you might consider secure offsite storage.

If you are allowed to destroy evidence, this doesn't mean you'll take the drive out and melt it or beat it apart with a hammer. Instead, you can permanently remove data from old drives, called "wiping," and reuse them. You can reuse old drives to store evidence or use them to send copies of data to other parties or internal reviewers. My favorite wiping software is BCWipe from Jetico, but other products are on the market as well.

We've Covered

We've covered a lot in this chapter. Building and maintaining a lab is a lot of work, but a good lab goes a long way toward helping you defend your work. Don't go crazy if you can't achieve 100 percent of the requirements in this chapter; just do the best you can and try to achieve 100 percent as you move forward and show value to those who are funding you. In the next chapter, we'll talk about how to approach an investigation so you start thinking like an investigator.

Choosing where to put your lab

- Access controls
- Importance of chain of custody
- Physical lab security
- Network security
- Electrical power and temperature
- Privacy

Gathering the tools of the trade

- Write blockers
- Drive kits
- Screwdriver kits
- External storage
- Antistatic bags
- Adaptors
- Forensic workstation

Choosing forensic software

- Open source for your budget
- Commercial for ease of use

Storing evidence

- How to store evidence securely
- How to organize and keep track of evidence
- How to dispose of old evidence and when it's appropriate to do so

PART II

Your First Investigation

CHAPTER 4

How to Approach a Computer Forensics Investigation

We'll Cover

- How to follow an investigative process

- How to test your hypothesis

- How to assess the forensic data landscape

- How to determine what you have the authority to access

Chapter 3 covered how to create a forensic lab. In this chapter, you will learn how to prepare for a computer forensics investigation. A computer forensic examination differs from most computer security work that you may have been asked to do. In a typical computer security project, you must try to implement some mechanism—whether policy, software, or hardware—to prevent an action from occurring. In a computer forensic examination, some type of action or activity has already occurred; it's your job to determine the what, when, where, how, and who.

The Investigative Process

If you've watched detective shows on television or at the movies, you might hear a lot of talk about following the investigative process. The idea behind the process is that when you approach an investigation, you are doing so without prejudging the outcome; you're open to the conclusion that the evidence will reveal. It's also equally important to stay focused on the questions being asked: If, for example, you are asked to determine whether someone e-mailed company secrets but you instead returned with embarrassing facts about that person's personal life, you might be the one facing an HR exit interview, instead of the suspect.

> **LINGO**
> Most computer forensic publications refer to the person whose activities we are examining as the **suspect**. This does not mean we believe the person is guilty, but merely that he or she is the focus of our examination. Your suspect may change, or other suspects may be revealed, over the course of your investigation.

What Are You Being Asked to Find Out?

This is the most important question to address when you are asked to perform a computer forensic examination. If, for example, you are asked, "We've been told that our suspect has been looking at offensive images during work hours; can you verify this?" then your investigation will be likely focused on the suspect's Internet activities during work hours.

If the suspect is taking his corporate laptop home at night and viewing offensive images from home, that may not be a violation of company policy.

Typically, you require internal authorization to perform an investigation. You will not have authorized yourself to analyze media to determine what has occurred, unless you are testing your own tools or using a honey pot.

> **LINGO**
> **Honey pots** are used in research and intrusion prevention systems. They are usually virtual machines that are configured insecurely to lure an attacker in. The attacker's actions are recorded outside of the honey pot, and their methods are analyzed.

Where Would the Data Exist?

The next question is one to ask of yourself: Where would I find data that would contain the evidence I need to answer the client's question? In the case of an employee viewing indecent images, you typically might look in the following locations for evidence:

- Any outbound proxy or web-filtering software log
- The computer from which the inappropriate access originated
- Firewalls configured to log outgoing web access

Other books cover how to read, query, and analyze firewall and proxy logs. Although other sources of evidence exist, and you should look at those sources, in a computer forensics investigation we will focus on the computer from which the access originated. We'll ask the following questions in each of our case examples:

- What applications might have been used in creating the data?
- Should you request to go beyond the scope of the investigation?

What Applications Might Have Been Used in Creating the Data?

Computer forensic evidence is generated either by the operating system or via an application that the suspect is using in his activity. The operating system can be easily identified, but knowing what application to focus your analysis on requires some thought. In this example, you are interested in the suspect's web site access, so you need to consider applications that the suspect could have used to access a web site—of which there are many, such as the following:

- Internet Explorer
- Firefox
- Opera
- Chrome
- Safari

Not only must you identify the types of application that might have been used, but you must inspect each application to determine which one the suspect has been using. Once you've identified the application, you must determine whether the forensic suite you've chosen supports it, either automatically or as a data type you can define for it to extract; this process is called *carving*. If your suite does not support this application, you'll need to extract out the suspect's activity using other methods (as discussed in Chapter 11).

> **LINGO**
> **Carving**, or **data carving**, is a term often used by examiners and computer forensic tools. Carving is the process of searching for blocks of data that match a *pattern*, either in the free space or in the unused allocated spaces of the disk, such as the slack space (explained later in this chapter). These patterns are normally called *file signatures*. A good example of this is an HTML document, which begins with an `<html>` tag and ends with an `</html>` tag. If we find a block of data in the free space or the slack space that contains this pattern, then all the data that falls between the two tags may be a deleted HTML document we can recover. That's data carving in its most simple form; it can quickly get more complicated as the file signatures do.

Should You Request to Go Beyond the Scope of the Investigation?

This question comes up a lot, mainly from internal corporate investigators, who in the scope of their investigations run across activity other than the one they were requested to find. The following considerations should provide you guidance here.

Child Pornography: Stop the Investigation

You can't read a computer forensic book or attend a computer forensic conference without the issue of child pornography coming up. (This will be the only time this issue is discussed.)

If you find what you believe to be child pornography on a forensic image, stop your investigation immediately!

Do not do anything further with the case. This is now a criminal case, and you are not allowed to investigate, possess, copy, or distribute the evidence, or you could face criminal charges yourself. You have a federally mandated obligation to report any discovered child pornography to the National Center for Missing and Exploit Children (NCMEC) at www.missingkids.com, and you should inform those who asked you to perform your examination of its existence.

Note

The law changed in 2008 with the introduction of the McCain SAFE Act (primarily aimed at ISP providers) from mandatory disclosure for all under federal law to the following:

Duty To Report. (1) In general. Whoever, while engaged in providing an electronic communication service or a remote computing service to the public through a facility or means of interstate or foreign commerce, obtains actual knowledge of any facts or circumstances described in paragraph (2) shall, as soon as reasonably possible, make a report of such facts or circumstances to the CyberTipline of the National Center for Missing and Exploited Children, or any successor to the CyberTipline operated by such center.

It will be up to the legal department to decide whether you are covered by this provision. Nevertheless, you should establish and follow written procedures incorporating reporting requirements under SAFE.

Ask the Person Requesting the Examination

Many examiners feel empowered to make decisions about what is and what is not relevant to an examination. Many times, however, they can be wrong. I recommend returning to the individuals who asked you to do this work in the first place, and ask them the following: If I find an indication of something other than the original action as requested, would you like me to go forward in examining that issue? Depending on your corporate environment, launching a new line of inquiry into your investigation without prior approval could get you in as much trouble as your suspect is in.

Testing Your Hypothesis

After you've identified the application your suspect used and you've found what you believe to be evidence, you need to prove that the suspect was looking at something horrible at work. You must ensure that what you believe to be true is, in fact, true!

If this is the first time you've found a particular piece of evidence—if, for instance, you've never recovered deleted Internet history records from Internet Explorer before—you should make sure that what you are seeing is correct. You do this by defining and testing your hypothesis—very scientific, don't you think?

Your Plan

In this section, I'm basically re-creating the scientific method for your forensic investigations. A more direct example plan would be the following:

1. **Characterization**   Observations of the subject of your inquiry—in this case, the digital artifacts of the investigation: "I examined entries in the suspect's index.dat file and have determined that entries there indicate that the suspect accessed inappropriate and/or offensive images using Internet Explorer."

2. **Hypotheses**   Theoretical and hypothetical explanations of what has been observed: "I believe these images were not random pop-ups, because they were found in the Typed URLs section of the index.dat file."

3. **Predictions**   Reasoning and deductions from the hypothesis or theory: "If I take a test machine and type a URL into the address bar, the history entries from the test machine's index.dat file for that location should be marked as being in the Typed URLs section. I will also open an HTML file that contains a link to a URL located at a different web site with Internet Explorer and click on that link to make sure that entry does *not* appear in the Typed URLs section of the index .dat file."

4. **Experiments**   Tests of the characterizations, hypotheses, and predictions to validate them: "The URL typed into the address bar of Internet Explorer did indeed show up in the test machine's index.dat file, while the URL accessed while clicking the link in the HTML file did show up in the log file, but not in the Typed URLs section."

Step 1. Define Your Hypothesis

In this example case, the hypotheses could be as simple as this:

I believe that the entry in index.dat for the offensive images I've located is not the result of a pop-up ad or other passive browsing, but of purposeful accesses to the site that hosted it.

Note that you don't actually have to write down your hypothesis, but it's important to frame it in your mind, because this will help you in determining how to test it.

Step 2. Determine a Repeatable Test

In this example case, you would create a clean virtual machine on which to perform your testing and then visit two kinds of web sites. The first would be testing direct access to a web site that allowed you to click and view multiple images. The second would be testing sites that have pop-under or pop-up ads to find out how their entries are recorded in the Internet history files. Once you've found web sites that satisfy both criteria, another investigator can run the same test to solidify your conclusions. If you are not required to use corporate funds to purchase access to a pornographic web site, you might be able to test this against the site the suspect actually visited himself.

Step 3. Create Your Test Environment

It's important not only to have a new virtual machine to test with, but to make sure the versions of the operating system and the application are the same as the versions used on the suspect's machine. You don't want a difference between Firefox 2.0 and Firefox 3.6.8 to throw off your testing. This may seem like overkill for a case involving viewing inappropriate images at work, but if this is your first real case, it's not too much to ask. This is a generic framework you can apply as you move into more advanced cases, where you may be breaking new ground in a computer forensic research area that has never before been publically documented.

Step 4. Document Your Testing

It's important that you document your testing environment, what you tested against, and your results. If you went through all the trouble of proving your findings, you should take the extra step to document these details in case someone else wants to re-create your work. The last thing you want is someone to challenge your results because of a simple miscommunication regarding what steps you took.

Budget Note

Rely on tests others have run. For most forensic imaging tools, and many other tools now in progress, NIST (National Institute of Standards and Technology) has produced a series of reports stating the results of their tests. You can find these reliable tests and their results at the Computer Forensics Tool Testing (CFTT) Project web site: www.cftt .nist.gov.

> **Note**
>
> It's important that you compare the version of the tool that NIST has tested against the version you are running. Changes do occur between versions, and they can affect your results. When in doubt, test.

The Forensic Data Landscape

When thinking about what will be examined in a computer forensic investigation, many people think about hard drives and stop there—but anything that stores electronic data may come under examination. For your first investigations, you will most likely see five sources of data:

- Active data
- Unallocated space
- Slack space
- Mobile devices
- External storage

Active Data

Active data refers to data that the user can see when he or she accesses a system. Any nondeleted files or data that are currently active on the disk counts here. Every operating system/file system includes active data, and all the parts that make it up (logs, registries, files, e-mail archives, file system objects such as $MFT, and so on) are files within it. Almost any search tool can help you find data in the active part of the disk, but forensic tools are purpose-built to break down the data into its subset chunks, allowing you to treat your search terms uniformly across all data. This process filters the different data types and compound files into plain text, so that when you are looking for data, you don't have to think of 100 ways to type in your search term.

> **Tip**
>
> Not all forensic tools support the ability to filter and normalize data for searching. Make sure that you understand your tool's capabilities before relying on its results.

Unallocated Space

Unallocated space is just that—the part of the disk that is currently not allocated to any active data. Many people think the unallocated space is a continuous section of the disk, as if data is written linearly to the disk. Instead, however, the unallocated space is a conglomeration of unused space located in various sections of the disk that most forensic suites will show to you as either a large blob of data or segmented into fixed sized numerical chunks of data. This means that depending on how the file system driver decided to write out and reduce fragmentation on the disk and the amount of space that had been used prior to that, you can potentially recover documents that date back to the first use of the drive.

To find, extract, and analyze data from the unallocated method, you first have to locate it within the unstructured blob of data. There are two common ways to do this: by finding file signatures or by using keywords. Neither of these methods is limited to finding data in the unallocated space. Either may also find data within large blobs of data, such as the pagefile, swap space, or slack space.

File Signatures by Data Carving Tools

All the forensic tools covered in this book include a utility you can use to examine the unallocated space to extract data that matches a known file signature. A simple example of this is an XML document. An XML document begins with `<?xml>` and ends with `</<tag here>>`. A carving program can search through the unallocated space for any piece of data that begins and ends with known patterns, such as these tags, and then extract out the data for your review. This simplistic example can be expanded for documents, pictures, e-mail archives, system artifacts, logs, and anything else for which analysts find a reliable file signature.

Keywords

There may be times when data you are looking for is partially overwritten by other data. In such cases, a data carve will fail, because it requires that the end of the known file signature exist within so many KB or MB of the beginning. In those situations, you can take some known piece of information, such as an e-mail address, and review search hits within the unallocated space to manually carve out these partial files to the disk. This is a manual and time intensive process, however.

Slack Space

The slack space is a byproduct of how data is organized on a disk. No matter what the size of a file, the disk is structured into fixed-size blocks that store the data. Any unused space within the block will still contain whatever existed there before. This is true for very small files as well as large files whose total size leaves the last block unfilled.

By definition, data that you recover from the slack space is almost always partially overwritten. There are times when parts of the data within the slack space may still match a file signature, such as a JSON (JavaScript Object Notation) object left over from web browsing, but keywords are usually the best way to find relevant data within it.

There are several types of slack space: volume slack, partition slack, and

LINGO
JSON or **JavaScript Object Notation** is a mix of XML and JavaScript and is used to transfer data between a web browser and a web server without having to reload a web page. These are the objects that Ajax uses in the websites we've come to know as Web 2.0. We talk more about this in later chapters.

basically anything that does fill up the entirety of the space allocated to it may contain slack. "Slack" is a term of art that refers to the loose, unfilled part of some preallocated space. To have slack, the storage must not be able to control the block sizes it is requesting. As long as the block size is fixed, there is potential for slack.

Figure 4-1 shows a single sector that has been allocated for a new file. Why a whole 512 bytes? Because that is the smallest sector that a file can be assigned. Whatever remains from the previous file write in the same sector will exist as long as the new file does not fill up the entire sector. Most files are larger than 512 bytes, but unless they are divisible by 512, their last sector will contain data from the previous file that occupied the space—that is, the slack space. The same concept applies to volume slack or partition slack. A file system or partition might contain data from a past file system in unused parts of the allocated structure. Files recovered from the slack space are almost, by definition, partial data fragments, because they occupy the end of a sector.

Tip
If you are still having trouble visualizing a slack space, Figure 4-1 shows a nontechnical example. Let's say you have an old cassette tape—good for this example because it's one long continuous piece of recording medium, so you can think of it as a sector. You previously recorded Elvis on the cassette tape, but now realize that the Beatles are more your thing. However, the Beatles recording was not equal in length to the Elvis recording, so there is still some Elvis left at the end of the tape. That remaining Elvis recording is the data we can recover from the slack space.

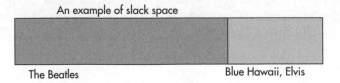

Figure 4-1 Understanding slack space

Mobile Devices

Cell phones, PDAs, tablets, i-Anything—all of these mobile devices that your suspect has written data to may become part of your investigation. EnCase and FTK both include modules that are able to acquire the contents of mobile devices, but more specialized suites are usually able to acquire a wider range of data.

Let's talk about what you can recover from mobile devices.

Standard Cell Phones

Even standard cell phones have internal storage for text messages and picture storage that can be recovered from the phone directly or the SIM card. What is recoverable from the cell phone will depend on the model, but the SIM card can be forensically imaged with any SIM card reader.

PDAs and Media Players

iPods, MP3 players, old PDAs—all of these devices have flash storage that has recoverable deleted data. What is recoverable will depend on the device and the operating system.

Smart Phones

iPhones, Androids, Symbian devices, Windows Phones, Windows Mobiles—all of these smart phones have flash storage and recoverable deleted data. All of them can be forensically imaged, depending on the OS version and your tool. You can recover not just text messages and images, but e-mails, documents, and Internet activity. The ability to recover not just what's on the device now but also what has been deleted from it depends on the software that you are using to acquire it. Check the vendor's product specification to know whether or not the tool you are using supports the type of data you are trying to get.

IMHO

I use Paraben's Device Seizure for its large support of phones, but I also use Oxygen Forensic Suite and Elcomsoft's IOS Toolkit along with other such specialized tools to get specialized data, such as a full forensic image of the flash RAM in an Android phone, that Paraben doesn't support. Know what your tools support before you promise anything.

In Actual Practice

Keep in mind that there may be issues with getting into a password-protected phone. Blackberries, for example, will wipe themselves if the wrong password is entered too many times. If you are trying to work with a phone that is password-protected, contact the requesting party for direction. In some cases, if the subject of the investigation is asked for the password, he or she will provide it. In other cases, if it is a corporate-issued device that syncs to a corporate server, the administrator may be able to reset the password for you.

Tablets

A number of tablets, such as the iPad, are on the market today, and even more are coming in the future. Running either a mobile or desktop operating system, they contain much the same information as a smart phone. They are also able to be forensically imaged with the same kinds of data you can recover from smart phones, with the exception of text messages or call records, as typically tablets do not have this functionality.

External Storage

External hard drives, DVDs, CDs, and thumb drives are examples of external storage. External storage can come in many forms, but all represent themselves to the operating system as a disk drive—meaning you can forensically image them with your existing tools.

What Do You Have the Authority to Access

Now that you understand the universe of data you can expect to run into during your first investigations, the question becomes, which of those sources do you have the legal right and authority to access? This book is not written for law enforcement, so you will not have a search warrant granting you the right to seize anything the suspect might have. We assume that you are either an employee of a company or are being retained by a company to investigate an employee. To determine whether you have the authority to access data, you should answer the following questions.

Who Hosts the Data?

If you are dealing with data stored on a server or an e-mail account, have you determined who hosts it? If the company you are working for does not directly host the data you are looking to access, does the company pay for and have the right to access the data of its employees on it? If the answer to both of these questions is no, you generally do not have the authority to access the data. If you answered yes to one or both of the questions, you are generally in the clear to access it.

In Actual Practice

Authority gets even more complicated with the new cloud hosting systems that are becoming more profitable. In a cloud-hosted environment, you typically do not have full administrative access to the underlying operating system that contains the logs and deleted files you might need in your investigation. In these cases, you have to work with the cloud-hosting provider to get the information they are willing to provide to you, possibly for a charge, and most definitely with some kind of restrictions of its use.

Who Owns the Device?

Is this a company-owned device or is it owned by the suspect? In general, if the company owns the device, you, as their agent, have the right to access its contents when instructed to do so. If the device is owned by the suspect, you may not have the legal right to access it, depending on your country, legal, and/or HR department's policies.

Tip

When in doubt, ask for authorization to access a device in writing, which in these modern days includes e-mail.

In Actual Practice

This will become a more common problem as the bring-your-own-device (BYOD) policies are implemented in corporate-land. BYOD might seem like a great cost-savings measure, but it becomes a nightmare when it comes to investigations, e-discovery, and data breach issues. Remember, though, that corporations can try to get the subject's consent in writing. It is amazing how often people will allow access when asked for it.

Expectation of Privacy

Before you begin looking into the private life of your suspect on a company owned, hosted, or provided device or service, you need to check with your HR and/or legal department to make sure their policies and your country's laws state that there is no expectation of privacy. If they have not formally stated this to the company's employees, then evidence recovered in your investigation may be ruled inadmissible.

Privileged Communications

Part of the expectation of privacy is *privileged communications*, which include e-mails sent between an attorney and a client. There is case law to support that even on a company-owned resource, e-mails between an employee and his or her counsel are still inadmissible, even if the company owns the device.

Personal Communications

Personal communications in the United States are generally not protected unless there is a reasonable expectation of privacy. This differs in the European Union, where data privacy laws require that a suspect provide written consent to having a forensic image made of any system on which he or she may have stored private data.

We've Covered

In this chapter, we've prepared you for your first investigation. Much more is going on in your forensic investigation than just the technical aspects of analysis. You'll be expected to be the expert in your work, and all of the tangential legal and policy issues will become part of your vernacular as you move forward. When in doubt, ask for written approval or authorization until you feel comfortable. In the next chapter, we'll talk about how to choose the forensic procedures and techniques you will employ in your investigations.

How to follow an investigative process

- What are you being asked to find out?
- Where would that data exist?
- What applications might have been used in creating the data?
- Should you go beyond the scope of the investigation?

How to test your hypothesis

- Define your hypothesis.
- Determine a repeatable test.
- Create your test environment.
- Document your testing.

How to assess the forensic data landscape

- Work with active data.
- Evaluate unallocated space.
- Search slack space.
- Assess mobile devices.
- Work with external storage.

How to determine what you have the authority to access

- Who hosts the data?
- Who owns the device?
- What types of privacy are expected?

CHAPTER 5

Choosing Your Procedures

We'll Cover

- Forensic imaging methods
- How to determine your comfort level with various methods
- How to create standard forms and a lab manual

Chapter 4 discussed how to approach and prepare for your first investigation. In this chapter, you'll learn how to decide what forensic imaging procedures (which are covered fully in Chapter 8) you are best suited to use. A wide set of established procedures and knowledge is available to you, but the choice of which you can use with the least amount of risk to your case is what this chapter is about. Your first decision, and one of the most important, is to choose which procedures you will make part of your standard practices when imaging and examining media for your investigation.

Forensic Imaging

The first step in any computer forensic examination is creating a forensic image of the media you are going to examine.

You'll need to choose which type of forensic imaging methods you will use, such as the following:

- Forensic imaging with hardware write blockers
- Forensic imaging with software write blockers
- Forensic imaging with dedicated devices
- Forensic imaging of live systems
- Forensic imaging using custom boot CD/DVDs

LINGO

A **forensic image** is not like what most IT people think of when they think of imaging. Unlike an image made with Acronis, Norton Ghost, or other system deployment tools, a forensic image captures not only the part of the storage media in use by the system, but also the rest of the media known as the *unallocated space*. The unallocated space is where deleted items reside for recovery using forensic techniques. In addition, forensic imaging requires a hash value that uniquely represents the data residing in the forensic image; this value allows a future examiner to detect whether even a single bit of data had been modified since the forensic image was created.

Each of these methods will create the same forensic image as an output, and all are equally valid. The method you choose will depend on which works best in your situation and your comfort level with them. Your level of confidence in explaining and defending your actions will determine which method you choose.

IMHO

When I first got started in computer forensics, in 1999 (ancient history I know), we didn't have write blockers. Instead, we had two options: we could boot up off of a DOS or Linux floppy and transfer the data over the serial or parallel port (network was available if you did crossover—we didn't have access to a lot of RAM from DOS), or we could buy a drive duplicator. Back in those days, the drive duplicators cloned the disk sector-by-sector, meaning that the data wasn't actually contained in an image when I was done. This is why wiping a disk before creating a clone became so important. If you didn't wipe the disk first, old data from a prior drive might still be on the cloned drive, confusing you about what existed. We don't have these problems today, and we have a large variety of cost-efficient solutions that we couldn't dream of in 1999 (although I still wipe a reused drive prior to use as a part of my sanitization procedure to counter accusations of comingling of data from old cases).

Determining Your Comfort Level

So how can you determine what forensic imaging method you are best suited to defend? Answer the following questions as your guide. Get out a pencil and mark yes or no to each question. In doing so, you'll have a quick self-assessment that will help you determine which forensic imaging method is right for you.

There is nothing stopping you from using all of the following methods. What you will want to do is try those that you are most comfortable with and use the method(s) with which you have achieved the most amount of success. Over time, your comfort level will grow and you can revisit methods that may have advantages you can make use of as your investigations grow more complex. Remember that your first goal is to pick the method that you feel most comfortable with and can explain/defend the best.

1. Are You Comfortable with the Linux Command Line?

Yes   Consider using one of the many Linux bootable CD/DVD options for forensic imaging. They allow for a read-only environment with the option of using any tool available; many tools are provided on these bootable CD/DVDs, all of which will make a forensic image. In Chapter 8, you'll learn how to use a Linux-bootable CD/DVD to forensically image a drive.

No   Many times when using Linux bootable CD/DVDs, you will have to drop to the command line to resolve unforeseen issues with some systems, such loading RAID drivers or dealing with new device types. If you don't feel comfortable working from the Linux command line, you should look at other options.

Note
Although a Linux bootable CD or DVD can be modified to be read-only by default for any media attached, not all of these CDs and DVDs are, in fact, forensically sound. If you plan to use one and will likely need to defend it in the future, make sure you choose one that either has documented testing that shows it does not modify devices attached to it or one that you can test on your own and show the documented results. These results, documented before you forensically image your first piece of evidence, will allow you to defend your process later.

2. Do You Have the Budget for a Write Blocker?

Yes   If you have the budget, consider buying something like the UltraBlock USB Write Blocker from Digital Intelligence. Using UltraBlock or a similar write blocker, you can attach different types of media (UltraBlock products are available for IDE, SATA, SCSI, SAS, USB, FireWire, and other types) to your computer as a read-only device. This will allow you to use any type of forensic imaging or forensic analysis tools without risk of modifying the original evidence. For many examiners who are uncomfortable with Linux or who do not think they have the technical qualifications to defend their choice of a Linux-bootable distribution, a write blocker can help create a great sense of comfort, because they are designed not to allow writes.

Budget Note
Write blockers used to be expensive, averaging $1000 each. Now, with the multitude of vendors offering write blockers, the cost has dropped to less than $400. This makes the relative low risk of a write blocker accessible even to those on a low budget.

No   If you do not have the budget for a write blocker, don't be concerned that you can't make a reliable forensic image. Three other options are available at no cost. Linux-bootable CD/DVDs, USB write block Windows registry modifications, and Windows bootable CD/DVDs are all forensically sound. Keep reading through this section to decide which is right for you.

In Actual Practice

Write blockers are not perfect. There have been issues in the past that showed flaws in some write blockers, so make sure that you stay informed by following postings regarding the manufacturer of your write blocker to learn of any issues or updates to firmware: register for support, newsletters, and support forums. Also, make sure that you test to be sure it works before you use it.

IMHO

You don't have to choose only one method. I use every method available to me, depending on what the case requires. I always prefer the method that will complete the forensic image the fastest, because all write blockers equally protect the integrity of the image when the process is performed correctly. Which method you choose depends on which machine you are forensically imaging.

3. Do You Have a Large Budget but a Low Tolerance for Risk?

Yes   This book is not meant for criminal investigations, for those who might face them, or for those who have a lower tolerance for risk. You can apply more funds to achieve a lower risk tolerance with self-contained hardware forensic imaging systems. These remove the operating system and user error from the picture in most situations. They can be quite pricey, at the time of this writing between $1500 and $4000 per device. An example of such a device is the HardCopy 3P, which can create a forensic image with speeds up to 6 GB a minute, with a very small opportunity for user error. That's not to say, however, that these units can't have their problems as well, and if you run into an issue, fixing it will require a firmware update from the manufacturer.

No   If you are not comfortable with either the Linux or Windows command line and you have a small budget with a low tolerance for risk, you may want to reconsider moving on. If you plan to perform forensic imaging for your organization or for a client, make sure that you can provide the services they are expecting and that you can defend your results.

4. Are You Comfortable Testing and Explaining Windows Registry Changes?

Yes   If you feel comfortable making, explaining, and testing a change to the Windows registry and you are not afraid of regedit, then this is a great and easy way to write block USB ports. Windows 8, the current version of Windows at the time of writing, and versions before it, have a registry change that can place USB devices into a read-only state. Many people have tested this registry change and found that it does, in fact, protect devices from being written to from the OS. Applying the change to the registry will render any USB device plugged in afterward as read-only, which will allow you to create a forensic image using any of the programs discussed in this book. When you are done with the forensic image process, you can remove the device and set the registry back to normal, which allows you to write to USB storage devices again.

Note

For versions of Windows prior to Windows 8 and 7, you may have to reboot between the application of the registry changes to have the change take effect. Always make sure to test your particular operating system to make sure that the write protection is working as you expect.

IMHO

One of the largest difficulties of this method is choosing where to store the forensic image when you are creating it. Since you can't write to USB storage, you will have to write to another type of interface such as FireWire, eSATA, network storage, or another internal drive.

No   Not everyone is comfortable changing registry settings if they haven't done them in the past. As you get further into forensic examinations, you'll do a lot of work within the registry to recovery your suspect's preferences and history. If you are not comfortable with the registry now, you will be in a couple of years!

If you've answered No to all of the preceding questions, there is still one remaining method that you should consider. See question 5.

5. Are You Comfortable with the Windows Command Line?

Yes   If you are comfortable with the Windows command line, another type of bootable forensically safe environment exists, a bootable Windows forensic environment. You start at a command line, not a GUI though, so make sure you are comfortable with it.

A bootable CD/DVD Windows distribution called Windows Forensic Environment (Windows FE) treats all attached media as read-only unless you specifically mark it to be written to. This is similar to the functionality you can get with a Linux CD/DVD forensic distribution, except you can use all the standard Windows forensic utilities. Windows FE works well for many examiners looking for the benefits of a forensically sound bootable environment without having to learn another operating system.

NO The command line can be confusing to those examiners who started working in a graphical user interface. Hopefully, you have the budget to get a write blocker so you can stay in the environment you are comfortable with.

Note

If you have not answered yes to any question in this section, I do not have a suitable forensically sound imaging method to offer you. That does not mean one does not exist for you, however. Consider waiting until such time you can say yes to one of these questions, or consider limiting your examinations to cases in which legal action is not an option and thus the defensibility of your actions is not a concern.

Your Choice

Congratulations, you've completed your self-assessment. Now, take your list of yes answers and create a list of methods you have available to you. Your next task is to test the methods you want to use in your investigation. These forensic imaging methods are detailed in the following sections in this chapter and in Chapter 8.

Note

This chapter discusses traditional methods of forensic imaging. If you are looking for nontraditional methods, such as live imaging and capturing system memory, Chapters 7 and 9 discuss these methods.

Into Action

Create your list of forensic imaging methods by answering these questions:

- Are you comfortable with the Linux command line?
- Do you have the budget for a write blocker?
- Do you have a large budget but a low tolerance for risk?
- Are you comfortable testing and explaining Windows registry changes?
- Are you comfortable with the Windows command line?

Forensic Imaging Method Pros and Cons

There is no one best method for every situation and as new interfaces, techniques, and equipment become available what works best changes. Every method has its pros and cons.

Hardware Write Blocking

A hardware write blocker is a physical device that sits between your computer and the evidence.

Pros

- Hardware offers reliable write protection with documentation and testing provided by the vendor.

- Any forensic imaging program, operating system, or analysis tool can be used without the risk of modifying the evidence.

- In some cases, device-specific imaging programs allow for optimized forensic imaging.

Tip

Tableau, for example, provides the Tableau Imager, which allows for multithreaded forensic imaging. It is free and can be downloaded at http://www.tableau.com/index .php?pageid=products&model=TSW-TIM.

Cons

- The number of devices you can forensically image at one time is limited by the number of write blockers in your possession.

- The types of devices you can forensically image are limited by the type of write blocker in your possession.

- Hardware write blockers are moderately expensive.

Software Write Blocking

Software write blocking offers control that is either built into the operating system by design, such as a bootable forensically safe environment, or via a change to a setting, such as the Windows registry change allowing USB devices to be read-only to prevent writes from affecting the evidence.

Pros

- The number of devices you can forensically image at once is limited to the number of bootable CD/DVDs or to the systems on which you can place a registry change.

- With a bootable CD/DVD, you can image any type of media as long as it has drivers allowing the OS to recognize the media.

- Software write blockers are free.

Cons

- Software write blockers can be slower than hardware write blockers or dedicated units.

- Without good prior testing and procedures, software write blockers can fail.

Dedicated Units

Dedicated forensic imaging units such as Logicube Talon or Hardcopy 3 allow even nontechnical users to forensically image a device safely. Liquid crystal display (LCD) touch menus allow the user to access the interface to capture forensic images without an operating system or additional computer.

Pros

- These devices are created for the sole purpose of creating forensic images.

- They are typically the fastest method of imaging.

Cons

- They are typically expensive.

- The number of devices you can forensically image at one time is limited by the number of dedicated units in your possession.

- Many types of media are not supported by dedicated units.

- Issues with the hardware require a firmware update to fix.

IMHO

When I started performing forensic imaging, I relied on Linux and DOS boot floppies. I've moved on to Linux boot CDs and hardware write blockers (now that they are so affordable). Having said that, I'm always looking for new methods and will always choose the method that gets me a reliable forensic image in the fastest way possible.

Creating Forms and Your Lab Manual

One of the most difficult things to get together when you are starting your lab and defining your chosen methods is creating the forms you will use. For years, people have been asking each other on forums, mailing lists, and conferences, "Hey, does anyone have sample forms?" Most people are hesitant to share their internal forms because they are unsure of their quality or they fear they will be revealing some kind of weakness.

IMHO

When you're starting out in computer forensics, it can be difficult to understand what kinds of forms you'll need. Many people latch on to any rumor, theory, or voodoo ritual they can find to create forms that prove that their evidence will be admissible in court. I've been testifying since 2003, and I've walked through the authentication and admission process for evidence many times; it is not as complicated as people make it. Here's a simple tip: After creating an image, fill out a form that identifies where it came from and how you forensically imaged it, that validates that your hashes match, and that indicates when the evidence is no longer in your custody. That's it! The notes about how you imaged it and validation of the image are not actually part of the chain of custody process; they are just there to help you remember in the future when you are asked.

A number of groups have attempted to put together a standard set of forms and documents, but I've seen only one that truly solves the problem, from the Scientific Working Group on Digital Evidence (SWGDE) at www.swgde.org. SWGDE is a combination of law enforcement, government, industry, and academia that works together creating standards and documents for anyone's use. These documents and this group's hard work are your best friends. They provide a set of peer-reviewed and approved forms that you can use today and have the security of their validation. The following sections discuss the need for specific forms and where to get them from SWGDE for your customization and use.

Chain of Custody Forms

The chain of custody form we adapted for *Hacking Exposed: Computer Forensics* (McGraw-Hill, 2009) was a popular download. Chain of custody forms, as simple as they should be, are easily the most feared forms to make for someone new to the field.

Although I have adapted our updated form at G-C Partners, LLC (www.g-cpartners .com,) for this book, you don't have to use mine. SWGDE offers a sample chain of custody

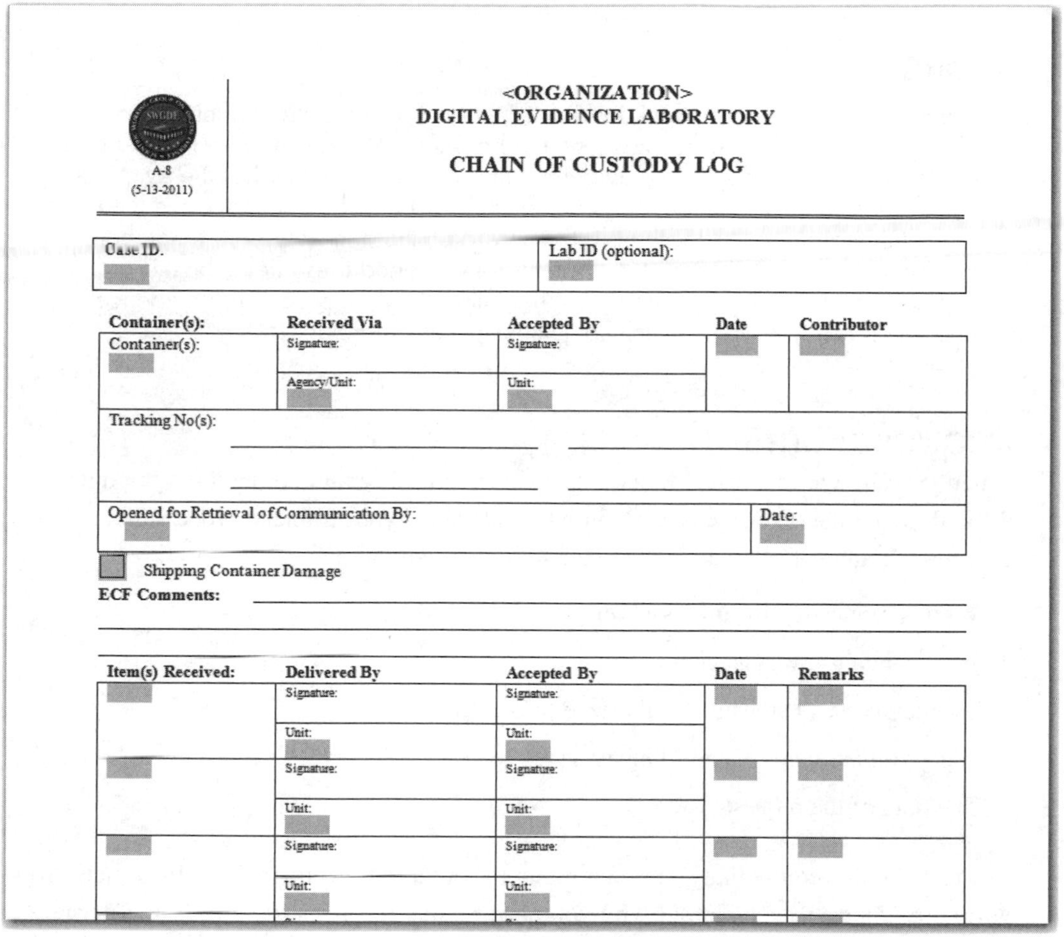

A-8
(5-13-2011)

<ORGANIZATION>
DIGITAL EVIDENCE LABORATORY

CHAIN OF CUSTODY LOG

Case ID.	Lab ID (optional):

Container(s):	Received Via	Accepted By	Date	Contributor
Container(s):	Signature:	Signature:		
	Agency/Unit:	Unit:		
Tracking No(s):				
Opened for Retrieval of Communication By:			Date:	

Shipping Container Damage

ECF Comments:

Item(s) Received:	Delivered By	Accepted By	Date	Remarks
	Signature:	Signature:		
	Unit:	Unit:		
	Signature:	Signature:		
	Unit:	Unit:		
	Signature:	Signature:		
	Unit:	Unit:		

Figure 5-1 The SWGDE sample chain of custody form

form that is simpler than mine, and you can download it from www.learndfir.com (the SWGDE link is too long to type).

The SWGDE form, A-8-ChainOfCustody-05132011.doc, is shown in Figure 5-1. It is true to the definition of what a chain of custody form should be: It defines what was taken into your custody, who it was received from, any defects, and who it was transferred to. At its most basic, this is all a chain of custody form needs to have. The *Hacking Exposed* form goes beyond this to help you as the examiner, but either form will hold up equally well in a court of law.

IMHO

I've said this before but I think it bears repeating. The additional fields in our *Hacking Exposed* form, available on the book's web site, are there for you and not to track the custody of the evidence. Information such as what the evidence was forensically imaged with, the name of the user of the computer, the time zone the computer was in, the BIOS time are all there to help you remember this information if you need it in the future. I've added these fields based on my experience in the field and find them helpful both when processing evidence and when testifying to it, which sometimes occurs years apart.

Request Forms

When you are working inside of a company as a forensic examiner, you may find it difficult to get the people you work with to understand your forensic process and needs. Creating a request form that captures the following will help:

- Who is requesting the information
- Who is being investigated
- The devices you are being authorized to access
- What you are being asked to investigate
- The date of the request

You should require that your coworkers fill out a request form. This information will help you easily recall later why you performed your investigation. If an internal investigation gets political, having this documentation can help protect you from unhappy executives.

Report Forms

Everyone looks for sample reports, and many forensic tools come with some kind of reporting option. In this book, Chapters 16 and 17 are dedicated to report writing. Our friends at SWGDE also offer a sample report available for your use if you are looking for an alternative trusted template to use. The form, A-1-REX-05132011.doc, provides a good baseline report that you can fill in. Your work will be judged by the report, so don't just generate a report from a forensic tool—take the time to fill out a report template like the one from SWGDE (shown in Figure 5-2) and explain in human terms what you've found. For more on this topic, read Chapters 16 and 17.

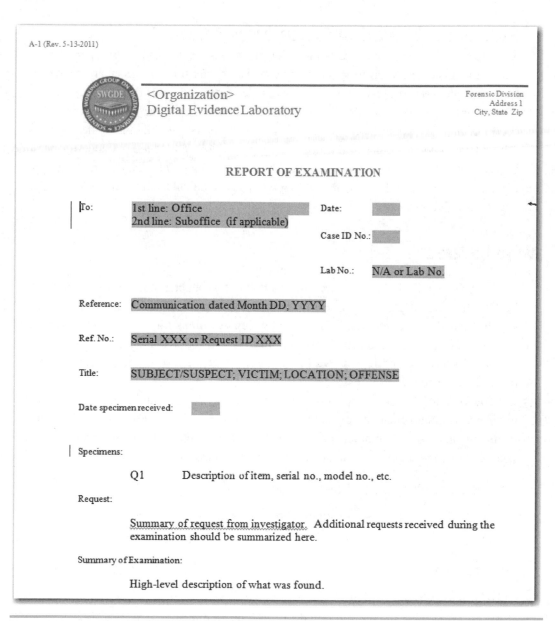

Figure 5-2   SWGDE Report of Examination

Standard Operating Procedures Manual

More labs are getting accredited, and more organizations are demanding transparency and repeatable processes. Many people have defended computer forensics as an art that cannot be turned into a series of processes; however, to be considered a true forensic science, our process must be repeatable. SWGDE has issued a framework standard operating procedures (SOP) manual that you can customize to fit your environment; it will quickly help you get started toward documenting your processes and procedures. The "Model Standard Operating Procedures for Computer Forensics" should be your starting point toward formalizing your lab and helping you scale it as your needs grow; you can download it from the web site www.learndfir.com.

We've Covered

You've been exposed to a lot of new information in this chapter, but we're not done yet. In the following chapters, you'll learn how to test your tools and handle nontraditional situations, and you'll be introduced to step-by-step directions for how to capture forensic imaging before we get into actual forensic analysis. This book is meant to get you started on your first computer forensic investigations; you have the rest of your career to master this field and become a success.

You've learned how to select processes, how to choose tools and procedures, and how to create the documentation you need. As you continue reading, we'll start getting into the technical areas of computer forensics, but the foundation of processes and procedures you've learned in these early chapters will form the foundation of your success.

Forensic imaging procedures

- Several risks are associated with different forensic imaging methods.
- Pros and cons are associated with different forensic imaging methods.

How to determine your comfort level with various methods

- Determine your comfort level with various methods.
- Be aware of the different traditional forensic imaging methods.

How to create standard forms and a lab manual

- Use example forms from Hacking Exposed or the SWGDE.
- Create a standard operating procedure manual for your lab.

CHAPTER 6

Testing Your Tools

We'll Cover

● How and when to test your tools

● Where to get test evidence

● How and where to access forensic challenges

● How and where to access tool testing images

In Chapter 5, you learned how to choose your forensic imaging method, and in Chapter 8, you will learn about forensically imaging a system. In this chapter, you'll learn about the tools and techniques you can use to test the forensic tools and procedures you use.

The first thing you need when you are going to test something is something to test against. If you already work in an established laboratory with ample evidence at your disposal, you can try to re-solve old cases, unless restrictions prevent you from accessing the evidence except for use in the original investigation. Alternatively, if you have the time to create sample images and know what you are trying to test for, you can set up test machines to image and look for what you have created.

The problem with both of these examples, however, is that they presume that you know the solution, or at least you know how to find the solution to the computer forensic puzzle before you. For this reason, many organizations—academic, government, and commercial—have created documented test images that will allow you to attempt to solve their scenario with supporting documentation when you need help.

In other cases, it's not learning a new forensic technique in a controlled environment for an examination you are preparing for, but rather testing to see if your tool is correctly interpreting an artifact. In such a case, obtaining a documented test image will allow you to compare the results of different tools so that you can cross-validate your results if you are unsure or challenged on a finding.

When Do You Need to Test

An investigator usually decides to look for test images for three reasons:

● To collect data for public research or presentations

● To test a forensic method

● To test a tool

Collecting Data for Public Research or Presentations

As you expand your skills and knowledge in the field of computer forensics, you may find new and novel ways to accomplish analysis, or you may discover new computer forensic methods. When you present you findings, however, the original evidence that you examined when you discovered the technique will likely be confidential. This means that you can't publicly disclose how you proved that the artifact existed and what it meant.

In such cases, you'll need to re-create your findings either on a test forensic image that you create yourself or on someone else's test forensic image that they've made publicly available. Presenting your findings, in the form of a blog, paper, or conference presentation, for example, means that you must grant other people the means to re-create your work. It would not be very helpful, of course, if you told them about some great thing you discovered but couldn't explain how they might re-create it for themselves. In addition, if you were to go to a court of law, you would have to disclose your method, since the opposing expert will be allowed to verify your findings.

Testing a Forensic Method

When you are testing a method you have never attempted before, it is wise to use it in a controlled environment first, such as a forensic test image. This can apply to a new forensic imaging method, artifact recovery, or analysis technique that you are attempting for the first time. For instance, if you are attempting to recover deleted event log entries from Microsoft Windows, it makes sense to create or obtain a test image known to contain deleted event log entries. This allows you to determine whether your method is working correctly, because if you were to apply the method incorrectly, you would not recover any deleted event log entries. If you were to use the new method without testing, you might think your method worked, but you may have actually missed additional evidence because you weren't yet adept at working with the new method. Whether you use a preexisting test forensic image or create one yourself, the important thing is to understand what is contained within it so you can create good tests.

Testing a Tool

In much the same context, if you are using a tool for the first time, being able to test it against a test image means you can assure yourself that you are operating the tool correctly. If you were using a search tool for the first time, or you were using a new search feature of a tool you already use, searching for data that you know to exist in different ways will allow you to discover how your tool supports different search syntax. Even testing new versions of tools to see if their behaviors have changed can be helpful.

In Actual Practice

I have an evidence room full of old cases that I can use for testing new tools. When I get a new version of software that includes a new feature or a change to an existing feature, I will typically test the tool using a previously solved case to see how it works.

Where to Get Test Evidence

Getting access to evidence to use in testing a new tool was problematic in the early days of computer forensics, when most investigators treated their research as a secret and barely even shared it on members-only web forums. In those days, we had to create our own test images—a time-intensive process—or test our own systems. Testing your own system can be a risky proposition if someone demands to see how you tested it and you expose your own data to them in the process.

In Actual Practice

Even worse than exposing your own data is exposing your clients' data. If you are working to re-create something that may be shown to people who are not authorized to review the client data, you'll find that making a new test image to work from is even more important.

Since those bad old days, life has gotten a lot easier. Today, you can use multiple public sources of test evidence in your testing. You'll find forensic challenges and collections of images that are made specifically for tool testing available to download for free. Most of these images are raw images, so you don't have to worry about what tool you are using for testing. You can still create your own test evidence, and there are times when that will be your only option.

LINGO
A **raw image**, also called a "dd image," is a forensic image that has no container wrapped around it.

Raw Images

The EnCase forensic image format called e01 puts the contents of a forensic image in a compressible form, with its hashes contained within the same image. Other forensic image formats, such as AFF (Advanced Forensics Format, an open source forensic image format), .S01 (a raw image in a compressed .gz [gzip] format with hashes and geometry in a separate file), or AD1 (AccessData's logical forensic image format), are also forensic images made to be loaded into a tool but not supported by every tool. Raw images are just the contents of a piece of media dumped into either a single file or a series of files segmented by a fixed file size. (The industry used to segment images into 640 MB because that is the maximum size file that could be burned to a CD-ROM.)

The most common tool used to create raw images is dd, which stands for data description; it creates copies of just about any type of data without trying to interpret or convert that data, unless told to, leading to reliable forensic images. dd is an open source tool that is available on every major platform. Because the images are just dumps of a raw disk or device, every tool supports the image format. The other added benefit of raw images is that they can be mounted as disks within tools such as VMware to experience the system as the user did.

Creating Your Own Test Images

There are times when you are trying to test something but you have no test image. This may occur because you are testing a server-based application that is not included in most test images, such as e-mail servers like Microsoft Exchange or database servers like Oracle. Or you might need to test a specific version of an operating system or application and no test image is available. In such cases, you can create two types of test images that involve different levels of effort.

Creating a Test Image from a Virtual Machine

If you do not need to test any results from the unallocated space, a virtual machine may be the best place to create your test image. Although you can create a fixed disk within a virtual machine that you can use to create a full image, a virtual machine is able to take snapshots of the active image as it changes. This will let you isolate system states for closer examination to see what changes occur as you interact with whatever artifact you are trying to re-create.

If you choose to create a test image from a virtual machine, you should do the following:

1. Install the operating system you are testing into a new virtual machine (using your choice of software).

2. Install the same applications and service packs/patches that are installed on the system you are re-creating. This is important to ensure that the same environment exists on both systems.

3. Create the type of data you are trying to recover or re-create.

4. Exit the virtual machine and either make a forensic image of it or feed it into your forensic tool directly.

Creating a Test Image from a Full System

Sometimes you need to test not only the functionality and artifact creation of an application or operating system, but you must also attempt to recover things from the unallocated space of the disk. In such cases, you can either work with a full image in a virtual machine or a fresh install on a new system that you can image afterward. Why a fresh install? Because you do not want software that may change or affect your results running on the system from an existing install.

If you create a test image from a full system, this is what you need to do:

1. Install the operating system on a new drive.

2. Install the same applications and patches that were running on the system you are trying to re-create.

3. Create the data you are trying to recover or re-create.

4. Create a forensic image of the disk. Unlike virtual machines, feeding in the drive directly to your forensic tool may change the state of your test evidence unless you hook it up via a write blocker. But even if you hook it up to a write blocker, we recommend that you create a forensic image.

Note
If you are using virtual machines for your test images, most forensic tools can now read the disk files directly, saving you a step on reimaging them as you try to re-create your artifact. EnCase, FTK, and FTK Imager all support reading virtual disk files, including VMware.

In Actual Practice

In addition to creating test images, you can create a bootable image out of an existing forensic image without modifying its contents. Using programs such as SmartMount from ASR Data or Live View, you can boot a forensic image inside of a virtual machine. Any changes you make will be stored in an "overlay" file, so they will never affect the forensic image itself. Obviously, it's a good idea to do this on a copy of the forensic image and not the original forensic image you made. With the original system booted into a virtual environment, you can try to re-create events using the exact configuration that your suspect used, which can yield very reliable results.

Forensic Challenges

Sometimes you are not looking to re-create an artifact but to test your skills or learn some new ones. To help you and others do so, many organizations have created challenges that help you test your skills. Some challenges are made to let you compete against other examiners, with points awarded for the speed and thoroughness of finding an artifact. Others will ask you to solve a puzzle with published answers so you can have a helping hand if you can't solve it on your own.

As you progress as an examiner, you might want to enter some of your own forensic challenges. Remember that they will not be easy, so don't be disappointed if you don't come out on top in your first attempt.

Learn Forensics with David Cowen on YouTube

http://www.youtube.com/learnforensics

You'll find sample images and challenges for each of the analysis chapters in this book at this YouTube site. You'll find videos explaining how to work through each of them. Come on by and subscribe to extend your learning experience!

Honeynet Project

The Honeynet Project was originally founded as an Internet security research organization that focused on creating and publicly releasing honeypots—purposely vulnerable virtual systems in which researchers could observe attackers who broke into these systems. This research has grown to include a variety of malware and attack analyses that led to computer forensic research as well.

Honeynet Project Challenges

http://honeynet.org/challenges

Here you'll find current challenges that range from malware analysis, to protocol analysis and computer forensic analysis. At the time of writing, three forensic challenges on this page have been answered and are available for you to test your skills. (Notice I said "skills," as luck will likely not help you.)

The Original Honeynet Project Challenge

http://old.honeynet.org/challenge/

The first Honeynet forensic challenge is also the most well-documented one. If you are looking to learn more about computer forensics or to learn more about Linux forensics, this is a great starting point.

Note

In the answers to the challenges, you'll notice that most people use open source tools. Remember that an artifact can be recovered with any forensic tool that supports recovering it. So, for example, if you are using EnCase or FTK, you can solve the same challenges being worked on with The Sleuth Kit or other open source tools. The steps to solve the challenge will be different, but if you understand what is being asked for and how your tools work, you should be able to solve the challenge using any tool. This applies to any forensic challenge and not just the original Honeynet project challenge.

DC3 Challenge

http://www.dc3.mil/challenge/

The Department of Defense Cyber Crime Center (DC3) has been hosting forensic challenges yearly since 2007. The DC3 challenges are made not only to test the skills of computer forensic examiners, but also to advance the state of the art of computer forensics. To compete successfully in an active DC3 challenge, you not only have to recover artifacts, but you also have to develop new tools that you provide to the contest to solve previously unsolved questions. Teams of up to four individuals can compete and win prizes for solving and developing solutions to the year's hardest problems.

If you don't feel up to the current year's challenge, don't worry. The past years' challenges are all online with their answers, so you can keep learning without having to worry about who is judging you.

In Actual Practice

If you are thinking about participating in the DC3 challenge, make sure you inform your employer first, because to enter the contest, you must agree to provide to the public the source code of all tools made for the contest and techniques used to solve the challenge.

DFRWS Challenge

http://www.dfrws.org/2010/challenge/

The Digital Forensic Research Workshop (DFRWS) is a yearly conference that brings together individuals who are researching new computer and other digital device forensic techniques. Researchers from academics, government, and commercial enterprises come together to network and share information. Along with the conference is a yearly forensic challenge that focuses on a digital device—in the 2010 challenge that you'll find at this

URL, the device is a camera. If you are looking to expand your computer forensics skills beyond standard file systems and out to the cutting edge, these challenges will help.

SANS Forensic Challenges

http://computer-forensics.sans.org/community/challenges

The SANS challenge is well documented and includes a full scenario to help you get into the investigative mindset. Although, so far, SANS has issued only one challenge (it was a contest at the time), look for more from them in the future.

High School Forensic Challenge

http://www.poly.edu/csaw-forensics#challenge

If you are looking for a more novice-friendly entry into forensic challenges, this is a good place to start. The Polytechnic Institute of New York University (NYU-Poly) runs this yearly competition that allows high school students to test their computer forensic skills.

Note

Unless you are part of a team of high school students, you can't compete, but you can view prior years' images and answers at http://www.poly.edu/csaw-forensics/previous-winners.

Collections of Tool Testing Images

If you want to test whether a tool is working as intended, you'll find a special set of forensic images created especially for that purpose. These images are purpose-built to determine whether the forensic tool you are testing can find data, keywords, or artifacts that were placed within the image.

Digital Forensic Tool Testing Images

http://dftt.sourceforge.net/

The Digital Forensic Tool Testing (DFTT) project is an open source effort to create small purpose-built forensic images that can test individual forensic tasks. Tests available at the time of this writing include the following:

- Detecting extended partitions
- Finding a word in a FAT/NTFS/EXT3 file system
- Correctly handling daylight savings when retrieving files from a FAT file system
- Correctly recovering a deleted file from a FAT/NTFS file system

This set of images is then tested against tools, and their results are submitted to the project for public viewing. The images are meant for tests that are smaller and less formal than those that NIST offers (more about NIST next), but they are equally as valid in their conclusions.

If you are looking to test a tool that is new to you or to test a tool you have developed, these forensic images can be very helpful.

NIST Computer Forensics Reference Data Sets Images

http://www.cfreds.nist.gov/

The U.S. government–funded National Institute of Standards and Technology (NIST) has devoted a project to creating test images for tool testing. The Computer Forensic Reference Data Sets (CFReDS) project currently offers 11 forensic images with answers on how they should be solved using any forensic tool. If you want to do a more extended test of your forensic tool, these images will help you more than the DFTT images.

The Hacking Case

http://www.cfreds.nist.gov/Hacking_Case.html

This forensic image is particularly useful because it is so well structured. The image provides enough forensic artifacts within it to allow you to answer 31 questions based on the user's activities and application settings. If you are looking for a good case to use for training or to perform an extended test of a forensic tool, this is a great one.

NIST Computer Forensics Tool Testing

http://www.cftt.nist.gov/

This site offers prewritten reports that thoroughly document specific tests performed on computer forensic hardware and software. As of this writing, the NIST Computer Forensic Tool Testing (CFTT) program is testing hardware and software that perform one of the following tasks, and it provides the results of these tests to the public:

- Forensic imaging
- Forensic media preparation
- Write blocking
- Deleted file recovery
- Mobile devices
- String searches

Note

Overachiever? Already need more? Good for you! An updated list of sample evidence files is maintained by the Digital Forensics Association. You can find their list at http://www.digitalforensicsassociation.org/evidence-files/.

We've Covered

In this chapter, we discussed how to solve the problems that most examiners encounter early on—how to test their tools and get the images for testing. Knowing where to obtain test images and how to test your own tools or techniques is an important step in your career. Keep this chapter handy as you progress in your skills; you'll want to come back to these images often. In the next chapter, we'll review forensic analysis of live systems and when to employ these techniques versus traditional postmortem forensics.

How and when to test your tools

- You learned why you need to test your tools.
- You learned when you need to test your tools.

Where to get test evidence

- You learned how to create your own test images.
- You learned about the differences among several test image creation techniques.

How and where to access forensic challenges

- What challenges are out there?
- Which challenges are friendlier to novices?
- Which challenges are made for more experienced investigators?

How and where to access tool testing images

- You learned about simple forensic tool testing images.
- You learned about complex forensic tool testing images.
- You learned about computer forensic tool test reports.

CHAPTER 7

Live vs. Postmortem Forensics

We'll Cover

● Advantages and risks of live forensics

● When live forensics is the best option

● Tools for live forensics

● Advantages and risks of postmortem forensics

● Postmortem memory analysis

Traditionally, and promoted heavily in this book, postmortem forensics is the recommended usual method of performing forensic examinations. Postmortem is a low-risk proposition to most investigators who are trying to solve crimes that happened in the past 6 to 12 months. However, with the growth of incident response methods and investigations of activities as they are occurring, the advantages of live forensics are swaying many examiners in that direction. A large and growing debate in the computer forensic and incident response community is focused on the advantages and disadvantages of live system forensics versus postmortem forensics. This chapter covers the pros and cons of both approaches and some live forensics–specific tools and techniques.

LINGO
As the name would imply, during a **live forensics** examination, you are examining a live system. In a live forensic scenario, you would log into the system, if you're not already logged in, attach an external storage device or network storage location, and begin dumping data from the running system. The main additional evidence in a live forensics examination, beyond the hard drives, is the content of the system memory. This information is quickly lost once the machine is powered off, so live forensics is the best way to access it.

LINGO
Postmortem forensics refers to the examination of a "dead" computer. Postmortem forensics indicates that at the time the evidence was captured, the system was powered off. The evidence you are reviewing is from a powered-off system.

Live Forensics

The biggest advantage of live forensics is that it offers the examiner the ability to capture the information stored in memory. Using the tools detailed in this chapter, you could preserve the contents of the running systems memory and map those contents back to the programs that stored them. Two major scenarios benefit the most from live memory analysis: The first is malware that resides only in memory (without live memory preservation, you may have never found it). The second is the potential ability to recover authentication and encryption passwords loaded into memory.

Live forensics can pose high risks, depending on the precautions that you take. For example, if you are preparing to perform live forensics on a system and you cannot disconnect from the network, you are risking an external user wiping information from the system before you can preserve it.

Another major risk in live forensics regards the tools or actions you use; these can have an impact on what is retrievable as well. The larger the tool you load into memory, the more you have overwritten data that was previously contained in the page file, and if you are saving data onto the local disk, you are overwriting potentially recoverable deleted files.

Always consider the impact of your tools on the system and what your ultimate goal in recovery is to determine whether these risk factors are relevant to your investigation. Also make sure to document all the tools and steps you followed when performing live forensics, because you'll need to show what changes your actions made to the system.

In Actual Practice

If you are performing live forensics from incident response, you more than likely are not interested in all the deleted data on the system. Instead, you are more concerned about what rootkits and other malware have been loaded onto the system, which memory analysis can reveal to you. When you know that deleted files are not going to be as critical to your examination, or that litigation will not follow your investigation, you do not have to be concerned as much about the changes you've made to the system in your live forensic review.

Just because you are examining the system live does not mean you shouldn't preserve a forensic image of the system. Being able to preserve the system as it stands in both memory and storage allows you to go back and look deeper if this is required in the future.

Caution

Remember that if you are going to preserve evidence, do it *before* you begin your analysis, or else you'll be changing files and/or dates you will want to rely on at a later date.

When Live Forensics Is the Best Option

In several scenarios, live forensics becomes a better option than postmortem forensics.

Caution

If we don't list a scenario you are facing and that you are considering using live forensics for, don't assume that you shouldn't continue down a live forensics path. Use your best judgment, and, when possible, inform whoever is requesting you to do the work of the risks involved in live forensics to make sure they understand them before authorizing you to use these techniques.

Live Imaging

If you are looking to investigate a production server, but you are mainly interested only in postmortem analysis, you can make a forensic image of the live system; we call this *live imaging*. Live imaging is ideal, for example, when you're working with a system with a large volume of data, and it can't be taken offline for the amount of time you require to forensically image it. In those cases, the burden of loss from the system being down outweighs the traditional benefits of powering off the system and creating a forensic image. A couple other valid scenarios for some investigations includes dealing with RAID or SAN storage that would be too difficult to re-create offline, or perhaps there are no drivers for your forensic software to use when you're trying to access it as a complete disk from a bootable forensic media.

When performing live imaging, make sure that you run your tools from external storage, and store your evidence on external storage as well to minimize your impact to the system.

> **LINGO**
> When we discuss **burden** here we mean it in the legal sense of the word. A court will usually not make you perform a task that is too burdensome to bear, unless there is no other option and the likelihood that it will deliver evidence relevant to the case is high. In the case of live imaging, the burden of downtime in a production environment is a good reason not to follow traditional methods, and that counts even in court.

Incident Response

When you are working on an incident response case, live forensics is really your only option. The only way to track down an attacker who is live on your network is by using live forensics to start analyzing memory and track network activity. In these cases, postmortem forensics may be something you do after the incident is over, but live forensics is the standard for your analysis.

Malware Analysis

Malware analysis requires live forensics as well. Oftentimes, you must quickly understand what a piece of malware is doing and you need to inspect the system memory, which is best captured with live forensics tools. Once you have captured the system memory, you can parse it with third-party tools that are outside the reach of the malware, preventing it from being hidden and allowing you to find all the files it is touching and actions it is taking.

Encrypted Systems

If you are dealing with an encrypted file system, live forensics can offer you two advantages. First, some full-disk encryption packages will provide fully decrypted physical disk access once credentials are accepted; this means you can live image the decrypted disk without having to obtain the encryption keys. Second, there is a chance that the encryption package has kept the encryption keys in memory, which you can extract with live forensics and memory analysis.

LINGO

Incident response is becoming a broad term that is used to refer to any activity for which you are starting an investigation in immediate reaction to a perceived security incident. Incident response follows, for example, a network breach by an external hacker, a situation in which targeted malware is threatening your system, or if a virus outbreak or a network outage occurs. Many times when incident responders are describing their work, they call it "DFIR," which stands for digital forensic incident response and shows that they live on both sides of the fence. When I talk about incident response in this book, I am usually referring to external attackers.

LINGO

With **full disk encryption**, the entire storage device is encrypted; this includes the partition tables and the free space of the drive. The only way to get access to the decrypted contents of the drive is to live image it or get access to the key or escrow key to decrypt it afterward. Both FTK and EnCase provide support to load encryption keys from most manufacturers for on-the-fly decryption.

In Actual Practice

Newer versions of full-disk encryption software show the physical disk as encrypted even when the system is booted into the operating system. In those cases, there is no getting around having to decrypt the image afterward if you are going to create a full forensic image.

Nonsupported File Systems

Suppose, for example, that an investigation leads you to a legacy system with data you need to review on a file system that no forensic tool supports. You could create a forensic image of the disks, but other than being able to perform a keyword search or carving for known file types, you won't be able to see the structure of the file system. In such situations, live forensics allows you to make a backup of the system to an intermediary form (tape, zip, tar, and so on), depending on what the operating system supports. This is often the only way to preserve data in a reviewable form from these systems.

There are exceptions to every rule, of course. If the operating system stretched the file system across multiple drives in a volume storage pool, even carving may have limited success, since the data could be written across multiple disks.

In Actual Practice

Sometimes what becomes a legacy nonparsable file system will suddenly be supported. Such is the case of IBM's Journaled File System 1 (JFS1), the non–open source variant of JFS (JFS2 is open source and widely supported). JFS1 was the default file system for AIX, and until the last few years, it was not supported by anything other than another AIX system. Since then, EnCase now offers support for JFS1. The lesson here: make sure to keep up with current tool capabilities to find out if legacy systems might actually have forensic tool support.

Enterprise Forensic Tools

Your forensic software vendor might not come out and say it, but any enterprise forensic tool that deploys agents to remote systems to collect data is doing live forensics. You will hear arguments that this tool is slightly different from standard live forensic methods since the tool is preloaded, and thus its execution does not change the system radically, but its methods of access and the risks associated with live forensics all apply.

Note

Enterprise forensic tools can include any type of forensic tool that can access devices over the network and pull forensic images and other types of data. A few examples of these are EnCase Enterprise, AccessData Enterprise, and Paraben P2 Enterprise Edition (P2EE).

Tools for Live Forensics

I've talked about the need for live forensics and when its most appropriate to use, but I haven't really talked about how to take advantage of live forensic techniques. The main advantage of live forensics is that it offers you the ability to gather data that you normally wouldn't have access to, specifically the system memory of the running device. This section discusses how to preserve the system memory, several tools that can analyze system memory dumps, as well as other live forensic utilities that you will find helpful. I do not go into depth on procedures or techniques for memory analysis, because that is a much wider topic covered by other books, blogs, and web sites.

Memory Dumping

Before you can analyze the memory from a running system, you need a way to extract information out of the system and into a file. Every operating system has a different method to provide access to the system memory, so this section will detail tools that can accomplish this for each operating system. For security reasons, you must be logged in as the administrator, root, or superuser to dump memory from most operating systems.

Tip

Always remember to match your memory dumping tool with the addressing scheme of the operating system. For instance, if the operating system is 64-bit, make sure the memory dumping tool you choose to run in it is also 64-bit if you want to create a full memory dump.

Windows Once you have administrator access to the system, you can acquire the system memory using a variety of tools. As long as you are dumping the system memory into a raw format, all tools should be equal in their result. Which tool you use will depend on the version of Windows you are using and which interface you feel comfortable with.

- **Memoryze** Memoryze is a free but not open source tool from Mandiant that is actively being developed. Memoryze can not only acquire a memory dump, but it can also analyze it. You can download it here: http://www.mandiant.com/resources/ download/memoryze.

- **Mdd** Mdd, or Memory DD, is an open source tool from ManTech that allows you to capture the system memory. However, the tool is no longer updated as of 2009 and may not support newer operating systems. It can be downloaded at http://sourceforge.net/ projects/mdd.

- **DumpIt** DumpIt by MoonSols is the current replacement for win32dd and win64dd by the same author. It requires no configuration or switches; just run the program and obtain a full image of the running memory. You can download it here: http://www .moonsols.com/ressources/.

- **FTK Imager** Not only can AccessData's FTK Imager acquire a physical image of a hard drive, it can also capture the system memory into a raw file. You can download it here: http://accessdata.com/support/adownloads.

Linux In earlier versions of the Linux kernel, you could just use dd to copy the contents of /dev/mem, although many advised against this. Since the introduction of the 2.6 kernel, that pseudo-device has been removed, which means we now need other tools to gain access to system memory.

- **Fmem** Fmem is free and open source, when compiled it will create a loadable kernel module that will create a device named, you guessed it, /dev/fmem. Once the device exists, you can use dd to image it as you would any other device. You can download it here: http://hysteria.sk/~niekt0/foriana/fmem_current.tgz.

- **Second Look** Second Look is a commercial product from Raytheon that is unique in that it can acquire memory locally or over the network. The network functionality adds a dimension to Second Look that may make the price worth it, depending on your environment and need. You can find out more about it here: http://www.pikewerks.com/sl/.

Memory Analysis

Now that we have the memory dump we can analyze it. Like the tools mentioned so far, memory analysis tools come in various states of license and cost, but in the end all should show you the same information. What will differentiate the tools is the level of automation that exists to identify areas of memory that are either known issues or known to be of interest to an examiner.

- **Volatility**   Volatility, from Volatile Systems, is a popular and free framework for memory analysis. The community behind volatility is constantly increasing the capabilities of the tool. If you are looking for a more hands-on analysis framework, Volatility may be your best choice. You can download it here: https://www.volatilesystems.com/default/volatility.

- **FTK**   FTK, discussed throughout the book, also offers a memory analysis function. You can load in the dump created by FTK Imager into FTK and visualize processes to memory locations for quick review.

- **Memoryze**   Memoryze not only captures RAM, but it provides tools for analysis as well. The Memoryze community is largely focused on incident response and malware analysis, but standard forensic investigations are also supported.

Live Imaging Tools

I've talked about memory analysis, but that is only half of what I would recommend you preserve in a live forensic investigation. If you are going to capture the memory of a running system, you should also capture the contents of the physical disk. Having this data can at least help you determine a key fact or recover a deleted log or sniffer log left behind by malware. Two tools are useful for live imaging.

Caution
If you do not trust the system you are analyzing (for example, you think an attacker/suspect may have replaced the standard binaries with his own tools), make sure to call tools such as dd and others only from a statically compiled toolkit on your own CD, thumbdrive, and so on.

- **FTK Imager Lite**   FTK Imager offers a version called FTK Imager Lite that was made for live imaging situations. It's packaged not to be installed, but to be run from external storage devices. If you are live imaging a Windows system, you'll like FTK Imager Lite. You can download it from http://accessdata.com/support/adownloads.

Note
You must be logged in as an administrator to access the physical disks in Windows.

- **dd**   If you are live imaging a Linux system, nothing beats standard dd. There are a few variants of dd, such as the popular dcfldd, but dd comes standard on almost all versions of Linux. This means you don't have to add any software to the system and can write out your forensic image to any available network or external storage location.

Note
You must be logged in as root to access physical disks in Linux.

Postmortem Forensics

The biggest advantage of employing postmortem forensics is its low risk. When you are doing any type of preservation or examination of a dead or powered off system, there is no risk that an external threat can change or destroy the system you are trying to preserve or examine. In addition, postmortem forensics typically requires no knowledge of a password or other credentials to access the system, unless the drive is encrypted.

In Actual Practice

Having said this, there are risks in postmortem analysis. The biggest risk occurs during the forensic imaging process, when modifications can occur to the original evidence during the process. Even after you've captured 100 forensic images, all it takes is one careless action to inadvertently modify number 101. When you are performing live forensics, people understand and accept that changes will be made to the disk before making the image and during the imaging process. When you are forensically imaging a powered-off system, any change will be much more heavily scrutinized—that's not to say the evidence is no longer valid, but it does certainly require much more to defend it.

Postmortem Memory Analysis

So you want to get all the great additional information that you get from memory analysis but you are stuck with a powered-off system, or perhaps the events you are investigating occurred in the past? Worry not, because there are two major sources of offline memory stored for your review: core dumps and hiberfile.sys.

Core Dumps

Core dumps in both Windows and Linux can be loaded or converted into most memory analysis tools. Core dumps are created when an application error occurs and the application can no longer continue. In an attempt to help the developer diagnose the error, the system will write out the contents of memory to a file on the disk. In Windows, look for files with a .dmp extension. In Linux, look for files named Core or core.

Hiberfile.sys

On any Windows system that has ever been put into Hibernation mode, a file called hiberfile.sys will be written to the root of the system drive. This file contains a compressed but complete memory dump of the entire system at the time of hibernation. To access it as a standard memory dump, you have to convert it first; the Volatility Framework and other software tools such as those provided by MoonSols can help you do this. Make sure that you match up the version of Windows and type (32-bit or 64-bit) to ensure that the tool you are using supports the hiberfile.sys file you are trying to convert. Once the file is converted, you can load it into any of the memory analysis tools mentioned in this chapter.

Tip

This book focuses on postmortem forensics, but that does not mean that you shouldn't learn more about live forensics. If reading this chapter has whetted your appetite to learn more about live forensics, check out *Incident Response and Computer Forensics, Second Edition* (McGraw-Hill, 2003). You'll also find a growing number of books, web sites, and blogs, such as the SANS blog mentioned in Chapter 2, dealing with the subject. SANS forensic courses also highlight these topics.

We've Covered

Advantages and risks of live forensics

- Live forensic makes it possible to capture the information stored in memory.
- You have to manage the risks that come with live forensics.
- You learned how to decide when to use live forensics.

When live forensics is the best option

- Use live forensics in incident response.
- Analyze malware using live forensics.
- Deal with encrypted systems and live imaging.

Tools for live forensics

- Capture system RAM with live forensics.
- Manage the capturing of RAM in different operating systems.
- Create forensic images of live systems.

Advantages and risks of postmortem forensics

- Postmortem forensic imaging is low risk.
- You can perform log and attacker toolkit recovery with postmortem forensics.
- You can understand an attacker's past actions with postmortem forensics.

Postmortem memory analysis

- You learned how to get access to the past states of memory in postmortem forensics.
- You learned how to identify Windows and Linux memory dump locations and names.
- You learned about getting access to RAM dumps made from suspending a running system.

CHAPTER 8

Capturing Evidence

We'll Cover

- Creating a forensic image of a hard drive
- Creating a forensic image of an external storage drive
- Creating a forensic image of a network share

This chapter discusses how to capture evidence, in the form of a forensic image, from various sources. We will also discuss what you can and cannot recover from each source. Because you should always try to create a forensic image with a forensically sound method, we'll discuss the best methods for capturing images. We'll also describe the methodology and tools available for capturing images of mobile devices and other devices where we don't have the ability to make a forensic image without modifying the original evidence. (Note that this chapter does not cover the steps required to capture such evidence, because those processes tend to change quickly as technology advances.)

LINGO
When used to create a forensic image, a **forensically sound** method does not alter the original evidence. This means that some kind of write protection exists to prevent or intercept possible changes to the disk.

In Actual Practice

There are times when forensically sound methods won't exist for capturing images from a device. In those situations, you must document in your notes the fact that no other reasonable alternatives were available and, if possible, document what changes your process will make to the evidence so you can exclude those changes from any possible analysis in a separate document.

Creating Forensic Images of Internal Hard Drives

Hard drives are the most common storage devices that you will forensically image. You can create forensically sound images of the entire contents of hard drives. The following

sections cover two options for creating
a forensic image in a forensically sound
matter with free tools: FTK Imager using
a hardware write blocker and FTK Imager
using a software write blocker.

FTK Imager with a Hardware Write Blocker

> **LINGO**
> In this chapter, the drive we are imaging
> is called the **evidence drive,** or original
> evidence, to indicate the hard drive we
> are imaging versus the storage drive to
> which we are writing the evidence.

If you have chosen to purchase a hardware write blocker, you can use the following steps to
create a forensic image with FTK Imager. Before you start, be sure that you have removed
the evidence drive from the suspect's computer.

> **Note**
> When you order a write blocker, as with all of your other forensic equipment, you
> should read its manual before you begin using it. Some write blockers can be
> configured to become read/write, so always know your equipment. If your write blocker
> supports read/write, make sure it's set to read-only before continuing! Otherwise, you
> could modify the evidence!

1. With the write blocker turned off but the power connected, attach the evidence drive to
   the write blocker.

2. Connect the write blocker to your forensics computer using the fastest port you have
   available—in this example, I use external SATA (eSATA).

3. Turn on the write blocker. Here you can see a powered on write blocker with status LEDs lit.

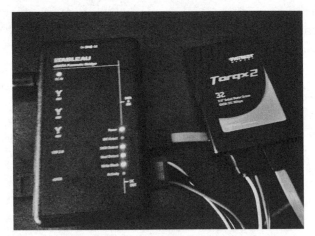

4. Run FTK Imager as Administrator.

5. From the top of the main screen, click the Create Disk Image icon, as shown here:

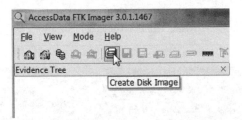

6. In the Select Source dialog, select Physical Drive and then click Next.

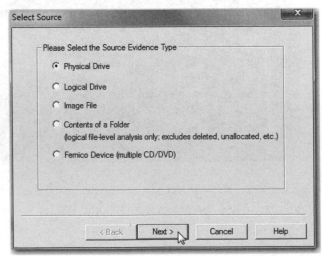

7. In the Select Drive dialog, select the hard drive you have attached from the drop-down list. Then click Finish.

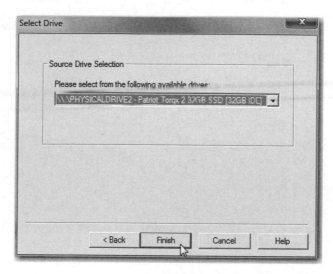

8. In the Create Image dialog, click the Add button to tell the program where to store the image.

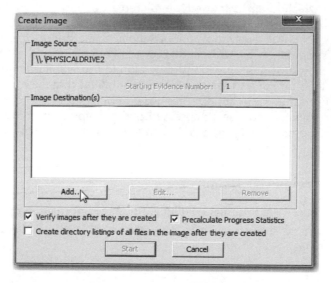

9. In the Select Image Type dialog, select the type of forensic image you want to make. I have selected Raw (dd). Then click Next.

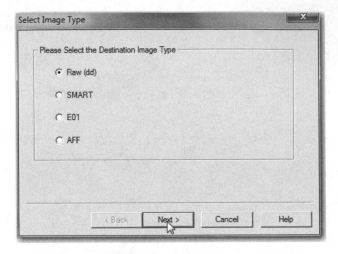

IMHO

Choosing which forensic image type to create depends on what you plan to do with the forensic image once you have created it. I like to create raw dd images because every tool supports them. Some people choose e01 (EnCase's format), AFF (Advanced Forensics Format), or s01 (SMART Format) because they know the only tool(s) they plan to use with the forensic image supports their format and they want the capabilities that the forensic image type supports. For instance, e01 images can be compressed and password protected. AFF files can be compressed and encrypted, and SMART images are just compressed raw images. When in doubt, choose Raw (dd) if you have the space to store it.

10. In the Evidence Item Information dialog, fill in the information to match your Chain of Custody form, as detailed in Chapter 5. Refer to Table 8-1 and Figure 8-1 to see how to fill in the fields.

Field Name	Description
Case Number	This does not have to be a number; it is simply an identifier of your choosing that represents the investigation.
Evidence Number	The evidence number starts at 1 for the first piece of evidence you capture and will go up from there.
Unique Description	I usually document the name of the custodian whose disk I am imaging here and what kind of computer it is.
Examiner	Your name goes here.
Notes	I will place any additional information here such as the serial number of the computer I took the drive from.

Table 8-1   Evidence Item Fields

Note

Just because you choose one type of forensic image does not mean you are stuck with it forever. FTK Imager can also convert between forensic image types, so if in the future you need the image in another format, you can change it without reimaging the original evidence. Migrating between forensic image formats will not change the forensic hash of the evidence contained within it.

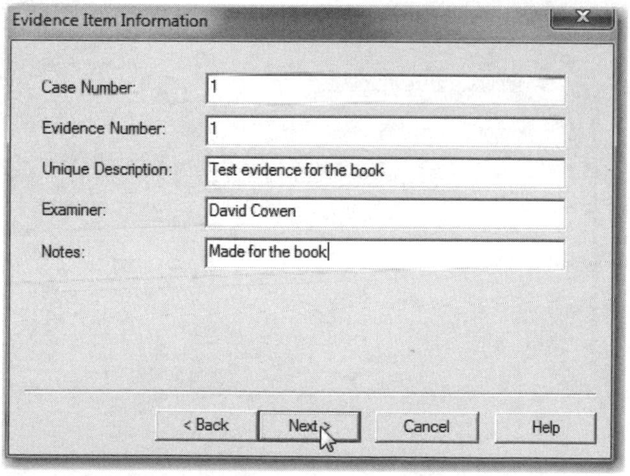

Figure 8-1   Filling out the Evidence Item Information dialog

LINGO
Message Digest 5, or **MD5**, is a 128-bit value that uniquely represents a data set of any size that is computed with it. Every time a piece of data is computed with the MD5 algorithm, it will have the same value unless the data has changed. Many people refer to these values as electronic fingerprints because they uniquely represent the content of a piece of data. If even a single byte of data is changed, the resulting hash will change.

LINGO
Secure Hashing Algorithm 1, or **SHA1**, is a 160-bit value, and unlike MD5, it has no known current weaknesses. The SHA1 hash and the MD5 hash provide additional validation that the data has not been altered. If even a single byte of data is changed, the resulting hash will change.

11. In the Select Image Destination dialog, choose the storage drive where you want to store the forensic image and type the name of the image, excluding the extension; this will be added for you depending on the type of image you have chosen. Then click Finish.

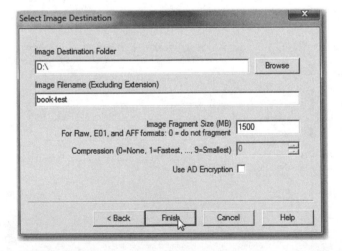

12. In the Create Image dialog, choose options at the bottom of the dialog. I usually select Verify Images After They Are Created and Precalculate Progress Statistics. Then click start. Figure 8-2 shows the forensic imaging in process.

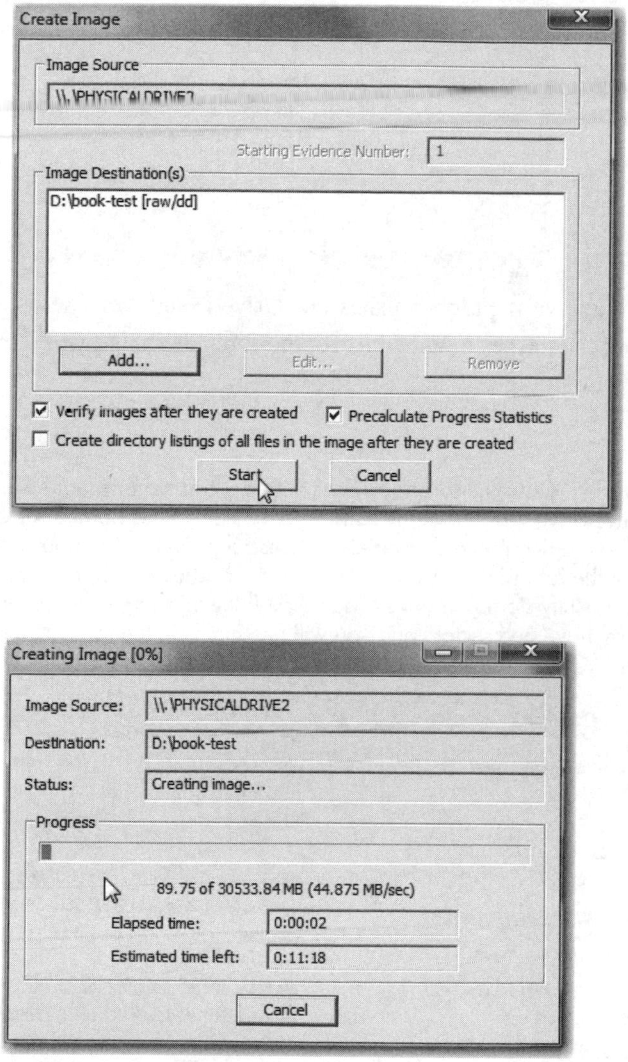

Figure 8-2 The forensic image being created

13. Once the image is created, verification will begin based on the options you chose.

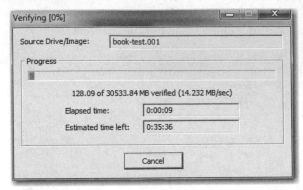

14. After the image verification finishes, the Drive/Image Verify Results screen will show you whether the hashes matched; if so, the forensic image was successfully created and stored on your storage device. See Figure 8-3.

Note

What are we verifying? As the forensic image is being created and data is being read from the evidence drive, FTK Imager is building two hash values named MD5 and SHA1. Once the imaging process completes successfully, we then compute the MD5 and SHA1 hashes of the forensic image we created. If the hashes match, then our forensic image was successfully stored on our storage disk. If the imaging process fails, the storage disk may have bad sectors and you will need to redo the forensic image.

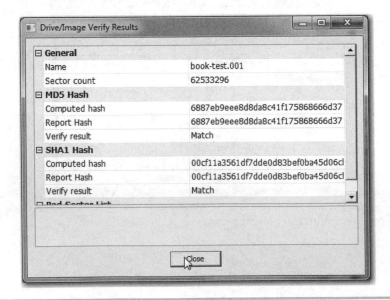

Figure 8-3   Verification shows that hashes match

In Actual Practice

If you are reading data from a bad evidence drive to begin with, you may not get hash verifications. The only way to know whether the evidence drive is corrupted is to attempt to reimage the evidence drive to a known good storage drive to see if you get the same error. If you get the same error, document the issue in your chain of custody form and do not return the evidence drive to service because it will likely die soon. If an issue is raised with the forensic image in the future, you have the option of having the evidence drive sent for repair with a data recovery company.

15. With the verification complete, click Close and you will see a dialog showing that the image was created successfully.

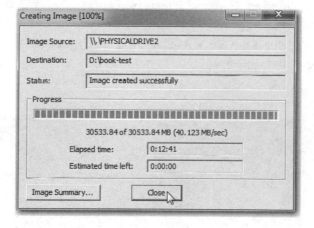

16. Update your chain of custody forms to indicate that the forensic image successfully complete and verified, and then power off your write blocker.

Note

All of the details about the drive's make, model, serial number, verification hashes, and options selected will be stored in a text file named after your image on the storage drive where the evidence was created.

FTK Imager with a Software Write Blocker

The only difference in methodology between software write blocking and hardware write blocking with FTK Imager are the first steps you take. This example assumes you are running Windows 7.

Note
All of your USB ports will be write blocked using this method. That means you must either have enough internal storage to store the forensic image within your system or another type of interface with which to attach an external storage drive to your system.

1. Download the disableusbwrite.reg registry modification from our web site at www.learndfir.com. Then double-click the file to start it.

2. Click Yes to indicate that you want to apply the change.

Note
If you are running Windows XP, you will have to reboot at this point. Windows 7 users can switch between USB write enabled and disabled between device plug-ins.

3. Your system is now software write blocked on its USB ports. Attach the drive to a USB port, as shown in Figure 8-4.

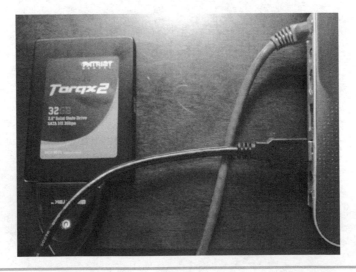

Figure 8-4   Attaching the drive via USB

4. Follow steps 1 through 6 from the hardware write blocking section to have FTK Imager create your forensic image. Instead of attaching a write blocker though, just attach the drive using a USB drive bay or USB-to-SATA kit.

5. In the Select Drive dialog, select a USB device to image.

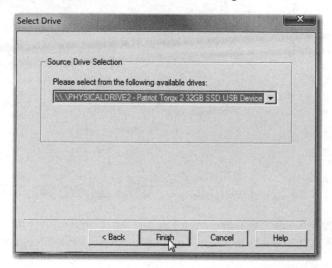

6. Fill out the Evidence Item Information dialog.

7. Save this image with a new name so you have both images created with two methods now on the D: drive.

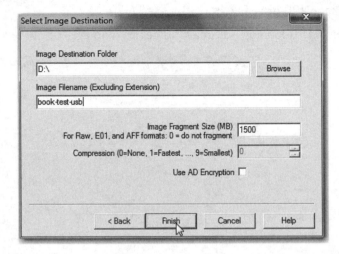

In Figure 8-5, you can see that the software write protection worked and our hashes are the same as the hashes produced from the hardware write blocking method.

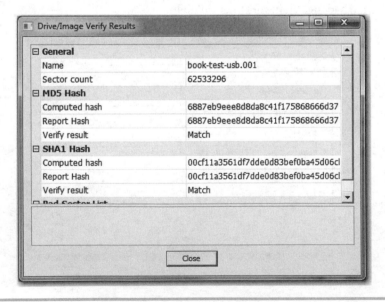

Figure 8-5 Software write blocking produces same hashes

Note

Don't forget that once your imaging is finished and successful, you need to apply the other registry key so that you can write to USB devices again (after you've removed the evidence from your system)—unless you want to leave your systems USB ports in a permanent read only state for external storage.

In Actual Practice

When working with methods such as software write blocking, which relies on the operating system to be successful, it is always wise to test your system before relying on it. Any service pack or system change can break a feature, especially one that is not well known or publically supported by Microsoft. When in doubt, test it out. Test that your system does not change the disk by running a test image of a drive with a known hash first to verify it does not write.

Creating Forensic Images of External Drives

If you have an external storage device and you do not want to remove the drive from its external enclosure for imaging, you can attach it to your system for imaging within the enclosure.

Note

Although there are multiple types of external drives, this discussion focuses on the most popular kind, USB, in this example. If you are dealing with an external drive for which you do not have either software or hardware write blocking support, consider Raptor (covered later in this chapter) or Win PE (not covered in this book) boot disks. Either solution allows you to have all connected and recognized devices be treated as read-only so that you can forensically image them.

We can create forensically sound images of the entire contents of external drives that appear as physical disks to the operating system. Here again you have a choice of hardware or software write blocking. When creating a forensic image in a forensically sound matter with free tools, you can use FTK Imager using a USB write blocker, FTK Imager using software write blocking, and write blocking with Raptor for Linux. The following examples will demonstrate how to acquire a USB thumb drive.

FTK Imager with a USB Write Blocker

Here you can see a USB write blocker with a thumb drive plugged in:

Figure 8-6 shows the Select Drive dialog, where a USB device has been selected to image. Other than the hardware device used to write block, the procedure for creating an

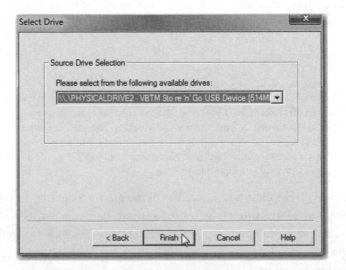

Figure 8-6 Selecting a USB storage device to forensically image

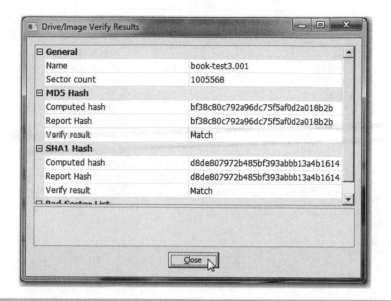

Figure 8-7 Hash verification results for USB write-blocked image

image from the thumb drive is the same as that for a hard drive. In Figure 8-7, you can see the hash verification for the USB write-blocked image.

FTK Imager with a Software Write Blocker

Using the same registry modification we used for software write blocking a hard drive, you can attach an external USB storage drive to our system and have it be write blocked. You would then follow the same steps as you followed in the preceding examples. In Figure 8-8, you can see that the hashes match between the methods.

Software Write Blocking on Linux Systems

If you are dealing with external storage that is not USB-based, or if you want to image a suspect's computer using her computer to do so, you can use one of the many customized Linux boot CDs that are configured to treat all drives as read-only until told otherwise. This example uses Raptor (http://forwarddiscovery.com/Raptor).

Follow these steps:

1. Download the Raptor ISO from the web site http://forwarddiscovery.com/Raptor.

2. Burn the ISO to CD-ROM.

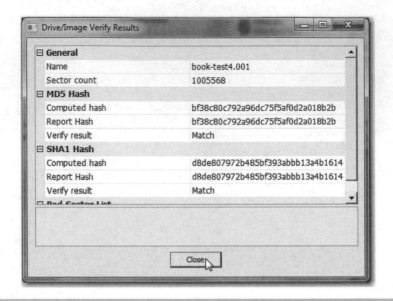

Figure 8-8 Matching hashes between the two write-blocking methods.

3. Boot either your system or the suspect's system off of the Raptor CD (depending on which system you are using to make the forensic image), making sure that the system is set to boot from CD-ROM in the BIOS.

Tip

If I am imaging with the suspect's computer, I will attempt to remove any drive cables from the evidence drive if it is accessible before attempting to boot from CD-ROM. Doing this prevents any accidental boots to the evidence drive.

4. Choose the default from the Raptor boot menu.

5. Click the Raptor Toolbox icon, which is the second icon from the top left and has a red border, as shown next:

6. Choose the drive you want to image and where you want to store the forensic image, as shown next:

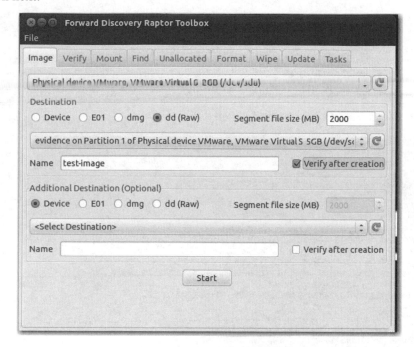

Notice that we are imaging the physical disk /dev/sda and writing it out to a dd (Raw) image located on a drive that was already formatted, with the volume name "evidence."

7. Select the Verify After Creation option to do the same hash verification we would do in FTK Imager or any other tool. Once this is set, click Start.

Note

As you can see, I am working within VMware in this example, so I can make good screenshots. The only difference in your system will be the names of the devices you are selecting.

8. The Imaging progress bar will appear:

9. The verification progress bar will start once imaging finishes:

10. Once the verification is done, a text file that has been written to your storage disk will be opened, showing the hash values generated in the verification process:

Creating Forensic Images of Network Shares

If you are being asked to capture the contents of a network share, I would recommend using a tool like FTK Imager to create an AD1 image. The AD1 image type allows you to store standard files and directories within a forensic image to prevent their modification and allow you to verify their contents at a later date by hash.

In Actual Practice

Other reasons to create logical images (such as AD1s or encases L01s) include dealing with encrypted data. If you find data within your forensic image that your tool can't decrypt within itself, you'll have to export that data out and then decrypt it. Since you want to bring that data back into your tool for analysis, putting it within a logical image prevents accidental changes to the data.

We can preserve all contents of a file or directory and its associated metadata, but we cannot recover deleted files from a network share unless we forensically image the server that is hosting it.

Capturing a Network Share with FTK Imager

To capture a network share with FTK Imager, follow these steps:

1. Load FTK Imager as you did in the preceding examples and click the Create Disk Image icon.

2. In the Select Source dialog, choose the Contents Of A Folder option, as shown next. Then click Next.

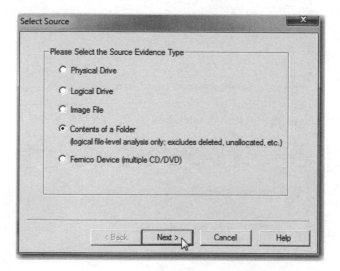

3. In the next dialog, click Yes to accept the limitations of the AD1 format.

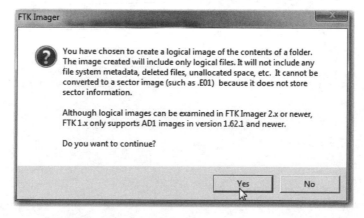

4. In the Select File dialog, click the Browse button in the Source Selection field to find the network share you want to collect:

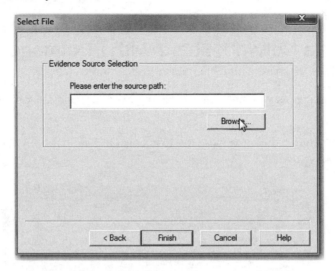

5. With the network path selected, click Finish.

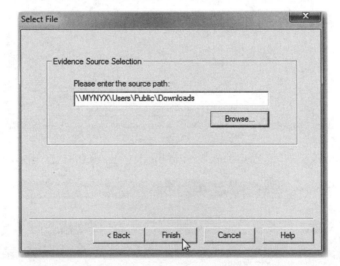

6. In the Create Image dialog, add a destination where the AD1 image will be stored, as in the preceding examples. In the same dialog, click the Add button.

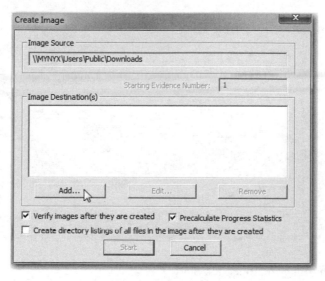

7. In the Evidence Item Information dialog, fill out the evidence information. Then click Next.

8. In the Select Image Destination dialog, choose where you want to store the forensic image, and then click Finish.

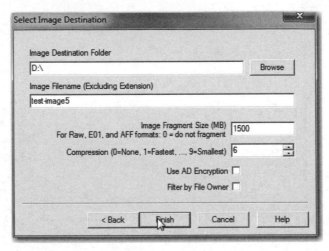

9. In the Create Image dialog, click Start.

10. Verify that the hashes matched, as shown next:

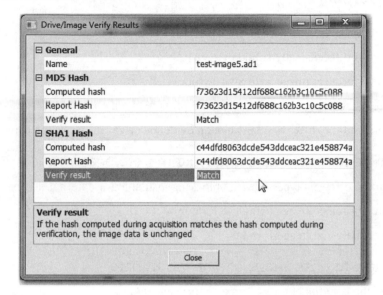

You now have created a forensic image that contains the contents of a network share. You can export data and copy the image as many times as you need without worrying about changing any of the data contained within.

Mobile Devices

Mobile devices include iPhones, Androids, Blackberries, tablets, and other devices being invented as we write this. Mobile devices change rapidly, as do the forensically sound methods that work with them, often changing with each version of the device. This means that any method we document within this book may no longer work with the newest device in your possession by the time you read this. With that in mind, we recommend looking to our blog (www.learndfir.com) and YouTube channel (www.youtube.com/learnforcnsics) to learn the current methods available to acquire the mobile device you are working with.

Servers

If you are dealing with servers and want to capture data without having to power off the system and remove the drives, we recommend turning back to Chapter 7 to learn about live imaging, RAID, storage area network (SAN), and network attached storage (NAS). To learn more, turn to the *Hacking Exposed Computer Forensics* books or our blog (www.learndfir.com).

We've Covered

Creating a forensic image of internal hard drives

- Understand forensically sound evidence.
- Create a forensic image with a write blocker.
- Use registry tweaks to make your USB ports read only.
- Understand the difference between an evidence drive and a storage drive.

Creating a forensic image of an external storage drive

- Learn the different types of write blocking available for external drives.
- Create a forensic image using the Raptor boot CD.
- Convert between image formats.

Creating a forensic image of a network share

- Know the benefits of logical images for data storage.
- Learn how to forensically image mobile devices.
- Learn how to image SANs and RAIDs.

CHAPTER 9

Nontraditional Digital Forensics

We'll Cover

- What is nontraditional forensics?

- When and why to use nontraditional forensics

- Understanding volatile system artifacts

- Memory acquisition and analysis

- Encrypted file systems and live system imaging

- Dealing with mobile devices

- Working with solid-state drives

- Virtual machine forensics

In previous chapters, you learned about building and equipping your lab, determining procedures, testing tools, and using the "correct" ways in which to conduct digital forensics collection as part of an investigation. I've stressed the importance of affecting the original evidence as little as possible during the course of your investigation, because under ideal circumstances you will make no changes to your evidence during the collection and analysis phases.

That said, there are times and situations in which you'll have no other option except to impact the system you are investigating to get the evidence you need. The constraints that require you to step outside of sound forensics practices may be technical, organizational, or an arbitrary whim of a client. In such situations, it is important that you have minimal impact upon the evidence itself, if you cannot have zero impact. This chapter addresses the most likely situations and scenarios that may require these types of collection and analysis and will provide you with specific steps and guidelines that you can follow to help minimize any contamination you might introduce to the system to help preserve the integrity of the evidence.

In many cases, a forensic practitioner will be given latitude to proceed in the best possible fashion during the course of an investigation. When it becomes necessary to deviate from accepted best practices in your approach to an investigation, it is important that you make sure you have authorization from the stakeholders to do so. You will generally be operating in such a way as to minimize any possible downtime of the computers you're investigating and without modifying the original evidence in any way. If you can't do the necessary tasks while satisfying both of those requirements, you need to make sure the stakeholders understand that, and you must work together to determine the best way to proceed.

If you're working in the corporate environment as a staff forensic practitioner, your management and legal department should be briefed on the situation to help them understand why you believe it is necessary to deviate from established digital forensic practices; they can help you make the appropriate decisions in a case. If you are working for a customer as a third-party provider of services, your customer must be made aware of the situation and then allowed to make an informed decision on how you will proceed. Never make assumptions about what authority you have; it needs to be explicitly stated.

Note

There are two areas in which digital forensics practitioners find themselves in trouble: overstepping their authority and failing to follow sound methodology during the course of an investigation without good reason.

Also remember that it's generally best to approach every investigation with the understanding that the evidence collected could end up being part of a civil or criminal case, and that being cautious and following proper digital forensic procedures will always hold you in good stead. If your investigation requires that you must break with accepted digital forensic procedures, make sure that you document the reasons for doing so and that you back up your actions and decisions with as much documentation as possible.

Breaking the Rules: Nontraditional Digital Forensic Techniques

Nontraditional digital forensic techniques are areas of digital forensic acquisition and analysis that come into practice when the tried and true methods of acquiring and analyzing static data from a system in a forensically sound way do not apply. As discussed in previous chapters, digital forensic examinations and investigations of computer systems are generally performed with the system powered off and focus on examining the stored data on a system's magnetic analog hard disk. This is accomplished with a hardware or software write blocker in place to prevent writing to the hard disk to avoid tainting the evidence and the state in which the evidence existed when the host computer was in its last running state.

Although this still makes up the bulk of most digital forensic work involving personal computers and servers, the ubiquity of network access, specifically to the Internet, has made the ability to gather information about running processes, existing and active network connections, and routing table entries a necessity during some types of investigations. And this introduces us to our first category of forensic artifacts that requires interacting with a live system and the use of these nontraditional techniques: volatile artifacts.

Volatile Artifacts

Volatile artifacts, to put it simply, are any system artifacts that exist only while the system is up and running. These include such things as system network routing tables, open and listening network ports, established network connections, cached login credentials of recently logged in users, running processes, passwords, and so on. The primary location for these types of artifacts is in system Random Access Memory (RAM), though they may also reside in the operating system page file or swap space. And because the purpose of a computer system's RAM is to store dynamically changing, nonpersistent data, it must be collected before a system is powered down. When power is removed from the running system to shut it down, whether that is by initiating the OS shutdown procedures or by severing the power connection from the AC outlet to the computer power supply, the power in the RAM quickly dissipates, removing any data that inhabited the RAM chips.

IMHO

In 2008, a team of researchers from Princeton University's Center for Information Technology Policy released a study showing flaws in full-disk encryption (FDE) products for Windows systems, where the encryption/decryption keys were stored in RAM. The attacks against FDE relied heavily on the persistence of data in the physical dynamic RAM (DRAM) modules used in modern computer systems for RAM. They found that many FDE products stored the keys in the system RAM, and the data could persist in the unpowered physical DRAM modules for seconds to minutes at room temperature before power completely dissipated from them and the data was lost. They also found that significantly lowering the temperature of the DRAM modules with readily available cans of compressed air could increase the amount of time that the data persisted in the unpowered DRAM modules. However, the longer the DRAM modules went unpowered, the more degraded the contents of the memory became until the power completely dissipated. So, although there are alternatives to taking a forensic memory image of a running system, they introduce complexity and increase the risk of losing a significant portion of the data over time. In this case, if a RAM image is necessary or desirable as part of an investigation, it is best to take it in the simplest way possible: when the computer is up and running. If you'd like to read more about this research, it can currently be found at *http://citp.princeton.edu/research/memory/*.

Incident response and *malware analysis* are two practice areas of digital forensics that rely heavily on the state of a running compromised system, and it is becoming common practice to take forensic images of the system RAM for later analysis as tools and processes become more commonplace for investigations in these practice areas. The reason for this is that although analysis of the static data from a hard drive can give you information of the state of the computer the last time it was running, it will not always give you a complete picture of the state in which the machine existed before it was powered down. There are some subtle and not so subtle differences here that are very important. As an example, the persistent routing table information for a Windows system can be rebuilt from the entries in the Windows registry by simply reading the key and value pairs listed under HKEY_LOCAL_MACHINE\SYSTEM\CurrentControlSet\services\Tcpip\Parameters\Interfaces\ and HKEY_LOCAL_MACHINE\SYSTEM\CurrentControlSet\services\Tcpip\Parameters\ PersistentRoutes\.

Running processes with elevated privileges, however, can make changes to the routing table of a Windows system, and these changes will be available only by examining the routing table of the system while it is running. On a Windows system, the routes in the routing table are manipulated and displayed via the route.exe program, which is executed from the command prompt. If someone, authorized or unauthorized, has added a route to the routing table of a Windows system via the command line using the route.exe program, it will be added to the permanent routing table only if the −p flag is explicitly used as part of the command. The −p flag indicates that the route is persistent across reboots and should be added under the last Windows registry key entry at one of the two locations mentioned in the preceding paragraph; the default behavior of the route.exe program is for any routes added to be nonpersistent. In the real world, you might see routes being added to the routing table with malicious software infections on Windows systems.

Malware

Malicious software, or *malware* for short, is a blanket term for several different categories of abusive software.

- **Computer viruses** Viruses are programs that embed themselves into files and spread on a computer system, just as biological viruses infect living organisms. Destructive behavior is not

> **LINGO**
> Wikipedia defines **malware** as programs intentionally "designed to disrupt or deny [computer] operation, gather information that leads to loss of privacy or exploitation, gain unauthorized access to system resources, and other abusive behavior."

a necessary characteristic of a virus, although many computer viruses are destructive. Mathematician John von Neumann came up with the concept of self-replicating computer code in 1949, although the first actual computer virus didn't appear until the 1970s and the term "virus" was not used until 1983.

- **Worms**   Worms are similar to viruses, but worms attempt to spread themselves to other systems via network connectivity. Newly infected systems also attempt to infect other systems. Worms usually target vulnerabilities in the software running on a computer that allows the malware to infect the system.

- **Trojan Horses**   Trojan horses, or Trojans, are programs that appear to be beneficial programs but actually cause harm. They tend to be gateways in which the various forms of malware listed here are installed on a machine. They are named after the Greek story of a large wooden horse that was given by the Greeks as a peace offering to the people of Troy. However, Greek soldiers were hidden inside the horse, and after dark they emerged and defeated the cities defenses, allowing the Greek army to enter and destroy the city.

- **Spyware**   These programs are used to gather information about a system and its users without the system owner or the users knowing the information is being gathered. Key-loggers, applications that record keystrokes on a computer keyboard, are one of the most common forms of spyware.

- **Scareware**   Scareware programs are designed to cause anxiety in users by misleading them to believe that their computer is suffering a problem or is infected with a virus; the program's owners want to charge you money to fix the "problem." These programs are designed to look as much like legitimate software or system messages as possible to fool people into paying to have their computers "fixed."

- **Crimeware**   This is a relatively new term coined to describe malware specifically designed for identity theft and financial fraud.

When malware is installed on a system, one of the first things it does is make sure that it will always be running when the system is running. This is most often accomplished by adding a key into the registry in one or more locations that causes the system to execute the malware program each time the system boots up or a user logs in.

The program's next step is to make it as difficult as possible for malware to be removed from the system, most often by disabling running antivirus software or at least removing the antivirus software's ability to update itself and its signatures. This is often accomplished by simply adding routes to the routing table that send all traffic for the networks used by antivirus companies or malware reporting sites into a black hole of sorts, making them unreachable by the computer. Because these routes do not persist across reboots of the system and get added when the malware executes on system startup or user login, there will be no evidence of the routing table changes performing a standard static analysis of the system hard drive. The only way to get to these types of volatile artifacts is via the running system RAM.

When I first started talking about volatile artifacts, I mentioned the Windows registry. It is important to note that when you're dealing with registry keys, some of the keys that are referenced by Microsoft in its technical documentation or visible in the Windows utility Regedit/Regedit32 may be volatile artifacts themselves. The HKEY_LOCAL_ MACHINE registry key is actually created by the Windows system kernel and exists while the system is running and is populated with data in subkeys that are derived from the various registry hive files. The HKEY_LOCAL_SYSTEM registry key is never stored on the computer's hard disk. However, if you look at the two referenced registry points previously mentioned for the location of Windows network interface and routing table registry keys, you will notice that they both reside under the SYSTEM subkey from HKEY_LOCAL_MACHINE or HKEY_LOCAL_MACHINE\SYSTEM. In addition to SYSTEM, other entries can be found under the key HKEY_LOCAL_MACHINE, including HARDWARE, SAM, SECURITY, and SOFTWARE.

With the exception of the HARDWARE subkey, each of these subkeys references a registry hive file of the same name that is located inside the C:\Windows\System32\config\ directory. HARDWARE is excluded, because much like HKEY_LOCAL_SYSTEM, it is another volatile hive that contains information about the current state of the computer hardware while the system is running. Fortunately, there is little to no relevant information contained in the HARDWARE subkey to be useful during a forensics investigation.

In Chapter 7, we discussed tools to capture RAM.

Encrypted File Systems

Previously in the chapter, I discussed a study about FDE products and the persistence of data in RAM that might expose those encryption products to attack. It just so happens that discussion of those attacks is apropos to this chapter. You see, encrypted file systems themselves can be considered volatile artifacts, at least while they are up in their running, unencrypted state.

Over the last few years, it has become common in the news to hear about some government contractor, health insurance company, or any number of other organizations that have lost control of a laptop with unencrypted sensitive information stored on it, exposing large numbers of people to identity theft. This is exactly the kind of scenario FDE products are designed to defend against. Often these products are used on laptop hard drives to help protect the data that exists on them should they fall into unauthorized hands. If someone attempts to look at a hard drive encrypted with FDE without having the keys to translate the data from its encrypted state, it would be unintelligible and meaningless. Essentially, it would appear to be completely random data.

In Actual Practice

Don't assume that because a computer is not a laptop, it won't have an encrypted disk. FDE products make good sense with mobile computing devices such as laptops, because laptops are exposed to greater risk of physical compromise due to their very nature of being mobile devices. However, FDE products are not limited to laptop use. I have seen FDE products used on desktop systems that were not mobile, especially in environments where physical access could not be easily controlled. It is also not uncommon for layers of encryption to be used in addition to FDE products, namely at the directory level with technologies such as Microsoft BitLocker or Apple FileVault, or at the file level with tools such as Pretty Good Privacy (PGP), TrueCrypt, or even WinZip, which allows you to encrypt a .zip archive file with AES-256 encryption. I've actually seen instances where a system had encryption at all the layers: full disk, directory, and file levels. This might seem like overkill, but there are those rare organizations that go above and beyond what is reasonable to protect data.

Typically with these products, the term "full disk" is actually a misnomer, because a small, unencrypted portion of the hard disk contains the Master Boot Record (MBR) and a simple boot loader that loads the FDE software and creates a software translation layer between the encrypted disk and the operating system. When the system boots up, the BIOS requests the data from the MBR, and the boot loader is read and executed. This presents the user with either a basic login screen requiring authentication credentials to allow the system to translate the encrypted disk for use, a challenge/response for authentication, or some other authentication method to unlock and translate the encrypted data.

With Check Point Software's Pointsec FDE product, a static username and password combination belonging to the user of the system must be used for authentication. If the user enters a correct username and password combination, or whatever authentication method the FDE software requires, the boot loader proceeds to translating the disk and loading the operating system, just as it would if the disk were not encrypted. If the user fails to enter a correct username and password combination, the system will eventually shut down or lock the user account.

Especially in corporate environments, it is not uncommon for some of these FDE products to include additional administrator accounts for desktop support personal to troubleshoot the hardware should a problem occur, or for methods for an administrator or technician to gain access. With Pointsec, this additional access is granted by using a hardware token, similar in appearance to a pocket desktop calculator, that generates a ten-digit number. This number is entered into a one-time login menu, and then the Pointsec software will return a ten-digit challenge code, which is then entered into the hardware token. Then it returns another ten-digit code, which, when entered into the login screen, will grant login access to the boot loader (see Figure 9-1); then the system will continue to load the operating system, bypassing the original username and password authentication setup.

In recent years, hard drive manufacturers have been working on implementing encryption schemes at the hardware level. This has led to the introduction of self-encrypting drives (SEDs), which allow for the same quality of protection of data as the software FDE products, but with a literal full disk of encryption and increased performance that uses the built-in encryption engines in the drives instead of being dependent upon the host computer's CPU. These disks are based upon the Trusted Computing Group's Opal specification and have the entire user accessible portion of the disk encrypted at all times. To access the drive, the disks follow a boot process similar in appearance as the software FDE products, but with notably different implementation.

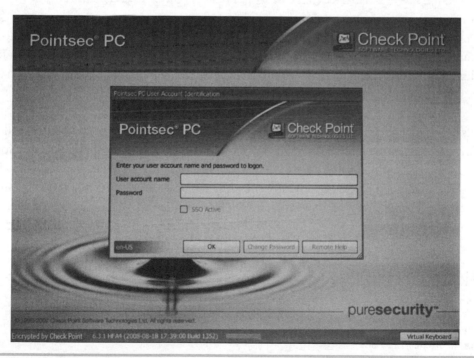

Figure 9-1   Pointsec login screen

When the BIOS of the machine requests the MBR of the disk, the disk instead returns a preboot record, which boots a complete but extremely restricted OS that starts the authentication process with the user. This is different from a software-based product in that the preboot data is actually stored in custom firmware outside of the user-accessible portion of the hard disk itself. If the user provides the correct credentials, the drive provides access to the encrypted data. Then the MBR is returned to the BIOS and the system loads as any normal system would. The background translation of the encrypted data is seamless and hidden from the user, and in many cases these drivers perform faster than their nonencrypted counterparts. Toshiba has taken this one step further and has created a line of drives that will actually deny access to the drive if it is removed from the host controller to which it is registered. This means any attempt to remove it from a machine and place it in another computer would result in the data being inaccessible, ruling out the possibility of traditional forensic imaging, even of the encrypted drive. With this feature enabled, the disk won't even be visible to a computer that does not contain the host controller to which the disk is assigned.

Challenges to Accessing Encrypted Data

So how do these encrypted disks affect digital forensic practitioners? As stated earlier, this layer of encryption between the disk and the rest of the hardware is designed to keep unauthorized people from reading the data on the disk, but it also causes problems for digital forensic practitioners. To get to the data on the disk in a usable way, we have to get past the encryption that obscures it.

Using traditional forensic methods, we'd first take a forensic image of the encrypted disk, and then we'd analyze the data inside our favorite digital forensics suite or with our favorite standalone forensic tools. However, as of this writing, few digital forensic tools provide good support for processing encrypted disk images, and what support is in place may be hampered by vendors slightly changing the way their encryption products operate between releases. You can find yourself with huge headaches because of a mismatch between the version of FDE software you're trying to decrypt and the library provided by your forensic tool vendor.

Note
More recent versions of software-based FDE make the disk appear encrypted at the physical level even after you have successfully booted into the operating system. This means we can no longer live image the system as mentioned in Chapter 7 to get access to the unencrypted data.

If we can make a forensically sound copy, we must then remove the encryption. If the FDE software supports bit-for-bit copying to another disk, we can always copy the data to another drive and then decrypt that, maintaining the chain of custody and integrity of the original evidence. However, in practical experience, some of the FDE products don't work when making bit-for-bit copies. Options for accessing the data are extremely involved, consisting of acquiring a forensic image of the encrypted disk with dd, converting the dd raw disk image of the encrypted disk to a VMware-readable image, booting a virtual machine with a Pointsec recovery boot disk in VMware, decrypting the raw dd image disk in the Pointsec recovery disk VM, rebooting the VM with an imaging Linux distribution CD, and then imaging the decrypted volume that way. That's a lot of effort.

In Actual Practice

Doing some informal polling of digital forensic practitioners, I found it interesting that many of them don't go through all of these steps and instead just decrypt the original drive with the recovery disk and then image it, though some do take an image of the encrypted disk as an added step before decrypting the drive. When asked as part of my informal polling, none of the practitioners who had performed this type of collection and imaging had experienced a problem with their data being used as evidence.

All of the mentioned effort relies on the assumption that you have the keys to decrypt the drive. In the corporate world, dealing with corporate assets, that will likely be the case. But what happens when you have to analyze a machine that's up and running and has FDE, but you don't have the keys to decrypt the disk? In that case, your only option is to create a live system image. To learn more about live imaging, refer back to Chapter 7.

Mobile Devices: Smart Phones and Tablets

In this day and age, it is very common for people to own and rely on personal computing devices that diverge from the average personal computer. I'm sure if you reach in your pocket or backpack, you'll find a smart phone or tablet device. (I have two that serve similar but segregated duties: one is for work, and one is for personal use.) Because these devices can do so much beyond just being a mobile phone or a network-connected e-reader, it makes sense that people use them in their day-to-day lives. And because they play such a large part in our lives, they also contain a large amount of data about us, from who we call or text, to where we've been and who we interact with socially. As the slogan goes "There's an app for that," and if there's an app, then there are probably digital forensic artifacts left behind, making for a rich environment for digital forensic analysis.

These devices, however, are just small computers in and of themselves, and it shocks most people to learn that Google's Android is actually built upon the Linux operating system and that Apple's iOS is based upon OS X. However, unlike PCs, these smart phones and tablets are integrated devices, where at least part of the flash storage, RAM, and processing is on-board; there is no effective way to perform digital forensics on these devices using traditional forensic methods of removing the persistent storage and imaging it without running the risk of damaging the device.

Most smart phones and tablet devices can connect to your PC using a USB interface and cable, so you can access the devices as a USB disk via a USB hardware or software write blocker under ideal circumstances, just as you would access an external storage device. You can also use standalone smart phone/tablet forensic acquisition software to acquire the device, or a standalone device such as a Celebrite universal forensic extraction device (UFED) or AccessData Mobile Phone Examiner (MPE), which are dedicated hardware devices for performing digital forensic imaging of phone and tablet devices. However, to take a full physical image of the device, many of the solutions require that the device be "jailbroken" or "rooted."

But there is still another major problem: The phone must be powered on to collect data from it, and when the phone is on, it's trying to connect to the mobile phone network and process information. All this activity is changing the state of the phone, whether you're actively interacting with it or not. Text messages or e-mails may be deleted due to age while you're imaging the device. Calls or text messages may arrive during the course of your imaging. Some smart phone platforms and add-on apps even allow for the remote wiping of a device by the authorized owner over the mobile network if the device is lost or stolen, and that could be disastrous to an investigation. The best way to combat this is to image these devices inside a Faraday cage. If you don't have access to a Faraday cage, low-cost Faraday bags or tents are available. These are a must have for doing mobile device acquisitions.

> **LINGO**
> A **Faraday cage** is a device that blocks electrical fields, including radio waves used for cell phones and tablet devices to communicate.

The point is that, unlike doing an image of a write-blocked disk, where the contents of the device are static and unchanging, the state of the phone and the state of the image you take of the phone are never going to be the same, no matter how you approach the acquisition. Even if you block out external radio waves and keep the device off the network, it will still have its own internal operations changing the system. To learn more about mobile device forensics, a large topic outside of this book, refer to our web site www.learndfir.com.

Solid State Drives

As an IT professional, you are probably very experienced with traditional magnetic hard disk drives, as the base technology has been around for almost 50 years and there are no indications that it will be obsoleted anytime soon. However, newer technologies have come about that show a vastly increased performance over standard platter-based magnetic storage hard disks. These devices are referred to as solid state drives, or SSDs for short.

Most SSDs available today are based upon NAND (Negated AND or NOT AND) flash memory, typically cheaper multilevel cell (MLC) NAND or in older units more expensive single-level cell (SLC), which is essentially an array of transistors used to store small amounts of voltage for long-term data storage. Since SSDs have no moving parts, they provide incredible read and write performance speeds. They also don't suffer from magnetic interference, because the data is stored electrically, not magnetically, like on a traditional magnetic-platter hard drive.

One interesting characteristic of these devices is that the technology used to store the data has some limitations when compared to their magnetic-platter based ancestors. First, the NAND flash cells support only so many write cycles before a cell becomes unusable. This is because every time the cell is used to store an electrical charge, it physically degrades, and with MLC flash cells are limited to around 10,000 write/erase cycles per cell. These cells are arranged into pages, typically 4096 bytes in size, which are the smallest allocation unit to which data can be read from or written to, and are analogous to sectors on a traditional hard drive. These are then grouped into blocks, usually 64 or 128 at a time, for a block size of 256 to 512 kilobytes. What's interesting to note is that while an SSD can read or write to the individual pages inside of a block, it can delete only entire blocks. Also, data on an SSD cannot be overwritten as we know it on a magnetic disk, because data can be written only to a blank page.

So, for example, let's say we have two files exactly 256KB in size that occupy the same 512KB block. And let's say we want to make a change to one of those files and save it. When we save the file, the contents of the block are read by the drive controller into a buffer, and then the changes to the specific pages where the file resides are made in that RAM buffer. Then, once that is done, the entire block is written back to the drive. Of course, due to wear-leveling schemes implemented by the SSD controller to reduce the wear of the NAND flash cells, the data would probably be written to another block on the drive, and the original block it was assigned to might be erased using TRIM or a controller automated garbage collection, or the block might be rotated into the pool of spare blocks that all SSDs have, taking it out of the pool of blocks available to be written to.

This is a very involved task, and this problem is referred to as "write amplification." Thankfully, just like magnetic hard disks, SSD drives have hardware controllers in them that handle the operation of the SSD drive. However, these controllers are much more sophisticated than those of normal magnetic hard drives and handle the tasks that are necessary to keep an SSD operating at peak performance. To combat the read/write life cycle of the NAND flash cells, the controller has a built-in wear-leveling system that keeps blocks from being used too often and distributes the read/writes across the entire storage area. SSDs also have a spare pool of blocks that may be rotated in and out of service as the drive controller sees fit to keep the drive running optimally. In addition, to ensure that operations that would appear to overwrite data appear fast to the end user, SSD controllers have a built-in functionality to keep the pages that are marked as unallocated empty so they can be written to without having to wait for an erase cycle. Initially, this was done with the TRIM feature set, which allowed the OS to tell the SSD controller which cells should be considered unallocated so that any data in them could be erased. But in order for TRIM to work on the drive, the OS had to have built-in support for TRIM. If your OS did not support TRIM, then performance of your SSD would definitely be degraded the longer you used it. Windows 7 natively supports TRIM, and other modern operating systems are becoming SSD aware, but TRIM is not available on all SSD drives.

Newer SSD controllers, specifically those made after 2008, can now identify NTFS file systems and interpret the file system allocation bitmap to clear out unused pages proactively and make them ready for new data; this is part of the controller's built-in garbage collection routine, which previously only handled data allocation across the storage device to help reduce fragmentation. This active deletion of data is a huge problem for digital forensic analysts, however, because it poses two problems.

First, the minor problem is that just like smart phones, tablet devices, or live systems, the data on an SSD drive is constantly changing when it's powered up. Unlike a traditional hard disk with a write blocker, which will not do anything to change the data on the disk, an SSD controller has the ability to make changes to the NAND cells on its own when it is under power. However, just as it has become accepted as an unavoidable issue with these devices, your best bet is to image as you normally would and document your collection to show how the device was handled. This will show that you handled the device in the best way possible, even if the inherent nature of the SSD's operation prevents the image from being perfect.

Second, with magnetic hard drives, overwrite operations are just that. Data simply gets written to the disk in a location marked as unallocated to a live file, even though the previous file's contents may still be there. When the data is overwritten, only the logical file size is written, so some of the old data may still exist in the slack space between the new data and the end of the logical sector or cluster. This has been a goldmine of data for forensic investigators, either allowing us to find data that has been marked deleted but hasn't been overwritten, or allowing us to find fragments of data that may be enough to help our cases. But with SSD hard drives with intelligent garbage collection routines, the likelihood of these nuggets of useful data being destroyed are high. By disabling TRIM or using an OS that does not support it for imaging, you can bypass any TRIM issues, but the background garbage collection routines that can identify the file system have no mitigating solutions. The instructions are built into the controller firmware and cannot be bypassed. The only perfect solution that makes sense is to physically image the NAND flash directly, which is possible but requires specialized hardware and training.

The problem with this perfect method is that it's destructive. Once you've removed the NAND chips from a device, it may not be possible to reconnect them. NAND flash removal and imaging, known commonly as *Chip-Off* forensics, is only done in those cases where you can physically destroy the device because the data that may be contained with the unallocated space is worth more than the drive being operational. I typically only see this done in high-profile law enforcement cases. For everyone else dealing with the imperfect world of SSD imaging, using traditional forensic methods is still the best practice.

Note

A study performed by Graeme B. Bell and Richard Boddington on this topic titled "Solid State Drives: The Beginning of the End of Current Practice in Digital Forensic Recovery?" appeared in the *Journal of Digital Forensics, Security and Law* (www.jdfsl .org/subscriptions/JDFSL-V5N3-Bell.pdf) and provides a lot of detail on their findings. One key point they noted is that these intelligent SSD controllers can start deleting NAND pages 3 minutes after power is applied to the drive. Another interesting paper that deals with the subject of flash drives and how software tools fail to sanitize data was developed by a group of researchers at the University of California, San Diego, and is titled "Reliably Erasing Data from Flash-Based Solid State Drives" (www.usenix .org/events/fast11/tech/full_papers/Wei.pdf). Although it deals primarily with the inadequacies of software tools to sanitize data reliably through the Flash Translation Layer, and not with garbage collection or TRIM, it is still a very interesting read.

Other special cases involving SSDs involve what forensic artifacts to expect within the operating system. For instance, in Windows 7, if the operating system was installed onto a SSD drive, then artifacts such as the UserAssist records (covered in later chapters) will no longer be populated. This prevents excessive writes to the disk.

Virtual Machines

When you are working on a case involving virtual machines, the best thing you can do is suspend the machines, if possible, and copy the contents of the directory they reside in. Why? Because in the suspend process, all of the RAM and disk contents will be written into the directory for easy access at a later date. If the machine cannot be suspended, then look for the virtual disk files that store the data: .vmdk, .vhd, .vdi, etc… You can then acquire the contents of RAM by using one of the memory capture tools mentioned in Chapter 7.

We've Covered

You saw some of this material before in Chapter 7, but in this chapter, we wanted to draw specific attention to areas that you may not have considered before. Every decision made by an operating system, hardware, and drive manufacturer affects digital forensics. It's important that you keep up to date on how those changes affect your cases and your ability to recover new data or lose some of your favorite artifacts. In the next chapter, we delve into investigations and what you bought this book for in the first place!

What is nontraditional forensics?

- How to know when you're dealing with a nontraditional scenario
- What makes something nontraditional

When and why to use nontraditional forensics

- When it's okay to change the original evidence
- When it's okay to go outside known processes to get the best evidence

Understanding volatile system artifacts

- Understanding the value of memory analysis
- The current role of malware analysis in nontraditional forensics

Encrypted file systems and live system imaging

- How to deal with encrypted devices
- The benefits of live imaging and decryption in dealing with encrypted disks

Dealing with mobile devices

- Understanding the realities of imaging an embedded system
- The impact of current forensic methods and how to best defend your work

Working with solid-state drives

- How SSDs store and delete data
- How to acquire the best image possible when imaging SSDs

Virtual machine forensics

- Best practices for preserving virtual machines
- How to find the data you need to preserve

PART III

Case Examples:
How to Work a Case

CHAPTER 10

Establishing the Investigation Type and Criteria

We'll Cover

- Determining what type of investigation is required

- What to do when criteria causes an overlap

- What to do when no criteria matches

Now that you've studied Parts I and II of this book, you are ready to investigate your first computer forensics case. After you prove your competency as an examiner, you can look forward to a continuing stream of investigations, because there will always be employees who misuse their employers' networks and networks that require forensic examinations. This book is meant to be a guide to walk you through time- and court-tested procedures, but we can't cover everything you might encounter. Remember that nothing goes "by the book" when you're dealing with human behavior!

In this chapter, you'll read about a set of common criteria that, when presented to you at the beginning of a case, should help you determine which set of procedures you should start with in your analysis. I'll cover the major types of cases you may encounter as a new computer forensics examiner, what to do when your case involves multiple types of criteria, and how to deal with a case that meets no established criteria.

Determining What Type of Investigation Is Required

You'll use a basic set of criteria to determine the type of case you're dealing with. Understanding the type of case you'll be investigation is important, of course, when you're deciding which forensic analysis procedures to use to find appropriate evidence. You could, for example, fully examine every artifact on every forensic image to determine everything a suspect has been doing, but then you wouldn't be able to finish your investigation in a timely matter or provide the results your employer is actually requesting. Always remember who is requesting that you perform an investigation, as it's rarely yourself, and try to meet their specific needs as you work.

Human Resources Cases

Chapter 11 covers common examples of HR investigations: an employee who is viewing pornography at work and an employee who is wasting and/or abusing company time and resources. These are, of course, not the only types of HR cases you will encounter—life is always stranger than fiction. Most computer forensic examiners begin their careers with HR cases, which are typically low risk and easy to solve. If your first case is an HR case, turn to Chapter 11 to read about example HR cases and how to handle the two most common types.

In Actual Practice

For many HR cases, you may not even need to use forensic tools and perform computer examinations; the logs from the company's firewalls, proxies, and e-mail systems may provide enough evidence to prove your suspect's activities. However, you should always try to create forensic images when it's allowed, because doing so allows you to perform a more thorough investigation if it's requested. Creating forensic images allows you to use traditional computer forensic techniques to recover deleted and hidden data from the disk to uncover more evidence of a suspect's activities.

Here are some examples of typical HR cases:

- Viewing pornography at work
- Wasting time on Facebook and other web sites instead of working
- Selling company property online
- Playing video games while at work
- Sexually harassing coworkers
- Threatening coworkers
- Having an affair with a coworker

Goals of an HR Case

Typically, HR cases do not end in civil litigation or criminal charges. The employee, aka suspect, may not have violated any law, but simply a company policy. The end result of a HR investigation is typically the employee's termination. Because an employee's job is being terminated, you need to produce enough proof and reporting to defend your work in case the employee tries to file a lawsuit against the company for improper termination.

LINGO

In an **improper termination** lawsuit, the plaintiff (typically the dismissed employee) alleges that the former employer fired him or her for false pretenses, in an unfair manner, or in a way inconsistent with how other employees have been treated. (This can also be used for a discrimination suit.) The employee could be suing to regain his or her position, but most often the suit involves lost wages and damages.

To defend your company from an improper termination lawsuit, we recommend that you follow all the procedures we've outlined in this book, when possible, and maintain your records related to the investigation until told otherwise by the company's HR staff. If your report is solid and your records are intact, most HR cases will not make their way to the courtroom, because when faced with the evidence, a former employee might not follow through.

In Actual Practice

I've experienced situations in which investigators didn't keep proper notes or didn't keep their forensics data after the employee was terminated. If you don't retain your notes and evidence, and an employee challenges the termination, you will at best have to re-create you work, and at worst you may be missing evidence to prove the claims. If you don't have room on your analyst system to keep your work product, copy it to an external drive or DVD for safe-keeping until told otherwise.

Administrator Abuse

"Administrator abuse" refers to the abuse of authority or access by an IT administrator into the company's data and/or systems. These cases can come to light via multiple sources, depending on the type of abuse that has occurred. The impact of an administrator abuse case depends on the nature of the abuse. In the best case, it involves an immature administrator who is just curious about

LINGO

Work product is a legal term that refers to documents, spreadsheets, databases, forensic files, notes, and so on that you produce during your investigation. If your investigation is being done by direction of an attorney, your work product may be excluded from being produced during litigation. To determine whether this is the case, ask your legal team for guidance.

what other employees are earning; in the worst case, someone is being malicious with the intent to harm, stalk, or blackmail another employee with the information they gather. If you believe you are entering an administrator abuse case, go to Chapter 12 to read an example of a real case and how such a case can be handled.

The following are some examples of administrator abuse cases:

- Reading users' e-mail
- Determining the salary of other employees

- Spying on other users using remote access tools such as Virtual Network Computing (VNC)

- Placing keyloggers and other spyware on users' computers

- Accessing other users' personal files and folders

- Stalking employees through personal information stored on company systems

- Running personal or side-job–related web sites and other types of network services on corporate assets

- Bypassing company policy by creating special methods of unfiltered Internet access for prohibited activities

Goals of an Administrator Abuse Case

Depending on the evidence you find, this type of case may end in civil or criminal charges. If nothing else, an administrator found to be abusing system access for personal gain will likely be terminated for these actions. The hardest part of an administrator abuse case is not to let the administrator know you are investigating them. An administrator may be reading the e-mails of the legal department as well as HR and possibly searching for mentions of his or her name to look for clues that he or she night be under investigation. It's important to take extra care with these cases to work covertly—that means making phone calls instead of sending e-mails, avoiding corporate instant messaging systems, and photographing the desk of the administrator before seizing evidence to make sure you can replace all the items where they were.

   If you learn that such a case may be referred for criminal prosecution, be sure to make a copy of the original forensic image you made to help as you work, and keep the original forensic image separated to show chain-of-custody issues when handing it over to law enforcement. You may hear your copy referred to as a "working copy" and the original as a "pristine copy."

In Actual Practice

As your vault of evidence builds, you'll need to develop an approved policy for disposing of evidence. In my work, I get rid of the forensic image and data collected only when either a) the case has been settled and my client no longer needs the data (sometimes this can be as much as a year later) or b) the case has run out of appeals and parties can no longer litigate, which can take as long as three to five years. Plan to keep and maintain plenty of evidence storage space and keep your images organized to prevent confusion at a later date.

Stealing Information

Other than HR cases, a case involving an employee who steals company information is the most common type of case you will encounter. These are not considered HR cases as they are usually originated by Legal and not HR. These cases normally involve a current employee who is planning to leave the company. Before leaving the company, the person takes with them some of the materials or information they may or may not believe is theirs and passes it on to their next employer. In the worst cases, the employee is bringing trade secrets requested by his or her new employer to gain an unfair advantage in the marketplace. Chapter 13 lays out an example case of stealing information and sample procedures to follow when working a common case of such employee theft.

The following are examples of cases involving stealing information:

- Sales person taking business contacts to use in another business
- Employee taking bid details on current, future, or former projects
- Taking trade secret business processes to a competitor
- Forwarding e-mails and files to a personal e-mail account
- Uploading data to file sharing sites for later access
- Wholesale backup of all data from company systems to personal hard drives
- External hacking into company systems

Goals of a Stealing Information Case

Cases in which former employees have stolen information typically end in civil litigation against the former employee who took the information and possibly the company they went to work for if the company was benefitting—or, worse, requesting—the information that was stolen. I've included external hacking cases in this category because they fit the definition of this type of case, but they are most likely incident response cases in which the actual attacker may be out of the jurisdiction of the court, such as in another country. You'll find many books on incident response that you can consult before embarking on an external hacking case, such as *Incident Response & Computer Forensics,* 2nd Ed., by Chris Prosise, Kevin Mandia, and Matt Pepe.

Internal Leaks

An internal leak case may seem similar to a stealing information case, except for one difference: the employee who is leaking the information usually is not leaving the company (unless the suspect hopes to gain a position after they are done leaking information to a competitor). If an employee is leaking information, they have to stay in their current position to continue doing so. In this kind of case, it can be more difficult to find your suspect, because you can't simply forensically image the devices of departing employees to find the evidence; instead, you must first have some idea that a leak is occurring, and then track down the source. If a data loss prevention (DLP) system is in place, it may offer you clues if it finds information on the system that possibly relates to someone sending data outside the company. Although this book won't go into all the ways you can find an internal leak, you will find procedures regarding how to review systems to find this kind of information in Chapter 14.

LINGO
Data loss prevention, or DLP, systems are typically network appliances that review all network traffic on your external network, looking for signs of improper data being sent outside the company. Examples of such data include credit card numbers, Social Security numbers, and other industry-specific terms. DLP products typically look for keywords or patterns of text to determine whether network traffic contains this type of data.

Note
DLP has expanded beyond the network appliance, and now the term's meaning can be extended to endpoint protection as well. Endpoint protection involves placing additional controls on a user's system to force full-disk encryption, limit and/or log any accesses to external storage, and so on.

The following are examples of internal leaks cases:

- Sending information related to internal matters to the press
- Sending information to competitors
- Sending anonymous e-mails to the company board of directors

Goal of Internal Leaks Cases
Once you've identified the source of information leaks, the person will be terminated from their position. Whether the leaker is also charged in a civil or criminal matter will depend on the type of offense—and whether the company wants to draw attention to the matter.

Keyloggers and Malware
Keyloggers and malware are cases that can involve an IT professional even before he or she has considered undertaking computer forensics. Any system—whether at work or at home—can be infected with malware, and large numbers of books, blogs, and web sites are devoted to information regarding how to detect and remediate these types of cases. This book reviews some good procedures for locating and identifying malware installed

on a system, but it does not go into determining the capabilities of malware other than showing you where you can go to get information about known malware.

The following are examples of keylogger and malware cases:

- Keylogger employed by an employee
- Keylogger employed by spouse
- Malware that enters a system through an employee's Internet usage
- Malware targeted at the company

Goals of Keylogger and Malware Cases

In the vast majority of cases, the systems of employees and possibly even family members are being infected with a wide variety of malware on a daily basis. Following are some examples of the goals of these cases:

- What was infected
- How it got onto the system
- What are the capabilities of the malware

These cases are the lowest risk, because once the malware has been identified, you can move forward to remediate the infection by removing the malware. If you can determine the capabilities of the malware (either because it is known publically or because you have the skills and knowledge to determine this through examination), you can also take the additional step of protecting your system or company data from possible theft by changing passwords to online systems or having credit cards reissued to prevent their fraudulent use, for example. Remember, however, that if the malware was found on your system, it means your private information has already been compromised.

In Actual Practice

Not all malware installed on a system can or should be taken lightly. Several malware packages aggressively attempt to steal your personal and financial information for use by third parties. In the scope of risk to you as an investigator, though, these are usually low-risk cases if something were to go wrong as there is no one to terminate, sue, or discipline within your country's jurisdiction.

Note

Malware analysis is a dense topic, and many books are devoted to it. Two major forms of malware analysis can be performed. The first, static analysis, involves researching the malware executable and files to determine known system libraries and possible reverse engineering to determine capabilities. The second, dynamic analysis, involves running the malware itself in a safe virtualized environment disconnected from the real network, so you can observe the malware's behavior to determine its capabilities. There is obviously much more to it; if you are interested, search for either term in your favorite search engine.

What to Do When Criteria Causes an Overlap

You'll also encounter situations in which the type of case before you is complicated and involves more than one type of criteria. Suppose, for example, that a suspect was initially suspected of administrator abuse, but the case turned into an HR case when the suspect was caught trying to sell information to another company. In this instance, you could add analysis procedures as discussed in this book and document your findings, keeping the suspect's actions separate. Why keep them separate? When you are reporting this information, it becomes easier to read and understand the context of what you are finding when it specifically relates to what has been done.

Because you should consider all the evidence you find when reviewing a system, keeping the evidence that relates to each type of case separate makes your job in explaining the cases much easier later on. You could, for example, create two sections (or more if appropriate) in your notes and bookmarks within your forensic tools to separate your findings for reporting reasons. Keeping them separate helps you organize your notes and/or bookmarks according to each case topic you are investigating. When you write your report, the relevant findings will naturally fit in their own sections, preventing confusion.

Caution

Before you decide to change the scope of an investigation, first inform the person who authorized your investigation of your findings and request their approval. This can prevent a lot of problems and misunderstandings moving forward.

What to Do When No Criteria Matches

So your suspect has done something outside the range of all of our typical cases? Well first, congratulations! You have an interesting case on your hands! This book was meant to assist you in handling the basics of computer forensics procedures. A complex case lets you take all the procedures and techniques you've learned and see how they apply to your unique scenario. The first thing to do is to step back and determine where to look for evidence.

For the criteria defined so far in this chapter, I've suggested where you might look for evidence; however, you should always ask yourself the following questions if you can't find the evidence you need:

- Where should the evidence be?
- Did this occur over the network?
- Did this occur on a local system?

Where Should the Evidence Be?

Being able to answer this question is a sign of your proficiency and maturity as a computer forensic examiner. Think about the activity that is suspected and draw out all the systems that could be involved when that kind of activity takes place.

Tip
Some people find that drawing out all the possible sources helps them determine sources they didn't think of initially. I like to write ideas on a whiteboard as I discuss a case with colleagues.

Did This Occur over the Network?

Consider all of the devices located in between the machines in question and the Internet. Which of those devices has logging capability?

- **Proxy logs**   If your network users access the Internet through proxies, look here for information about their web activity.

- **Firewall logs**   Depending on the firewall logging rules, you may gain some insight into network traffic here.

- **IDS logs**   The early signs of probing and known attack patterns can be helpful if you are dealing with an external breach.

- **IPS logs**   Much like IDS logs, IPS logs may be useful in finding IP ranges to look for in your local system.

- **Router logs**   Usually this is not a helpful source, but it's always worth considering, depending on the logging and functions utilized, such as a VPN.

- **Local firewall logs**   Most systems now also have a local firewall that keeps its own logs.

- **Domain authentication logs**   The suspect may be utilizing multiple systems, so tracking their logins within the domain can help you identify those systems.

- **Internal webmail (OWA/Outlook web access) servers**   Webmail is often utilized by suspects who hope to keep their activities off the company e-mail system.

- **VPN servers**   Suspects' activities often occur on remote servers.

- **DHCP Logs**   Check those logs to determine which user had an IP address at the time of the offense.

Did This Occur on a Local System?

Determine what software was installed on the system. Things you might not normally consider may create logs or artifacts that are out of scope for other types of defined cases.

- **Antivirus logs**   Use these logs to determine what files were on the system before and to look for any possible past infections.

- **Desktop search indexes**   Both Windows and Google provide these services, which include an index of all the files that existed on a system.

- **Event logs**   These can be helpful not just when you're looking for direct evidence of the incident, but they can also show errors that may have occurred because of the incident.

- **Flash cookies**   Sometimes data may exist here even if your suspect used some kind of private browsing function.

These are just a few examples. Your own understanding and ability to collect information about your environment will always be more valuable than what I can suggest here. The more you know about your own systems, networks, and applications, the better equipped you are to handle the unknown.

Nothing Working? Create a Super Timeline

Consider creating a *super timeline* using the SIFT log2timeline tool. Often, when you can't find any related evidence to the case you are working on, you may not be aware of everything the system is doing. While I'm not an advocate of creating a super timeline with log2timeline for every case, many cases are simple enough to be solved with the usual artifacts; in those situations where you need guidance in what else could have happened, these artifacts are a great way to see a large amount of information gathered from throughout the system. Remember that a super timeline is only as good as the information you populate it with. Make sure to utilize all the modules that your operating systems support with log2timeline to get the most complete picture.

Once you've constructed this timeline, you may feel overwhelmed by the amount of information and not sure where to start. You can consult a diagram that was created to help you find likely patterns in the timeline at http://computer-forensics.sans.org/blog/2011/12/16/digital-forensics-sifting-cheating-timelines-with-log2timeline.

For me, super timelines are a good way to find a new source of evidence or to double-check that I haven't missed anything. The number of examiners who use super timelines is growing thanks to SANS, and I believe you will see more and similar intelligent tools being developed in the near future.

Note
For more on creating a super timeline, read the SANS blog here: http://computer-forensics.sans.org/blog/2011/12/07/digital-forensic-sifting-super-timeline-analysis-and-creation.

What does a super timeline offer you that your forensic tool's timeline feature does not already do? Good question! A super timeline goes beyond the traditional timeline created by a forensic tool. A super timeline lays out files and some system events in a sortable list and can break out data into timestamped events. This means that all of the following, and more, can be brought together into one large (super) timeline to help you find what you are looking for:

- File system metadata
- Event logs
- Application logs
- Internet history
- Registry files
- Antivirus logs
- Exchangeable image file format (Exif) data
- Firewall logs
- .LNK files
- Restore points
- Recycle Bin entries
- Prefetch files

You'll find more uses every day as new modules are written.

Note

This huge amount of information can be quite overwhelming if you don't know what you are looking for. This is why I recommend starting your investigation first and then going back to the timeline to find what you might have missed.

We've Covered

This chapter is your first look into the breadth of investigations that await you and how to determine what to do next. The industry has come to be known as Digital Forensics Incident Response (DFIR) because the spectrum of cases an examiner could work on continues to grow. No matter what type of case we are working, we all use the same forensic artifacts to make our conclusions, so the next chapters will help you with your work regardless of what case you end up on.

Determining what type of investigation is required

- Understanding the differences between the most common cases
- Understanding the goals of each type of common investigation

What to do when criteria causes an overlap

- How to combine your forensic methods for a case that crosses boundaries
- How to segregate your results for easy review and tracking

What to do when no criteria matches

- How to find out where the evidence exists
- When to bring in a super timeline

CHAPTER 11

Human Resources Cases

We'll Cover

● Results of a human resource case

● How to work a pornography case

● How to work a productivity waste case

Chapter 10 showed you how to identify the type of investigation you are dealing with. This chapter discusses typical investigation criteria when working with human resource cases. This chapter covers the concepts and artifacts for you to review. If you want to view step-by-step guides, go to www.learndfir.com to watch the videos for this chapter. You'll read about several different types of real-world cases and the approaches to analysis each presented. This chapter covers the easy stuff—pornography and productivity waste. In later chapters, we'll move on to more challenging issues such as theft of proprietary information. This information will be most useful for corporate forensic analysts; however, analysts working outside of the corporate environment will find the implications and challenges of working in a networked environment of particular interest.

In my experience, the average HR-related cases end up being fairly straightforward. You may encounter the occasional oddity, but the essential questions to answer are the same: Has an employee violated a policy or otherwise wasted company resources?

Results of a Human Resource Case

In 99.99 percent of all the human resources cases I've worked, I've been asked to determine whether enough evidence is present to support the termination of an employee for a violation of company policy. What activities violate company policy varies by the company, but for most companies, an employee who views online pornography instead of working is typically on the road to termination, while an employee who plays games instead of working may warrant a reprimand or counseling.

Of cases that involve a terminable offense, the most common issue is the unauthorized surfing of pornographic web sites and other types of adult media. In other cases that end in immediate termination, the issue often involves employees making threats against others via company e-mail or instant messaging—all of which involve risk to the employer.

Of the cases that do not involve immediate termination, the most common is the waste of company time or resources for personal enjoyment. This most often involves seemingly endless web surfing, playing games, using Facebook, and spending time in other distractions.

In some cases, such as in pornography, it can involve both waste of company resources, violations of established company policy, and/or cause of personal discomfort or harassment of other employees.

Note

Although I am covering the most common human resources cases in this chapter, there are other examples of HR cases, such as sexual harassment, threats of physical violence, and affairs in the workplace. Your work in all of these types of cases can involve the same methods discussed in this chapter—that is, reconstructing the user's Internet activity to find evidence of his or her actions.

How to Work a Pornography Case

Pornography is the easiest of all types of HR cases to analyze and investigate. What you're looking for is obvious when you see it. (If it walks like a duck and quacks like a duck, guess what? It's a duck!) This section focuses on a case study of a real-life pornography case. Then you'll learn a few tips on how to perform an analysis of a pornography case yourself.

IMHO

A pornography case is almost always the first type of case a new corporate investigator will examine. Viewing pornography at work is not only the most common unsavory activity that an employee will do if they think no one is monitoring them, but it is the easiest type of evidence to detect. In most cases, just the existence of pornography on the work system is enough evidence to warrant termination. And most employees will not try to sue for improper termination if they are fired for viewing pornography for fear of embarrassment, so this is a very low risk case for you and for the individuals who request it.

Pornography Case Study

An employee surfing pornography while on the job can occur at almost every company in today's always-connected work environments. Some employees will waste an hour a day or more surfing pornographic sites. These cases are easy to investigate, because a simple review of the user's Internet history and a view of the images on his or her hard drive will quickly reveal any pornographic images. And related information you may uncover can take investigations to the next level, and that will challenge you to do some more creative analysis. These investigations occur when the employee is generally aware that someone may be monitoring his or her web browsing and may be using privacy features to prevent evidence of it being created. This leads us to the following scenario.

Note

According to Neilsen Online, as of October 2008, approximately 25 percent of employees visit an Internet pornography site during working hours. It used to be one of the most common types of internal investigations, though today's implementation and thorough tuning of web content filtering has reduced the vast majority of access. As you work other HR cases, ask whether you should also check for pornography use. Other types of HR cases can incorporate pornography issues if you look for it.

The Sluggish Network

An employee was surfing pornography sites while on the clock at a regional retail company. However, this man wasn't an average company employee—he was the corporate IT director.

The matter began as all seem to, with an everyday work issue. In this case, the IT department received multiple complaints over a few days' time that "the Internet sure is moving slowly." The IT director received the complaints through the company's trouble ticket system and assigned the task of troubleshooting the problem to a member of his staff. The employee reviewed the bandwidth consumption report on the firewall and identified the users who were using up the most bandwidth. He found the usual list of activities—streaming music, video, and so on—but when he viewed the list of host sites being visited, he noticed that a particular user was visiting obvious pornographic sites, for anywhere from five to seven hours a day!

This was very unusual, because at this company, policy emphasized that employees were prohibited from surfing pornographic sites. In fact, the company had purchased a content filter appliance and installed it in the infrastructure to prevent such activity. The company also paid for continuing updates to the content filter database.

The IT staff member assigned to the task looked up the static internal IP address assignments in the DHCP server and determined that the offending user was his boss, the IT director. After compiling a thorough list of activity from the firewall, he took the information to the company's HR department.

After receiving the logs from the IT employee, the HR director contacted in-house counsel. The next day, the in-house counsel contacted outside counsel after determining that the termination of a director might end in litigation. Later in the week, the outside counsel contacted my company.

LINGO

In-house counsel or **inside counsel** refers to a lawyer who works in your company. Most large companies have legal departments, and the head of the department is called the "general counsel." Smaller companies might employ one in-house lawyer or an outside law firm that is retained to make legal decisions for the company. In either case, as long as the lawyer is providing advice to the company for internal matters, he or she is considered in-house counsel for the examples presented in this book.

LINGO

Outside counsel refers to law firms retained by companies that desire a third-party opinion of a company decision. The company usually asks for the opinion in writing, which can be referred to at a later time if challenged, or if the company is seeking a lawsuit. Why does a company need outside council for a lawsuit? Typically in-house counsel is not actively practicing law in court, so companies rely on law firms that regularly bring matters to the court and know the rules and have licenses to do so.

The company asked us to conduct this investigation and create all imaging covertly, during the evening when the employees were gone. This is a typical scenario when you investigate a key employee and an outside firm is brought in to perform the analysis. If this investigative work was performed during the work day, the company would have to explain not only why outside consultants were in the building, but also why they needed access to the IT director's computer.

In Actual Practice

Today, many companies and consultants are making use of enterprise investigation software, such as EnCase Enterprise, AccessData FTK Enterprise, F-Response, and more. These packages allow you to install an agent over the network and create a forensic image of a computer over the network. This works especially well when the examiner is working on the same LAN as the suspect—meaning fast transfer speeds and covert investigations. If this software is set up (and the IT director or another suspect is not in charge of it), it can be used to capture imaging during the work day without the suspect's knowledge.

In this case, evening data collection was necessary because the IT director was known to have a somewhat aggressive personality and was very paranoid about people going near his work area. (In retrospect, the company should have been suspicious.) In fact, on a few occasions he chastised the cleaning crew if he noticed that they moved items on his desk while cleaning up. To ensure that it didn't appear as though we had touched the computer, we conducted a "black bag" style job. We were asked to take photographs of his desk before we took the drive out of the computer, so we could put everything back in the exact place we found it.

LINGO
A **black bag** job refers to a nighttime operation that leaves no evidence of your forensic imaging. This term is based on the military/intelligence community's technique of grabbing a suspect off the street and placing a black bag over his head to prevent him from knowing who grabbed him or where they are going. I often call this a "covert collection."

After imaging the system, we began the analysis, and we found evidence of the pornographic web surfing activity. The Internet history file (index.dat) documented all of the suspect's surfing activity and showed that his pornography surfing activity amounted to approximately three to five hours per day. After documenting all the activity and copying pornographic images and movie data that we could recover from the forensic image, we presented our findings to the HR director. These findings showed the HR director conclusive proof of daily accesses to pornographic web sites—this was not a one-time event—and the long extended sessions of access to pornographic materials—this was not the result of a random pop-up ad.

Afterward, we were informed by the HR director that because the company feared an improper termination lawsuit, this was insufficient for her to terminate him. She said that he would surely fight the conclusions, because he would argue that someone else had obtained his password and logged onto the system under his credentials to explain why the images would appear under his user profile. After I explained to her that this would involve the offending party literally logging on while the IT director was there, at work, she said she believed that she would still need further evidence to confront him with.

IMHO

You'll often encounter nontechnical people who are in a decision-making position in your investigation. It's important that you understand their fears and learn how to explain your report in plain, simple layman terms to help ease their concerns. In this case, the HR director was considering terminating a member of the company's senior staff, and her decision would lead to scrutiny from both the other executives, who may be feeling vulnerable themselves, and the legal department, which will be looking at the liability that the termination would expose the company to.

In such cases, it's understandable that a HR director would be overly cautious about pulling the termination trigger. When you are providing results that, to you, show complete proof of a terminable action, don't be surprised if you are asked either to explain it further or provide even more evidence that proves the identity of the suspect creating the artifacts you recover. And remember that the HR director may decide to take no action whatsoever, and, if so, there is nothing you can do as a forensic examiner.

At this point, to support our efforts to gather definitive evidence of our suspect's identity, we were given permission to review the corporate firewall and content filter appliance during another late evening on site, with the HR director advising IT staff to assist us and give us access. We were met that evening by the HR director and the employee who initially found the logged data. Can you already guess who set up the content filter appliance? The IT director, of course, turned on the pornography filter and then wrote a rule that applied to all IP addresses on the network—except his. Thus, his IP was specifically exempted from the pornography filter, and he could go wherever he wanted. That was the specificity—the exemption rule that the IT director had created—that the HR director needed to take actions against the suspect, because it was a known fact that the IT director was the person who set up the content filter and thus could not deny his knowledge of either the setup or the static IP address in use.

In Actual Practice

As you can see, this case involved a bit of overlap in the end. We moved from what began as a simple pornography case to a blended case of pornography and abuse of administrative privileges in the IT director's actions with the content filter. Keep in mind that there is no rule that says that one type of case can't lead into another type of case, or a blended case. What is important is that you look at how the case starts and make a plan on how to deal with issues as you discover them, and then handle whatever you discover—because you'll never know.

How to Investigate a Pornography Case

For those cases not quite as quirky as the preceding example, an average pornography investigation is fairly straightforward. You will find pornographic images in the Internet cache when you review them; some pornographic videos might have been downloaded onto the hard drive and can be located by file signature; and the Internet History file will detail the URLs of the pornographic web sites and date and time the suspect visited them. Let's look at how you can get at this data.

The following examples use FTK, but you can use whatever tool you're comfortable with. If you are a new FTK user, we recommend you go through the product's user manuals first to learn how to add evidence—this book is meant to show you techniques and procedures, but it doesn't offer individual tool instructions.

In Actual Practice

Almost every commercial suite and many open-source tools support analyzing Internet history files. If you are using EnCase or FTK, they offer built-in support for the major browsers: you simply locate the history files and review them. If you are using SIFT, you need to run either the log2timeline tool or another tool that supports the history files created by the browser.

It is important to answer the following questions:

1. What browser is the suspect using?

2. What tool in your tool kit supports analyzing the history files that they create?

3. Can you analyze the history file?

4. Can you recover deleted history records, either with the tools you have or with specialty tools that you can find on the Internet?

Budget Note

If you have some extra cash for a tool that specializes in Internet history file analysis and can carve out more deleted records that most tools, you should look into Digital Detective's NetAnalysis tool (www.digital-detective.co.uk/netanalysis.asp)—a great specialized tool for the job. If you don't have extra cash, multiple open-source and/or free options are available as well. Once you've identified the browser being used, you can search sites such as the SANS blog to look for entries of free and/or open-source tools you can use to analyze history files.

Analyzing Internet History

First, we'll look at obtaining URL and date/time information from the Internet history file (index.dat). Figure 11-1 shows how FTK renders the history file for hits to the keyword "purplepornstars." To get to this point, I let FTK process the drive, which means it found and analyzed the Internet history entries, and then searched for a keyword of the suspected pornographic web site. All of the entries in the history file that match the keyword are located, and the data in the parsed index.dat file can be bookmarked for inclusion in the FTK report.

Note

Index.dat is a history file specific to Microsoft Internet Explorer. Each browser has its own way of storing the history of a user's web activity. You must identify which browser the user is using and then determine where that browser stores its Internet history files. You must also make sure that your forensic tools support that history file type for analysis.

Although providing the date/time that the pornographic web site was accessed is often sufficient for most simple investigations, once in a while you'll be asked to gauge, as best as possible, exactly how much time a particular employee has been surfing web sites. In such a case, you can find great tools that will process all recoverable index.dat files and allow you to parse them and run statistical analysis. Taking that refined and recovered data, you can create a cohesive picture of the amount of time the suspect spent on particular sites. Another approach may be to export all the data to a delimited format, which can then be imported into a relational database such as Microsoft Access and queried as needed.

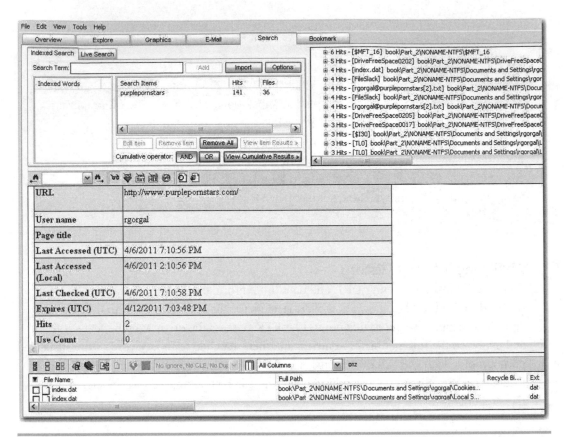

Figure 11-1   Viewing an Internet history entry from a search result in FTK

In simple cases, you may not need to go through the trouble of identifying every pornographic web site the suspect accessed. Instead, providing samples of pornography stored on the system might be enough.

Figure 11-2 shows the EnCase Forensic gallery view that can display all images in a selected folder, group of folders, or the entire drive image. Almost every forensic analysis tool has a similar function, which makes them great for investigations involving pornography. With EnCase, all you have to do is scroll through all the pictures and find those specific to the matter at hand.

Along with finding the images and movies on a user's hard drive, you should also consider another method of content transfer that is becoming one of the most widely used in the world of Internet pornography: streaming video—more specifically, streaming via Flash. Recently, a slew of new web sites have emerged that stream movie content in both short preview and full length via Flash; these movies have the same look as YouTube

Figure 11-2   Reviewing images in the EnCase gallery view

video. Streaming is starting to far outpace other methods of pornography distribution. In fact, according to a 2009 *Forbes* article, "The Challenge of User-Generated Porn," by Oliver J. Chiang, "Five tube sites—including Youporn, Pornhub and RedTube—are among the top 100 web sites in the world, according to web analytics service Alexa.com. Conversely, the mega pornography movie distributor, Vivid.com, which charges for its content, is ranked 12,718."

Examples of "tube" style Flash movie sites include these:

- http://www.xxxduck.com/
- http://www.3tube.com/
- http://www.8tube.com
- http://www.flvtube.net
- http://www.porntube.com

If you are working an HR case with a streaming video component, be it pornographic or not, you'll probably at one point be asked to show what it was the employee saw. Keep the following in mind when you're dealing with video streams:

- Images are often downloaded to the browser cache, or links to videos download to the cache and start instances of a media player, but streams don't work that way.

- You will usually find the HTML remnants of the page the video was embedded into.

- If you need to reconstruct the session as it was viewed, the original stream content must still be on the same server that was used when it was originally viewed by the user. This differs from data that is downloaded to the hard drive as part of the rendering process.

The most reliable way to find these HTML remnants is to search for the domain names of the web sites you discovered that the suspect was visiting from parsing their Internet history. The HTML remnants have to link to pages within the site or load JavaScripts, Cascading Style Sheets (CSS), and other elements that should have the name of the domain embedded within them. Once you've found all the pages—both active and deleted—available, you can move on to the next step.

After finding the HTML remnants, you'll need to examine the page source code to get the stream identifier. The simplest way to do this is to remember that the embedded video is just another object, and thus it has properties, including dimensions on the page. If you search for the object properties, what you find will ultimately identify the stream content source. The easiest properties to search for in the remnant HTML are the most obvious. In this case, the video stream has to fit within the confines of the page that's being viewed, so width and height are the two most obvious properties.

After exporting the artifact HTML found on the image, and going through the source code for the object property of width, we ultimately find the source stream, as shown next:

```
<div class="img-holder">
<a href="/en/Made-in-Xspana-05-Scene-1/film/28577">
<img src="http://edge04.images.famedownload.com/movies/7701/7701_01/
    previews/2/128/top_1_185x135/77_01_01_01.jpg" alt="Made in Xspana
    #05, Scene #1" title="Made in Xspana #05, Scene #1"  height="135"
width="185" />
</a>
<a href="/en/Made-in-Xspana-05-Scene-1/film/28577" class="clip-link" >
    <strong>Made in Xspana #05, Scene #1</strong>
    </a>
</div>
```

Since this artifact HTML page is from the Evilangel.com web site, all you need to do to reconstruct the stream session is to combine the domain and path to the video content in the browser window, http://www.evilangel.com/en/Made-in-Xspana-05-Scene-1/film/28577. This will show the content as it was viewed by the user. Why is this important? Often, having what was being accessed is not enough; HR professionals may require proof of what was being accessed in order to determine the type of disciplinary action that may be appropriate.

How to Work a Productivity Waste Case

Here are a few statistics that show how much time one "productivity waster" spends each day on things other than their work:

- Thirty to forty minutes setting up recipes and getting them out on time, in order to be named the undisputed champion of Café World

- One hour spent posting and reading postings on the PC

- Fifteen to thirty minutes reading updates on a smart phone

Many articles have been written recently about the average productivity loss as a result of unrestrained access to social media sites at work. An August 20, 2007, article by Andrew West, published in the *Sidney Morning Herald*, gave statistical estimates that Australian business lost approximately $5 billion a year to this type of activity. "The report calculates that if an employee spends an hour each day on Facebook, it costs the company more than $6200 a year. There are about 800,000 workplaces in Australia."

This is not to say that having a presence on a social media site isn't profitable for most businesses; however, more and more, HR personnel have to contend with employees spending too much time using social media when they're supposed to be working. The forensic analyst is typically faced with providing the HR department with a context for how much non-work activity may be going on during business hours. As with pornography investigations, some information is easy to get at, and some takes a little work.

Although there certainly are more social media sites than Facebook, I'll focus on Facebook for now in terms of the ramifications for the forensics analyst, because it is the largest social network and because there is a greater statistical chance that you will deal with a case involving Facebook. The techniques described here are equally valid for other social media sites.

Note

I focus on Facebook Chat here because it's the world's most popular social web site at the time of writing this book. Many other instant messaging software packages are available for time-wasting. The best way to make sure you know what the suspect could have used is to review their installed programs and their Internet history, and then look for artifacts of their chats. For some applications, they will be in self-contained log files for easy recovery. For web-based chats like Facebook, you will have to search the forensic image as I do in this example.

Examining how much time employees spend playing games or viewing their page or a friend's page on Facebook is easy. All the information is contained in the Internet history file, with URLs, timestamps, and so on. This is very simple stuff already covered in this book, so I won't waste time here. What is a little more difficult is to analyze the amount of time spent on Facebook Chat, the site's instant message (IM) service.

But analysis of IM on Facebook is fairly straightforward, once you understand the components. The first thing to remember is that there are forensic artifacts of the chat, and the complete chat sessions are actually cached on the user's system. Each message thread is cached in its entirety every time the page is refreshed or the user returns focus to the chat window.

When searching for Facebook IM sessions, you'll find it easy to search for text that's found in every session. For me, that is the keyword `"msgID"`. Yes, you'll also get a lot of false positive results, particularly in e-mails; however, you can very easily sort the resulting filenames or extensions to streamline the review. I like to sort by filename because all that remains to be done is to look for the telltale naming conventions of the chat artifacts, which are characterized by long numeric filenames. In some cases, they could be TXT files, or they could be HTML files.

Tip

If you are having no luck with searching for Facebook chat messages because of a change in Facebook's format since this book was published, or you are looking for other chat tools, you might want to look into tools that specialize in the recovery of instant messaging. Belkasoft's Evidence Center and Magnet Forensics' Internet Evidence Finder are two such tools, but there are many others. Or you can do the research yourself to find the identifiers and search out the chat remnants.

I recovered Facebook Chat messages after searching for the keyword `"msgID"` and sorted by filename to find the following two files in the Temporary Internet Files (Figure 11-3):

```
p_100002240784811=2[6].txt
Book\Part_2\NONAME-NTFS\Documents and Settings\rgorgal\Local Settings\
    Temporary Internet Files\Content.IE5\4DQGH2BF
\p_100002240784811=2[6].txt
```

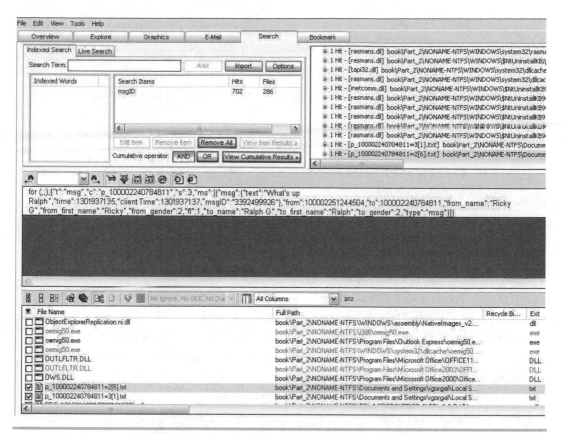

Figure 11-3 A recovered Facebook chat message

```
p_100002240784811=3[1].txt
Book\Part_2\NONAME-NTFS\Documents and Settings\rgorgal\Local Settings\
     Temporary Internet Files\Content.IE5\
M9DZHCV3\p_100002240784811=3[1].txt
```

Examine the following contents and you can see the IM session in its various parts. In the first TXT file, p_100002240784811=2, you see the opening part of the thread:

```
for (;;);{"t":"msg","c":"p_100002240784811","s":3,"ms":[{"msg":
{"text":"What's up Ralph","time":1301937135,"clientTime":1301937137,
     "msgID":"3392499926"},"from":100002251244504
,"to":100002240784811,"from_name":"Ricky G","from_first_name":"Ricky",
     "from_gender":2, "fl":1,"to_name":"Ralph
     ","to_first_name":"Ralph","to_gender":2,"type":"msg"}]}
```

Let's break it down:

- On the first line, the text message "What's up Ralph" is recorded.

- On the second line, the time the message is sent is recorded, as well as the `"msgID"`. You can see that the sender is user profile 100002251244504 and the recipient is user profile 100002240784811.

- On the third line, the aliases of the two user profiles are recorded.

Thus, Ricky sends Ralph the message, "What's up Ralph", at Time: 1301937135. The timestamps are Unix time code.

In the second TXT file found on the image, p_100002240784811=3, you see the reply:

```
for (;;);{"t":"msg","c":"p_100002240784811","s":4,"ms":[{"msg":
    {"text":"Not much Rick","time":1301937187,"clientTime":1301937193,
    "msgID":"2095800751"},"from":100002240784811,
"to":100002251244504,"from_name":"Ralph G","from_first_name":"Ralph",
    "from_gender":2,"to_name":"Ricky G","to_first_name":"Ricky",
    "to_gender":2,"type":"msg"}]}
```

Notice that the two filenames, p_100002240784811=3 and p_100002240784811=2, correspond to the Facebook profile number of the user alias Ralph. That means the image being worked on was Ralph's computer.

To discover the date/time of the text message thread, you'll need to convert the Unix time codes. There are lots of free Unix time converters out there, but the one I prefer is at www.onlineconversion.com/unix_time.htm.

Note
Although I specify that these chat artifacts can be found in HTML or TXT files, the file type makes no difference to the underlying data. As long as the data you are looking at more or less matches the examples just shown, you know you're viewing Facebook chat messages.

We've Covered

We've talked about two types of the most common HR cases and how to approach them. The biggest commonality between these two types of cases is that the user's Internet activity is the source of the evidence we start with. So if you are starting a HR case, you should begin your investigation by recovering deleted Internet history records. Finding porn and users wasting company time on the Internet are fairly straightforward cases. It can get complicated if the user is trying to hide their tracks; if you encounter this, visit our blog for the newest techniques for identifying and recovering what the suspect is trying to hide.

Results of a human resource case

- What to expect a HR case will need to reach a conclusion
- When to expect termination versus discipline for your suspect

How to work a pornography case

- Recovering active and deleted Internet history
- How to recover streaming video usage

How to work a productivity waste case

- Understanding what makes a productivity waste case
- How to recover chat messages between social network users

CHAPTER 12

Administrator Abuse

We'll Cover

- Dealing with challenges in administrator abuse cases

- Investigating an administrator running his own business out of his employer's network

- Investigating an ex-administrator spying on his prior employer

Chapter 11 covered how to work human resources cases. This chapter covers the challenges in administrator abuse cases, as well as how to investigate theft and espionage. In my experience, cases involving administrator abuse are as bad as it gets, especially in terms of challenges presented from an analytical perspective and damage that can be inflicted upon an organization. Make sure to go to www.learndfir.com to watch videos on working the cases in this chapter and download images to work on your own.

An administrator as a suspect presents a challenge unlike others, because an administrator has the access and the technical ability to wipe out the forensic evidence you rely on. If this person is cautious, they will also be watching the e-mail accounts of those who could investigate them to get advance notice to wipe the evidence. When an administrator is your suspect, make sure you advise those you are working with not to use corporate-owned or controlled systems to communicate about the investigation. Examples of internal systems to avoid include Voice over IP (VoIP) phones, e-mail, corporate instant messaging, and anything else your rogue administrator can monitor.

The Abuse of Omniscience

Administrator abuse is the abuse of omniscience. Why? Because administrators know *everything*: they are paid to know everything. They know how everything is configured—remember the IT director from Chapter 11 who created the rule on the content filter that allowed only his IP address to access pornographic web sites? Beyond allowing themselves access to restricted web sites by exempting themselves in the systems meant to restrict them, administrators also have the network credentials that will grant them access to whatever information they desire on the network. As we'll see later on in this chapter, admins can also use those privileges to change evidence and hide their tracks.

Knowing how everything is configured and having unlimited access results in a one-two punch that most often means the forensic analyst must fully understand how the interconnected networks operate in order to find the evidence.

LINGO
Network credentials refers to such things as the username and password required to log into a company computer as the administrator, or the password to network routers and security appliances, for example.

LINGO
Security appliances can be firewalls, content filters, data leakage prevention systems, and so on. Any type of dedicated system that is made to secure the company's network applies here.

While participating in an expert panel, I was asked, "What makes a good forensic investigator?" My answer was, "Someone who not only understands how to reverse a user's actions while thinking as an investigator, but who also understands how a network operates." Computer forensic examinations of a single system are essentially straightforward, because all the data you need to review is contained in a single place: the hard drive of the system(s) you're working on. Yes, finding evidence of pornography, chat sessions, and e-mails is important, but when compared to the investigation of a network and the activities that span it, these types of cases are simple.

If you want to step up your game in terms of a challenge, performing a forensic investigation across a corporate network is the place to do it, and networks are the world of the administrator. In most of your investigations, you will be reviewing the activities of a user who may or may not have technical knowledge. An administrator suspect will have gained a large amount of technical skills and configured the systems you will be investigating, which means they will know the systems far better than you do. Your advantage will be in your specific knowledge of computer forensics and forensic artifacts—knowledge that, hopefully, the suspect will be lacking. This knowledge and the element of surprise are what you will have to even the playing field.

IMHO
In my dealings with administrator suspects, I've found that their greatest weakness is usually their confidence in their abilities. One ex-administrator who was assisting another in spying on his former company never thought of deleting the logs he left behind, because no one, in his opinion, was smart enough to find them. Other administrators assumed they knew how to hide or delete data but then failed to wipe it, making it easy for simple recovery. The worst thing that can happen is if the administrator becomes aware of your investigation, because they will focus their efforts on hiding the evidence. Most administrators leave the evidence of their actions in place because they think it's "their systems" and no one else will look at them, or know how to.

The world of the administrator is much broader than a group of machines you might have to image as part of your normal investigation. The admin's world is about routers, firewalls, databases, e-mail servers, authentication mechanisms, physical and virtual machines, and the list goes on. And you have to know how it all works together.

In Actual Practice

It's important that you find out what other potential sources of evidence exist on the network. Although you may start your review with the current network infrastructure, it's important that you determine what kind of network logging and correlation systems are in place already. Security Information and Event Manager (SIEM) is one such system that maintains all of the events and logs generated from systems across the network, and they are a goldmine of evidence when you're looking to determine the actions of a network user. Recorded historical log information can be overwritten quickly if it is stored within a network appliance, especially firewalls, so examining where a suspect might be sending those logs can help you tremendously. Just make sure that you don't tip off your suspect to your investigation when you inquire about such information.

Suppose you know how to find evidence of pornography, chat sessions, and e-mails; how would you even begin to work a case in which an unauthorized person is reading the e-mails of the top executives in your company? In such cases, the suspect may reveal himself, because top executives get suspicious when the only place a specific piece of information that was leaked to your competitor exists is in a single confidential e-mail sent by the CEO to the CFO just the day prior. With the mandate of identifying where the leak came from, can you discern whether spyware has been installed on potentially every computer in the organization, or whether an insider working against the company?

For a larger list of the kinds of administrator abuses we've come across, look back at Chapter 10.

Scenario 1: Administrator Runs a Pornographic Site Using Company Resources

This real-life scenario begins with, of all things, spam. A woman received spam via e-mail at home on her personal computer. She clicked on the link included in the e-mail and was immediately redirected to a pornographic web site. She was paranoid about reporting spam and knew how to track down domains via the IP in the message header. After she identified the domain, she discovered that the IP was assigned to a management company. She called the company, and she talked directly to the company owner. She explained to him how the originating IP address came from his company's domain. The company owner requested that the woman forward him a copy of the e-mail and explain to him how she obtained their IP address.

The woman later sent the requested information, and when the company owner clicked the links, he saw that they did indeed redirect him to a pornographic web site located on his company's network.

The company owner then assigned the task of investigating the matter to the company IT director. A few days later, the IT department reported that they could not find any evidence that their servers had been compromised, and they also reported finding no unusual content on any of the web servers.

After the meeting with the IT director, the company owner decided to take the IT department's report at face value; he determined that no further action was required. Several days later, the company owner was watching a news report about network hacking and how tracks are typically hidden; he decided to have a thorough threat assessment made of his company's network, so he contacted a private investigator. At that point, the PI contacted me to consult on the investigation.

IMHO

It's a "special" type of suspect who thinks he or she can get away with something as brazen as running a business out of his employer's systems. Although these cases are not common, when they do occur, it's almost always the case that someone at an executive level is involved to ensure that your overall investigation activities and resource usage can be hidden from others. Keep this in mind as you talk to your contact person; they need to be aware that they must not communicate to anyone involved with the systems—executive or otherwise—of your presence, or else the suspect(s) may get tipped off and destroy the evidence before you have a chance to preserve it.

Beginning an Investigation

As you begin an investigation that may span an entire corporate network, you need to know that, ultimately, you'll be dealing with many different pieces of equipment. You should understand that you are responsible for putting all those pieces together to access all the evidence you are looking for. If you don't feel up to the task, ask for help early on.

You might assume that the first place to start, when dealing with a rogue web site, is the web server. However, it's very important to keep one thing in mind as you work with one of these systems: Any web server, regardless of the host operating system, needs to be considered for what it is primarily designed to be—an *interface* to *other* systems and services.

In Actual Practice

As you begin your work on a complex case, you can create a list of all of the possible evidence you may want to review and the artifacts you know should exist. As you work through the case, keeping this list and updating it ensures that you don't miss anything and helps you keep your eye on the big picture.

The Web Server's Role in the Network

A web server is usually considered a static system that provides pages after a browser requests them. However, a web server can also be an interface to other systems and services, connecting to databases and business applications that feed it data to display on those pages. In this case, the web server is not the only piece of forensic evidence you must preserve, but it's your starting point in determining what other systems are involved. But first, you have to find the web server.

LINGO
A **web server** provides web pages to web clients. The amount of systems and processing involved in generating a web page depends on the developers and the underlying code that exists in the page.

A web server can be designed as a doorway, or an interface, to the world, exposing data stored on other systems in the network. In that capacity, more so than with other kinds of servers, web servers present unique challenges both to administrators who must secure them and to investigators who must put the pieces together to solve a case. If you look at the statistical measures for network breaches or exploitation of other system or service vulnerabilities, the web server is often used as the point of entry, or system penetration vector.

Accessing Other Systems

In our pornography scenario, the suspect web server was a Microsoft Internet Information Services (IIS) server. As an interface to other systems and services, IIS provides a functional set of methods for accessing system resources, such as the file system. This can be accomplished by using HTTP GET and PUT commands, directory browsing with WebDAV, and so on. Web servers do not necessarily store the content they access on the local system. They can rely on something as simple as a network drive or as complicated as a Distributed File System (DFS) for that. So, for example, even though the physical web server may be in Miami, the actual web content (that is, pages, images, and so on) can be in Los Angeles, or overseas, or anywhere within the corporate network.

> **LINGO**
> Any network of servers in which shared data is replicated and stored can be considered a **Distributed File System (DFS)**. Microsoft uses the term to describe its implementation of this technology within Windows Servers. Multiple systems appear to have local storage, which is actually mapped across multiple systems across the network. To recover any deleted data or create a forensic image of the physical disks that make it up, you must track down those servers.

From a computer forensics perspective, instead of imaging just one system, you may need to image multiple systems in diverse locations (and with differing laws in other countries) to perform the analysis of a single web server if you're looking for deleted files and other artifacts. That's much different from standalone PC forensics, in which each system is its own island; even if that system has a RAID attached, it's still a limited set of drives that contain the evidence you need to preserve and analyze. In contrast, with a DFS, you may have to forensically image multiple systems and then re-create the network back in your lab to examine how it functioned. Add in the complexities of virtual machines, and you realize you'll need to make sure you understand the environment you are examining before you decide what to preserve and what not to.

Accessing Other Services

Certainly, web servers can interface with relational databases such as Microsoft SQL and e-mail servers such as Microsoft Exchange. In both cases, "other services" are being accessed, and the web server is acting as the interface to those back-end services. This means the evidence you need to preserve isn't limited to the servers where data is physically stored, per se, but it also includes the underlying data contained in the services to which the data is connected.

Web pages can be coded to interact and access databases in myriad ways (such as server pages, ASP.NET, Java, PHP, and so on), but the framework is always essentially the same. This is important to keep in mind when you're trying to understand the source of the data being presented in your examination. Consider the following:

1. A user connects to a web server via her browser, the web client.

2. The web server takes the request and executes the code in the web page to query the back-end database server.

3. The database server runs a query with the provided information and returns the results to the web server.

4. The web server builds a new web page on the spot and inserts the query results on the page, and then sends the page back to the web browser, where it is presented to the user.

In Actual Practice

I am discussing an example of a web site whose pages are being created from the database dynamically for every access. Common web platforms, known as content management systems, such as WordPress, ConcretePlatform, Joomla!, and others work in similar fashion. That does not mean that a web platform is the only way that a web server can interact with a database—that depends on what the code in the web page is written to do.

Investigating the Web Server

A database server itself may not store its database on a local disk. Instead, the database may be located on a DFS drive or a SAN drive. Remember that assessing the configuration of the service is not limited to any one service, such as the web server, to determine where the underlying data is stored. You don't want to make an assumption about where data is stored only to begin your analysis and then realize that you are missing data and have to redo your work.

As we began our investigation into the rogue pornography web site, my team was able to establish that, indeed, the company web server did not contain any of the pornographic material described. However, during our network analysis and documentation, we discovered that all five of the servers on the network were default installations of Windows 2000. Each of these servers came with Microsoft IIS version 5 running by default; therefore, there wasn't just one web server on the network, as you would infer from the stated purpose of the systems; there were five.

After imaging all the servers, we found that the pornographic site was actually being run on the company's file server, where no one was looking for it. All of the pornographic site content (graphics, HTML, and ASP) were found in an obscure folder inside the Program Files folder of the machine being used as the file server.

In Actual Practice

I wish I could report that we made the discovery by examination of some grand technically challenging search scheme to trace network traffic in real time, but in fact we just mounted the images into our forensic tool and went over to the graphics tab and scrolled through looking for dirty pictures until we found them. That's why the existence of porn is so easy to investigate. Remember, however, that in your investigations, you may be limited regarding what you are being asked to review. If there are privacy concerns in your investigation, you may not be allowed to review any pictures stored on the system.

Directories

Web servers use directories to restrict what data a remote user can request to files and folders beneath its web root. In most cases, those files are HTML documents; however, web servers can provide access to any type of data that it's configured to allow. In addition, in modern web servers, what often appears to be a page is actually a program executing on the web server and returning content instead of just the content of a file in the directory.

LINGO
The **web root** is the first folder in the hierarchy from which the web server will return data. For instance, if you configured your web root as C:\web, then the web server would not serve up any information from the C:\ directory, because it is outside of the C:\web path.

In this case, we were dealing with IIS, so I'll discuss some of the directory issues with IIS. IIS sets up two directories when it is installed: One is in the %systemroot%\ System32 directory called Inetsrv, which contains configuration files related to running and administering the IIS server. The other is the web root, in the %systemdrive%\Inetpub directory by default, but administrators have the option of changing the web root location during installation. It has several directories that may contain some sample HTML files and includes the default web root directory named wwwroot.

When users connect to the web server without any specific request for a page, such as a request to www.google.com, the web server follows its configuration to load the default page. In the case of IIS, the default page would be located in the wwwroot directory. The web server then returns the default page for that directory (that is, the home page).

In Actual Practice

Because IIS can host virtual servers and virtual directories, these web root locations can be modified. (Surely you didn't think it would be that easy after getting to this point!) A web server can be configured to host multiple web sites with different web roots and different default pages all from one IP address; each of these web sites would be hosted in what's known as a "virtual server." To determine what page to display, the web server looks at what web site has been requested. To determine whether virtual servers exist, you must examine the configuration of the web server.

Virtual Servers

Like most web servers, IIS can be configured to host multiple domain names on the same computer—such as sales.mydomain.com, marketing.mydomain.com, mydomain. com, yourdomain.com, and so on. This can be accomplished by assigning a separate IP address to each site and having the web server configured to respond to each IP address differently—or, more commonly, the web server can take the domain that the web client has requested and determine which virtual site should be accessed. This can make analysis confusing when you are trying to locate a particular virtual server and you don't know the hostname, so, again, you'll need to go back to the configuration to determine what exists.

Virtual Directories

IIS allows the files used by web sites to reside either on the local computer hosting the web site or on shares located on other systems, as shown in Figure 12-1.

In the IIS Manager interface (Figure 12-1), you can see that several web sites are being run on this single physical server. Some of the content is local, but the ProFolders, Exchange, and Exadmin folders are not.

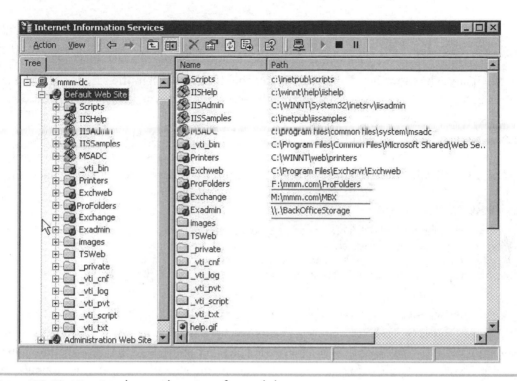

Figure 12-1   Viewing the true location of virtual directories

During my team's analysis of the source code for the pornography site, we discovered a database call to a sample database on the company SQL database server. The call was to the Northwind Traders sample database that is installed with Microsoft SQL Server 2000. The next logical step in the investigation was to determine what part the database server played in this matter. Examination of an SQL server is fairly straightforward if you are interested in the actual raw data contained in the databases. Because forensic tools do not mount relational databases or allow you to search them efficiently, the easiest way to examine the server, in the case of a SQL server, is to export the pertinent data file (.mdf) and the related log data file (.ldf) from the forensic image.

After extracting the data and log files from the SQL Server forensic image, my team mounted the database on a separate SQL server and found that the pornographic web site user and credit card information was being maintained in the Northwind database. So all the client data for the porn site was intermixed with all the sample data that ships with the Northwind database from Microsoft, and it looked as though it was sample data, too. This was a very clever way of hiding data in plain sight.

The next step in the investigation was to follow the data packets, which meant we needed to backtrack the route a packet would travel. This led us to the firewall.

Examination of the firewall revealed that the company had four external IP addresses, as provided by their ISP. One of them was assigned to the porn site, according to the DNS record, and the mail server was on a completely different IP range at a commercial hosting company. The firewall had a rule configured that forwarded all traffic associated with the external IP of the porn site to the internal IP of the file server, and when the request was received by the web server, it served up the site.

Obviously, when you discover a firewall configuration like this, it points toward internal IT resources being complicit with the web site's operation. Our examination of the firewall rule didn't reveal any further relevant information or configuration anomalies.

Note
In this case, the firewall didn't have good logging enabled to capture what changes were being made by which user, and it was not configured to send its logs to another system for long-term storage. If we had this information, we could have determined which internal resources were allowing the traffic to be routed to the file server and capture those systems.

After we found the pornographic web site on the file server, the customer and payment records on the SQL server, and modifications to the corporate firewall, we were granted permission to image all of the company computers for analysis to find out who internally was involved. During our review of the network administrator's computer, we found several hits to the offending pornographic web site's domain. The first hits were not out of the norm, since he had been tasked with finding out whether a breach had indeed occurred. Later keyword hits came back to the webmail interface for the porn site, located at an external web hosting company, which only someone who was operating the site would know to access. As a result, we were able to recover remnant copies of the porn site's inbox, including e-mails generated by the online payment system and those from customers.

After exporting the files, the network administrator was interviewed by human resources, and he admitted he owned the site.

Scenario 2: Exploiting Insider Knowledge Against an Ex-employer

Of all the cases I've been involved with since I first got into this type of work in 1999, what follows is by far the worst and most damaging in terms of scope. It would not have been possible without the key knowledge of several former network administrators, who used their in-depth knowledge of systems they themselves installed to plan and execute a relentless series of spy and sabotage attacks against their former employer. In the end, tens of millions of dollars were made and lost. This case took more than a year to investigate and then settle in civil court; as of this writing, the suspects are facing criminal charges.

A Private Investigator Calls...

This case began when my team was called by a private investigator, who had been contacted by a local company to check for listening devices in their offices. The company was suspicious that one of their competitors had been listening to their conversations. Why? Because a large portion of their customers had been lost to a brand-new company in their service space. After the private investigator had not been able to locate any listening devices, he suggested they have their computers scanned to determine whether they had been compromised in some manner and gave them our contact information.

As if They're Reading Our Minds...

My team initially received a small group of computers for imaging and analysis. Some of these computers belonged to five former long-term employees who had very recently resigned—and had gone to work for a new competitor. It turned out that the new company had been started by one of the former employees less than a year earlier. In that short amount of time, the new company managed to take several of our client's longest standing and most profitable customers.

In Actual Practice

At the beginning of any case, you may find it easy to be led toward a conclusion by the person who brought you in. It's important that you keep perspective and always let the evidence be your guide when you're making conclusions. Sometimes, you'll find that what started off as one type of case turns into something else completely before you are finished!

For some reason, the new company always seemed to be one step ahead of our client and *somehow* had knowledge of highly confidential information relating to business dealings. Things just didn't add up (not ethically, at least). During my initial meeting on site, the in-house legal counsel said it was as though the competitors were reading their minds. Now, with no listening devices found anywhere in the office building, they wanted to make sure their network had not been compromised.

We were given several computers for imaging; these belonged to several high-ranking former employees encompassing sales, management, logistics, and network administration. The initial scope was to determine whether the systems contained data indicating that these former employees had accessed critical client information to take with them to the competitor, as well as any communication with the new company while they were still employed.

LINGO

The **scope** of your investigation is always determined by the person requesting it. I've talked about this in previous chapters in the book, but you are rarely given free rein to review a system for what *you* believe is pertinent. Instead whoever asked you to perform your investigation will explain what they are looking for and what they are asking you to determine.

In addition, we received computers from the highest ranking current staff to determine whether they contained data that would indicate they had been compromised in some fashion, via keystroke loggers or other malware. After imaging and analysis, we found no evidence of system compromise on the current employees' computers. We then recommended a network vulnerability assessment, which was approved.

In Actual Practice

This case began as a civil investigation, but at the end of the civil case, a criminal investigation was commenced by the FBI. It's important to remember that your case can also turn criminal, so always make sure that you keep good case records and chain-of-custody records to assist law enforcement in their use of your forensic images.

What a Network Vulnerability Assessment Can Reveal

It was at this stage, during analysis of the Microsoft IIS system that hosted the corporate webmail, where we found the first indications of a compromise.

During the analysis of the web server Outlook Web Access (OWA) logs, we found various instances of a defined group of network service accounts, including the corporate voicemail server account, Blackberry Exchange Server account, and database server account, had been accessing and reading the e-mails of the company president, CFO, legal counsel, marketing director, and more. We found that more than 50 high-ranking staff members' e-mails had been read.

Tip

I remember explaining to the company executives and attorneys that it's not normal for voicemail servers to log into webmail sites. You should not assume that whoever is requesting your work is technical enough to understand why that's funny. Take the time to explain not only what you found, but what it means and why it's important.

Further review of the Active Directory records revealed that all of the service accounts that had been used to read the mailboxes had network administration rights and were given administrative rights to the mail server, so they could read any user's mail. Thus, whoever was using these service accounts was logging onto the domain with full network administrative privileges.

After exporting all the web server logs from this forensic image, we imported them into a relational database for further analysis. This revealed that someone had been using these service accounts to access the e-mails of company executives approximately nine months earlier.

Additionally, the source IP addresses were both external and internal. This meant that in some of the sessions where e-mail was read, the web browser that did the reading was assigned an internal IP address. The logical conclusions at that point were that insiders were involved, or a VPN or other remote access was used.

We then captured a forensic image of the VPN server and analyzed the logs, which indicated that the external IP addresses that were documented in the webmail server logs had also connected to the VPN server. The VPN session logs revealed that the assigned internal IP addresses correlated to the IP addresses found on the webmail server logs. We were then able to re-create the complete series of events, from the external client logging onto the VPN server, being assigned an internal IP address, and then starting a webmail session to read the executives' e-mails. In other cases, the intruders simply went to the webmail server's external interface and logged on. The logs also indicated that after the messages were read, they were then remarked as unread.

After we documented all of the relevant external IP addresses from the logs, our next step was to determine their origin. In some cases, the IP addresses were tracked to the new company—where the former employees now worked. In other cases, the ISP data indicated that the users accessed the webmail via their home accounts.

The next phase of this investigation was to determine the scope of damage by documenting which e-mails had been accessed and what sensitive company data had been compromised. When dealing with Outlook Web Access data, as we did in this case, the best place to get that kind of information is in the web server logs. That's because OWA logs are configured to record the title of each e-mail that's accessed and every attachment that is opened. The attachments are stored as objects in the Exchange Server database (EDB), and they are documented in the URL column of the OWA server logs. So if you simply copy and paste the URL into a web browser that is currently running an OWA session, you can access the e-mail and attachments exactly as they were read by the user.

Figure 12-2 shows the formatting of the OWA log file and the order in which viewing occurred. In the cs-uri-query column (at right) of the database containing the imported OWA logs, the commands shown were `preview`, `open`, and so on, when the message was being previewed, opened, and so on. In the cs-uri-stem column, notice the objects that were accessed, as shown in the figure.

In the log, we focused on e-mails titled Super*XXXX* Info.eml, or FW: Layne *XXXX* .eml. We also found that an MS Word attachment, Dance Flyer.doc, had been accessed. Immediately after the filename of the Word document is the object reference in the Exchange database, which must be passed to the server.

We didn't enter this investigation with an awareness that the OWA logs could be analyzed to determine what e-mails were being accessed. Instead, we found the evidence of the accesses and then began testing ways to determine how to re-create what was being viewed at the time.

E-mail Data Review and Server Restoration

We found thousands of e-mails to review. Over the span of several months, we restored incremental backups of the Exchange Server to our re-created working environment and passed the e-mail and attachment URLs through an automated process to a web browser.

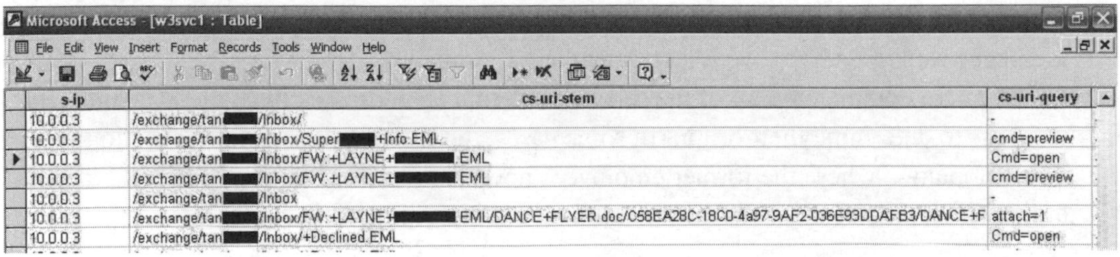

Figure 12-2   Reviewing a OWA log in MS Access

This allowed us to provide the client with copies of every e-mail and attachment that had been read, for which the data still existed on the backup tapes.

The former employees took client lists, read highly sensitive marketing and strategic partnership agreements, as well as closely guarded deal information, and used that information to take customers away from our client's company. All of this would not have been possible if the former IT managers, who now worked for the new competitor, had not exploited their in-depth knowledge of their former network:

- They used their personal knowledge that those obscure service accounts all had domain administrative privileges.

- They knew how to log onto the VPN, and once inside they used the pcAnywhere tool to take over client systems to access subsystems and try to cover their tracks.

- They knew where the front door was, and, more importantly, where the backdoor was.

We learned that the ex-network administrator set up all of the administrative permissions to the network and e-mail systems on these service accounts before he left the company. When training his replacement, he agreed to be recorded via audio tape as a means to keep better notes that would help in the transition. In that audio recording, he informs his replacement that he should never change the passwords on those service accounts "because no one knows what it would break," although the truth was that changing the passwords would have closed the backdoors he had opened to the network.

Stepping Up Your Game: Knowledge Meets Creativity

Earlier, I said that a case that involves administrator abuse across networked systems is where you really step up your game, because it will pit your personal skills against those of someone who has a greater technical knowledge of the network you are trying to analyze. That is true; however, both of these cases illustrate an essential point: When dealing with administrator abuse, you must exercise patience and approach the investigation in a methodical and logical manner. Just because they know more about their network doesn't mean they can't make a mistake or become complacent with their own systems. The administrator who took the time to think of a creative way to hide his porn site by putting it on a back-end server and storing his client transaction records in a sample database didn't bother to clean his own computer, and he left behind all the Internet history files.

The administrators who took the time to think of using service accounts to read e-mails, and hid their tracks by using the VPN and pcAnywhere, overlooked deleting the simple IIS log of the very service they were exploiting.

In Actual Practice

There is no such thing as a court approved tool, as mentioned in previous chapters in this book. What matters is that you created sound forensic images of the evidence you are preserving and can replicate the evidence you've found to another examiner who can reach the same conclusion as you.

In both cases, forensic tools and methodologies were used to obtain and preserve legally defensible data. However, most of the real work was done outside of a forensic tool. Don't limit yourself to the closest and/or most convenient forensic tool. Nothing says you are a better forensics investigator if you spend days reviewing log files with a forensic tool, painstakingly, one line at a time, versus dumping all the service logs into a database so you can query it in two minutes. There is nothing that says your case will stand up better if you spend days going through IIS configuration files trying to decipher the Inetsrv data using a forensic tool instead of just going to the web server, opening up the administrative interface, and documenting where the web site is storing its data.

We've Covered

In this chapter, you got to see how to approach two scenarios involving rogue administrators. We focused mainly on procedures and techniques and not as much on artifacts, as in network investigations the logs usually become the centerpiece of the investigation. Log analysis is a big part of large forensic investigations, especially because you often do not have access to examine the offending system or the administrator wiped the evidence.

Dealing with challenges in administrator abuse cases

- Deal with the unique challenges of investigating those people with access to do what they choose presents the investigator with unique challenges.
- Work outside the view of the rogue administrator who may be watching.

Investigating an administrator running his own business out of his employer's network

- Detect and track down network abnormalities.
- Track down the true location of your evidence.

Investigating an ex-administrator spying on his prior employer

- Detect espionage and find the source of the leak.
- Determine who is involved and find previously unknown evidence sources to prove your case.

CHAPTER 13

Stealing Information

We'll Cover

- How to look for patterns and identify artifacts
- How to determine where the data went
- How to detect which data has been taken on external devices

The theft of information can involve a lot of diverse activities, but in this chapter, we will cover the most common example: the theft of corporate information by a (soon-to-be) ex-employee. We'll look at how to determine where the stolen data has gone and how to recover evidence after information has been stolen.

What Are We Looking For?

We are looking for evidence of an employee stealing correspondence, customer contacts, drawings, contracts, spreadsheets, e-mails, source code, and other company-owned information—whatever they consider of value to them or a future employer. In a nutshell, you're interested in determining whether an employee transferred files to some external media or otherwise transferred the data out of the control of the original owner or employer to make the information available to use in the future.

These cases typically involve certain patterns that you should keep in mind as an investigator. For example, you'll usually see increase in user access to files, which occurs in large blocks. A large number of files may be accessed on a specific day; then, perhaps another set will be accessed the day after. These files may be copied on to external storage devices (USB, FireWire, eSata, and so on) or uploaded to file hosting/webmail web sites. Typically, if the employee is transferring data via e-mail, he or she rarely uses the corporate e-mail system. Most people understand that the corporate e-mail system is, or can be, monitored and backed up. The user obviously doesn't want to have their activities intercepted by corporate IT personnel, or otherwise preserved for posterity. Most employees will use a corporate e-mail alternative such as Yahoo! Mail, Gmail, or Hotmail to send the data they consider valuable out of the corporate system.

In the vast majority of these cases, the suspect believes that their personal web-based e-mail leaves no trace on the actual computer. Luckily for us, that's not the case. Most commercial forensic tools have webmail analysis and carving features, and they work in the same way. They search the drive image for the unique headers used by the various webmail systems across both active HTML files and searching for valid header/footer combinations across the drive for deleted files. This has changed somewhat with the wide usage of Asynchronous JavaScript and XML (AJAX), which does not require a new HTML page to be created for each request. We can still recover the e-mails the suspect has viewed, but the artifacts that contain them are more likely to be overwritten more quickly as they typically exist only in the pagefile/swap. These artifacts are encoded in JavaScript Object Notation (JSON) and are well documented.

> **LINGO**
> **Asynchronous JavaScript and XML (AJAX)** is the magic behind the ability to update part of a page without reloading the entire page. AJAX is used in almost all Web 2.0 applications. It works when a JavaScript function at a set interval or action makes a request to a web site that replies to the request in XML. The XML is then parsed and the updated data is shown to the user. The parsed XML objects returned from a AJAX call are normally stored in **JavaScript Object Notation**.

Data that can help you work a case involving stolen information can be varied and can come from diverse types and locations. Consider all the forensic artifacts available to you when trying to determine whether a suspect has taken data with them. Table 13-1 shows some places you should check (most of these artifact sources are discussed in this chapter).

Combining these artifacts tells a compelling story about what was taken, how it was taken, and when it was taken. Putting these stories into a report (as discussed in Chapter 16) may be enough to convince an ex-employee to return stolen information or to get a judge to grant an order forcing him to do so.

Type of Artifact	What It Tells You
Webmail	Whether your suspect was attaching files from his computer and sending them through his personal e-mail
LNK Files	Whether your suspect was accessing files copied onto other drives
Shellbags	What other directories exist on other drives identified from the LNK files
USBSTOR	The make, model, and serial number of an external storage device, as well as when it was last plugged in
Setupapi logs	The first time a storage device was plugged in
Log fragments	Activity showing what the suspect was taking

Table 13-1   Artifacts and What They Tell You

Tip

Two popular products can help you find the most popular kinds of webmail for review. Internet Evidence Finder from JAD software and Evidence Center from Belkasoft will search a forensic image and find all of the known webmail fragments on the disk for you. You can do this by hand as well, but using these products can save you lots of time.

I won't go into webmail analysis in this section, because in a best-case scenario, one of the recovered HTML pages will be the user's Inbox, which will have columns identifying the sender, date, subject, and whether an attachment is included. Inbox views are typically static and written to the disk in their entirety, which makes it easier for us to recover. The individual e-mails will either be static pages for older webmail systems or JSON objects. A static page will be written to the disk in the cache folder and will be recoverable in its entirety. If parts of the page are dynamic—aka JSON—they will typically exist only in the pagefile and memory dumps. Attachments are handled separately and typically have their own static page or JSON object created, indicating their successful uploading and possible virus scan.

LINGO
The **Inbox view** refers to finding a page viewed by the suspect when he viewed the webmail. The page is typically static and can be recovered through standard data carving.

In Actual Practice

Remember that you can recover only what the suspect received from the web server. Text typed into a form, such as sending or replying to an e-mail, is not usually sent back to the sender but is instead directly submitted to the web server. You can't forensically recover what is not viewed and stored on the suspect's system.

When it comes to webmail, it's either there or it's not; to determine whether you should look for it, use the Internet history records (see Chapter 11). If you can find Internet history records showing access to a webmail site, you should begin trying to find the artifacts it created. Using tools like NetAnalysis to rebuild cached pages helps with this, and using the suspect's e-mail address as a search term is a great way to find all the Inbox pages, because it is normally displayed in the header of the page.

If by luck the corporate e-mail system is used, the e-mails are usually routine correspondence. The user includes his home account as a blind carbon copy for the purpose of "archiving" important information in case something happens to the corporate e-mail system, or if the user begins to forward e-mails to a personal account. This is simple to detect: search for the suspect forwarding or BCCing (blind carbon copying) any messages to a personal account. If you can't locate their personal accounts, a quick review of the suspect's Internet history should help you identify them.

Determining Where the Data Went

Another common way that suspects take data is via USB flash drives or USB hard drives. The USB flash drive has made it easy to take large amounts of data. Luckily, established procedures of forensic artifacts to inspect can help us determine whether this has occurred.

LNK Files

LNK (or .LNK) files are created whenever files or folders are opened on a Windows 95 or later system through Windows Explorer. The following information is contained in a LNK file:

- The full path to the file, which can be the local drive, network share, removable media, and so on

- The type of drive the file is being accessed from: removable media, CD-ROM, local drive, or network share

- The size of the file in bytes

- The volume name and serial number of the drive from which the file is being accessed

- The MAC address of the system where the file is stored if it's being accessed over the network

- Date information related to when the associated file was created, modified, and accessed: it will also have its own date information, identifying when the .LNK itself was created, modified, and accessed

LNK files are found in both the active file system as well as free space on the drive. Most commercial forensic tools have the built-in ability to recover LNK

> **LINGO**
> **Windows Explorer** is the interface you work through on your desktop. If you are viewing files and folders through My Documents, My Computer, or any other graphical interface to your files, you are using Windows Explorer. Don't confuse Windows Explorer with Internet Explorer, which is a web browsing application.

data from the free space. LNK files have the same names as the files they are accessing, so if an MS Word document named Document1.doc is accessed, for example, the corresponding LNK file would be named Document1.LNK.

Note

If you recover, or data carve, a LNK file from free space, you will not have the name of the LNK file or the metadata of the LNK file. You will still have the contents of the LNK file, however, so you'll know what file it was pointing to and the relevant metadata. Although some investigators will downplay the importance of LNK files, they are some of the most important pieces of evidence provided on any Windows system. They offer detailed examples of specific file access, especially when you can use them to determine what files existed on an external storage device you no longer have access to.

In Actual Practice

LNK files don't just matter for external devices. For example, I worked on a case where a single LNK to a SQL Server application led to further investigation of a server not originally in my investigations scope. On review of the transaction logs, I saw that after logging on, the user ran a query of all the company client information. The resulting data was then saved to a CSV file, which I found by following any files that were created after the time in the transaction log. Back on the suspect's system, I found a LNK to the CSV, which identified the file as residing on a USB flash drive. These separate LNK files brought the user activity into contextual meaning, where I could re-create what happened first, second, third, and so on.

In most forensic tools, the easiest way to get to the LNK files is to filter the files for the LNK extension. The LNK files associated with a user's recent folder will be found at the following locations:

- **Windows 95/XP/Vista**   <Path to User Directory>\Recent
- **Windows 7**   <Path to User Directory>\AppData\Roaming\Microsoft\Windows\Recent

You can also find LNK files in the following places:

- The Microsoft Office directories in the user's profile directory for files opened within Microsoft Office
- The Start menu directory tree for each user for every executable
- The Desktop folder found in the user profile for any desktop shortcuts and for any other application that decides to make use of LNK files

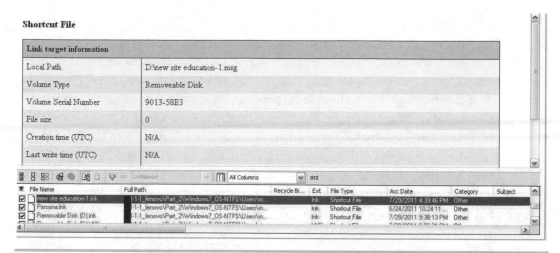

Figure 13-1   LNK file showing access to a .msg file on a removable disk

As shown in Figure 13-1, FTK parses LNK files for you and presents the most forensically relevant portions of its contents. In this example, you can see that an e-mail .msg file was accessed from a removable disk.

Before moving on to the next section, you need to understand the significance of the dates found on a LNK file and within it. Table 13-2 explains them.

If you clearly explain the meaning of a LNK file timestamp in your report, you can much better explain when and where a file or a series of files was copied to an external storage device.

Type of Date Timestamp	Located on the LNK File	Located Within the LNK File
Creation	The first time this file, located at this path, has been accessed on this computer	When this file was created/copied to whatever directory the LNK file is pointing to
Modification	The last time the file was accessed from this computer	The last time the file being pointed to was modified, at the time it was being opened by the LNK file
Access	The last time the file was accessed from this computer, but it can also be changed by other processes	The last time the file being pointed to was accessed, at the time it was being opened by the LNK file

Table 13-2   LNK File Dates

Shellbags

Shellbags can reveal information about external devices that few other artifacts can. Shellbags are found in the Windows Registry and store user preferences for folder display in Windows Explorer, such as the size of the window or how items were listed. For a folder to exist in the shellbags, it must have been opened in Windows Explorer at least one time by the user. The shellbag subkey information is specific to each user and can be found in their NTUSER.DAT registry file for Windows XP and later and also in the USRCLASS .DAT registry for Windows 7, both located within the user's profile directory.

Like LNK files, shellbags contain specific information regarding when a folder was first accessed and last updated, plus the folder name, full path, and so on. Why, then, do

we need to locate shellbags for review? Although LNK files show us only which files and possibly directories have been opened, shellbags show us every directory a user accessed, whether they opened a file in it or not. When you are attempting to understand the scope and breadth of what files may have been copied onto external storage devices or what other contents an external storage device contained, this is incredibly useful.

> **LINGO**
> **Shellbags** are a series of registry keys that keep track of a user's preferences on how each directory he or she has opened should be displayed. They allow us as investigators to determine which directories a user has accessed using Explorer and their creation, modification, and access dates.

The registry files are located in the following folders:

- **Windows XP/Vista**   <User Profile Directory>\NTUSER.DAT

- **Windows 7**   <User Profile Directory>\AppData\Local\Microsoft\Windows\ USRCLASS.DAT

You can use several tools to analyze shellbags, including Paraben's Registry Analyzer and TZWorks' ShellBag Parser (sbag.exe). For this example, we will use the sbag.exe, a command-line tool available for download from www.tzworks.net/prototype_page.php?proto_id=14.

Parsing the contents with sbag.exe involves three steps:

1. Export the user's NTUSER.DAT, and/or USRCLASS.DAT for Windows 7, from the forensic image into a directory where sbag.exe is located.

2. Execute sbag.exe, as shown in Figure 13-2. You can see we redirected the output of the program to a file named ntuser.csv instead of to the screen.

3. Open the CSV file into a spreadsheet program such as Excel to review the contents.

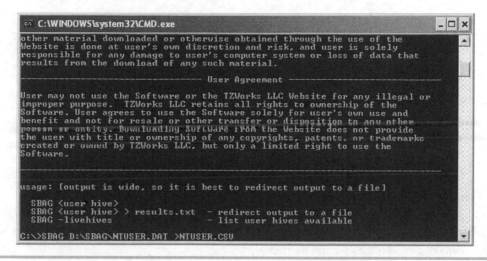

Figure 13-2   Running sbag.exe

In this case, the NTUSER.DAT file is located at D:\SBAG\NTUSER.DAT, and the output file, NTUSER.CSV, will be created in the same folder, as illustrated in Figure 13-3. We will have to repeat the process for USRCLASS.DAT, which is located in the same directory if this came from a Windows 7 image.

After the shellbags data has been parsed and exported by the SBAG.EXE, it can be opened natively by any application that can interpret the CSV data. Note that for sbag .exe, the field separator is actually the pipe symbol (|) and not a comma. In Figure 13-4, the CSV is being opened in Microsoft Excel. You can see the entries for D:\ drive, the removable disk, in lines 388–395. In addition to the directory path, you can also see the creation, modification, and access dates of the directory last captured by the system.

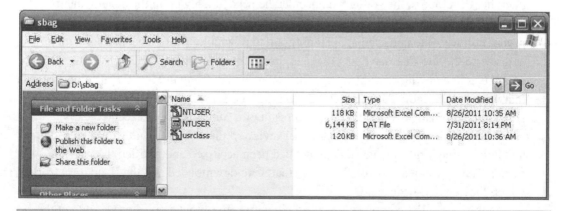

Figure 13-3   The resulting files stored in the directory

385	25	07/30/11 02:18:59.649	D:							Desktop\(CLSID_MyComputer}\D:\
386	62	07/30/11 02:18:59.649	Q:							Desktop\(CLSID_MyComputer}\Q:\
387	94	07/30/11 02:18:59.649	D:							Desktop\(CLSID_MyComputer}\D:\
388	107	07/30/11 01:42:49.809	Account Management	01/26/2011	04:06:44	01/26/2011	04:06:46	01/26/2011	04:06:46	Desktop\(CLSID_MyComputer}\D:\Accd
389	108	07/30/11 01:42:49.809	Recordings	01/26/2011	04:06:46	01/26/2011	04:07:44	01/26/2011	04:07:44	Desktop\(CLSID_MyComputer}\D:\BD Cal
390	123	07/30/11 01:42:49.809	Seagate	11/22/2010	21:31:36	11/22/2010	21:31:38	11/22/2010	21:31:46	Desktop\(CLSID_MyComputer}\D:\Seagate\
391	124	01/26/11 20:14:22.968	SeagateDashboard	11/22/2010	21:31:38	11/22/2010	21:31:38	11/22/2010	21:31:46	Desktop\(CLSID_MyComputer}\D:\Seaga
392	126	07/30/11 01:42:49.809	Products	01/26/2011	05:48:42	01/26/2011	07:13:26	01/26/2011	23:47:16	Desktop\(CLSID_MyComputer}\D:\Products\
393	127	01/28/11 17:50:59.669	Lead Generation	01/26/2011	05:50:38	01/26/2011	05:58:48	01/26/2011	23:47:16	Desktop\(CLSID_MyComputer}\D:\Product
394	128	01/28/11 17:50:59.669	Compensation Planning	01/26/2011	07:10:52	01/26/2011	07:13:06	01/26/2011	23:47:16	Desktop\(CLSID_MyComputer}\D:\Prod
395	129	01/28/11 17:50:18.173	Research	01/26/2011	07:12:04	01/26/2011	07:13:04	01/26/2011	23:47:16	Desktop\(CLSID_MyComputer}\D:\Products\

Figure 13-4   Reviewing the contents of the parsed shellbags in Excel

Equally as useful is the registry modification time; this shows the last time the directory was accessed by this user.

To put the last two sections together, make sure to read Chapter 14 and learn about the USBSTOR registry key and the SetupAPI logs to be able to tie your external devices to their makes, models, and serial numbers.

Scenario: Recovering Log Files to Catch a Thief

Sometimes, the only evidence that data has been copied comes from text fragments in partially overwritten logs. A great example is a case I worked a few years ago: a soon-to-be-former employee saw the writing on the wall and decided to pull the ejection handle before his boss had a chance to fire him. In this case, a web development firm had one big customer comprising more than 70 percent of its business, but it was going to be replaced by another web development company in 90 days.

One of the developers knew his position would soon be eliminated, so he applied for a job at the company that was taking over the contract. However, the new company would deal with him only as a contractor on a probationary basis.

Eager to impress his new bosses with his productivity, and to get a head start on all the other developers, the young man decided he needed a leg up in the development cycle. Using his inside knowledge of how the web site was configured, he logged onto the production web site and used an FTP program to download files he needed for a major upgrade to the site that was being planned. In doing so, he also selected the entire site contents in the download, which happened to include more than 100,000 customer records that were kept in individual archival files on the web server. The archival files were generated automatically at midnight, as a result of a subroutine that executed daily.

The next morning, the hosting provider reviewed their firewall and web server logs and noticed the large amount of data that had been accessed and notified the web site owner. They provided lists of all the files that were downloaded and the IP address from which they were downloaded.

At this point, the company contacted a law firm to obtain a court order and get the customer information associated with the IP address on the date in question from the ISP.

After being contacted by the legal team, the developer denied accessing the web site and downloading the files. He then agreed to allow examiners to take a forensic image of his laptop.

All of the customer records that were on the web server had a standardized naming convention that always started with the same set of characters, so those were used as keyword search criteria. During the search, thousands of hits to the standardized naming convention were found in a partially overwritten log from the FTP program he used, WSFTP. This log recorded that the files had been downloaded directly from the company web server to a USB hard drive that was attached to the laptop that evening.

After presenting the findings to the client, the legal team feared that the 100,000-plus customer files and web site code might have been copied onto other media. They presented their arguments to the court, and a judge authorized a seizure of all media at the developer's residence for analysis. The U.S. Marshals Service served the order on the developer, and all media in his home was taken into custody for review.

After confronting the developer with the log, he admitted to the download.

During our analysis of the media seized from his home, we discovered that the USB hard drive that the files had been copied onto originally had by then been reformatted. We were able to recover more than 70,000 of the customer files and provided the findings to the legal team that there was no additional evidence of the files having been copied onto any other media.

In Actual Practice

Recovering log files can be as easy as finding them deleted in the directory they were created in or as complicated as recovering them from the free space. However, to do either, you have to know what kind of logs you are looking for. For example, if you are looking for FTP server logs, you would find a current log on the system and find some unique term within it to search for to find other deleted partial logs in the free space. Tools such as the scalpel utility can be helpful in log file recovery, because you can define a pattern that matches your log file entry and have it export out all the entries that match it.

You might notice that I've gotten specific regarding a specific log type. This is because log types vary widely, depending on what made the log. Even saying an FTP server log is not very specific, because there are Microsoft FTP Servers, FileZilla FTP servers, Serv-U FTP Servers, and so on, each with its own log format. The important thing to remember is that you need to find out what types of logs you could be interested in, find samples of the log entries, and then search to find them so you can review their contents and reconstruct the suspect's activities.

We've Covered

In this chapter, we've gone over the most common ways that employees take information with them when they leave an employer. These cases make up the bulk of our case load, and most companies are surprised to discover who the thief ends up being. The best-case scenarios involve a former employee taking contacts and knowledge to try to stay in contact with customers they are forbidden to solicit based on signed agreements. The worst-case scenarios involve employees stealing decades of intellectual property and trade secrets to compete unfairly and steal business away.

How to look for patterns and identify artifacts

- Identify the most likely sources of data exfiltration.
- Track down webmail to recover files being e-mailed out or sent to the cloud.

How to determine where the data went

- Review Internet histories to find webmail and cloud storage sites.
- Review user activity to determine data transfer and access.

How to detect which data has been taken on external devices

- Use shellbag data to identify which external storage devices have been connected and when they were connected.
- Determine what existed on external storage devices.

CHAPTER 14

Internal Leaks

We'll Cover

- Why internal leaks happen

- How to investigate internal leaks

- Using file system meta-data to track leaked or printed materials

One of the most common and easiest ways organizational information is leaked is by someone working inside an organization. This chapter will prepare you to conduct a post-mortem investigation—that is, after an internal leak has occurred. I'll cover how to investigate internal leaks and simple scenarios to get you started with an investigation.

IMHO

Most IT professionals are likely to think they know the obvious ways information can be leaked from an organization, but they may not fully understand the mechanics. I worked in IT for years before entering the computer forensics industry, so I am familiar with how IT professionals think. My eyes were opened to an entirely new perspective when I entered the computer forensics world, and I am far more paranoid now than I was when I was in IT. Electronic information has become so ubiquitous that it is difficult to know where to begin looking for misconduct.

Why Internal Leaks Happen

The reasons and causes leading to an individual leaking internal information are numerous. An internal leak is a great threat to an organization precisely because it comes from the *inside*, where critical data is often far too easy to access, because all the protections in place are focused on outside intruders. Many threats are present in the age of the Internet; however, the easiest way to get information is still to "walk it out the door," and this is easiest done by someone on the *inside*. This chapter does not present a case study on how to prevent internal leaks; instead, it will educate you regarding the ways internal leaks can occur and offer techniques you can use to identify credible forensic evidence.

Following are some examples of types of internal leaks.

- Corporate espionage:
  - Intellectual property theft is extremely valuable, and litigation can be very costly.
  - Stolen business processes can provide a competitive advantage to another company.
  - Stolen pricing schedules, vendor agreements, and customer relationship management (CRM) data are valuable; undercutting based on these stolen documents happens more than you might think.
  - Finance and accounting information can offer insider information when applied to a public company.
- Disgruntled employees may have bad feelings or malice toward the organization and may steal information as revenge.
- Poor information security practices can lead to theft. Organizations should use strong group policy settings, digital rights management, and strong Active Directory (AD) auditing, as well as some form of Internet usage tracking in conjunction with a firewall.
- Negligence or incompetence can lead to theft. Laptops can be stolen from cars, for example.

It is amazing what some people think they can get away with, and often do, because of poor security practices and limited internal reviews and auditing of business practices. Performing a security review and audit and keeping people on their toes can help keep dishonest fingers out of the cookie jar; a competent and outside consultancy is best suited for such a job. Letting people within the organization know you have the tools, training, and processes in place to be able to track or discover what they have done if they choose to abuse their corporate privileges, even if moderately exaggerated, is a valid method of deterrence against the potential criminal.

In Actual Practice

The burden is on you to analyze the evidence to determine the facts pertaining to the matter. Once you are notified or have knowledge of an internal leak, you should deal with the matter promptly and according to *commonly accepted forensic practices*, or you could be in for trouble if the evidence and/or your findings regarding the matter

(continued)

make their way to court. This is especially important for the first responder who first handles the evidence. Even if the first responder is not trained in forensic techniques, getting them to document their actions can be enough to assure that the evidence is acceptable in court. Chain of custody starts with whoever first possesses the evidence; your ability to explain what happened to it while you were interacting with it is just as important. If you can't explain how things came to exist before forensic imaging, your evidence may be excluded in court. For some commonly accepted forensic practices, go to www.swgde.org.

Investigating Internal Leaks

Forensic artifacts are time-sensitive, because normal usage of a computer can and will overwrite information that can be critical for the investigation. This is why it is so important to act in an expedient and proper manner to preserve the hard drive, external devices, file server, cell phone, e-mail, tape backups, and other relevant data and storage devices without arousing the suspect's suspicions. If you can gather the evidence without the suspect's knowledge, the suspect will not be able to cover their tracks and hide or destroy evidence.

In Actual Practice

Avoid the temptation to examine a suspect's PC to look for smoking guns before taking the proper forensic route. For example, one of my clients asked an IT person to examine the files on a PC of a suspected employee. Unfortunately for this client, the IT person moved and/or copied files on this computer and then opened the files. By doing this, the IT person changed *meta-data* and possibly *overwrote* data in drive free-space—data that is critical to the investigation! Such activity could destroy the very evidence you are trying to find.

In addition, if a judge has issued a protective order to preserve the person's computer, and you go snooping around after the order has gone into effect (even if you merely boot the PC), you have violated the court order and the judge is not going to be happy. A computer hard drive should be preserved when possible as a forensic image before you go snooping around.

In any forensic investigation, when looking for files that might have been copied to external media, you must take the following basic steps:

1. Review the registry files: Look for user activity in UserAssist and RecentDocs in NTUSER.DAT. Look for the use of external storage devices by examining USBStor in SYSTEM.

2. Look for file activity by reviewing LNK (Windows shortcut) files.

3. Wrap up the investigation by obtaining and examining any involved external storage devices.

> **LINGO**
> **Meta-data** is data about the data. It commonly contains information such as the creation, modification, and access times of a file. However, on an application-by-application basis, the meta-data can also contain things like the author's name, the name of the computer that created the file, which printer the file was sent to, who the file was e-mailed to, what the original name of the file was, and more! Understanding what kind of meta-data is kept by your company's applications is important so you know what to look for.

Reviewing the Registry Files

You'll typically start an investigation by reviewing registry files to search for user activity and externally attached devices. This multiple-step process involves the review of each user's NTUSER.DAT on the system—not just the primary user—and documenting the individual details. It is also important that you look at create dates for important system directories such as \Windows, \Users, and \Program Files and compare those to the create dates for NTUSER.DAT. This helps you establish the age of the system and user profiles. You can add evidence using Forensic Toolkit, EnCase Forensics, or SANS Investigative Forensic Toolkit (SIFT) software suites.

Following are Microsoft Windows registry file locations as of 2011:

- c:\users\<userdir>\NTUSER.DAT (Vista/Windows7)
- c:\Documents and Settings\<userdir>\NTUSER.DAT (Windows XP and Windows 2000)
- c:\windows\system32\config\SYSTEM
- c:\windows\system32\config\SOFTWARE

User Activity: UserAssist and RecentDocs in NTUSER.DAT

In the user's NTUSER.DAT file, the UserAssist key will allow you to see recent user activity and the Start menu jump list, and RecentDocs will show recently used documents by file extension. Sometimes this artifact can be a gold mine; other times, not so much. The RecentDocs registry key holds recent activities performed by the user—unless the user cleared the activity, disabled the RecentDocs feature, or used another tool such as CCleaner or SIFT Workstation's Forensic Log Analysis GUI (FLAG) to clean it out.

Tip

For the following examples, I created a text file using Notepad and saved it to a USB thumbdrive. In Figure 14-1, you can see that I used Notepad; Figure 14-2 shows the reference to a LNK file; notice the timestamps used in these figures. Keeping track of date-time's correctly is critical to the success of your analysis. Keep notes of what you are doing and when you did it. Good notes also help with justification for your work later on.

CCleaner   CCleaner (or Crap Cleaner) is a popular free tool that can be used to clear out a user's activity from a system. We frequently find this program on suspect systems and often the registry keys are empty because of its use.

The UserAssist and RecentDocs entries are found at the following locations:

- [HKLM]\SOFTWARE\Microsoft\Windows\CurrentVersion\Explorer\UserAssist
- [HKCU]\SOFTWARE\Microsoft\Windows\CurrentVersion\Explorer\RecentDocs

In Figure 14-1, you can see (under Value Properties at the lower left) that I used Notepad on May 13, 2011.

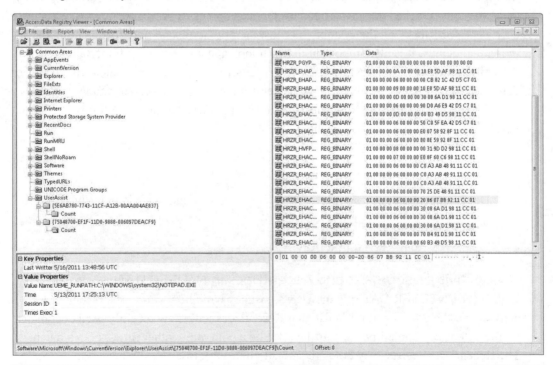

Figure 14-1   Viewing Notepad's execution in UserAssist

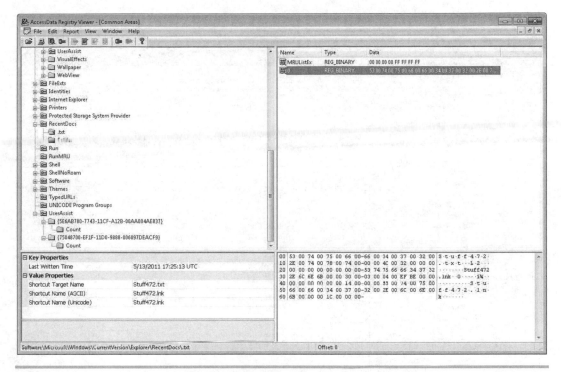

Figure 14-2   Viewing a LNK file access in UserAssist

In Figure 14-2, under Value Properties, you can see an entry for a text file with a corresponding LNK file value, which indicates that we might be able to find an LNK file that will tell us more on the drive.

FLAG   Using FLAG in Mozilla Firefox in SIFT Workstation did not properly decode UserAssist (as shown in Figure 14-3). (Note that as of this book's writing FLAG is still in beta preview.)

> **Tip**
>
> I like to review the registry using at least two tools to limit the risk of missing something obvious or running into a nuance in one of the tools. It slows me down a little, but I'd rather be sure than miss something important! A free registry parsing tool that provides easy to read output is RegRipper (http://regripper.wordpress.com/regripper/) by Harlan Carvey.

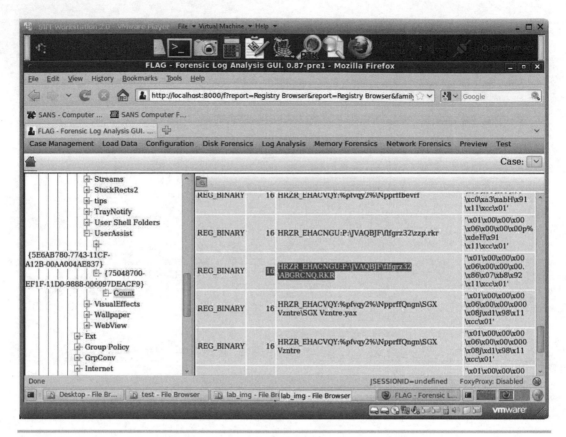

Figure 14-3   Examining UserAssist records in FLAG for SIFT Workstation

External Devices: USBStor in the SYSTEM Registry

Let's review USBStor in the SYSTEM registry file to look for possible external devices. The USBStor contains information for devices attached via USB and can have a large number of entries in older systems. The USBStor can be found at [HKLM]\SYSTEM\ CurrentControlSet\Enum\USBSTOR\.

The following examples are from three forensic kits: AccessData's Registry Viewer, EnCase Forensic, and SIFT FLAG. Figure 14-4 shows an example using AccessData's Registry Viewer component. Figure 14-5 shows how EnCase Forensic renders the USBStor. As you can see, both packages show consistent information regarding the external device. FLAG, shown in Figure 14-6, shows consistent information regarding the USBStor.

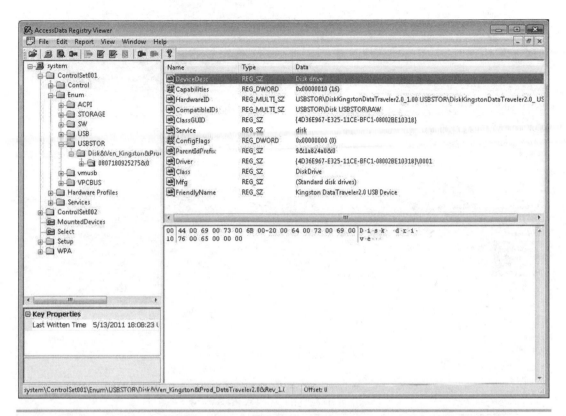

Figure 14-4   Viewing the USBStor key in Registry Viewer

Analysis   As you can see, a USB thumb-drive was attached on May 13. The internal serial number assigned to it by Windows is 0807180825275&0, and we have the "friendly name" for the device: Kingston Data Traveler. Now we have something specific to look for when we're identifying LNK files, in addition to the file Stuff472.txt that we are interested in tracking down—which we found being accessed in the LNK file.

Tip

If a user has restore points enabled in Windows 7 or Vista, you can convert the forensic image to a virtual machine and use a tool called Shadow Copy Explorer to open the shadow copies to retrieve previous versions of the registry and files! You can test this on your machine for fun and see what's been stored over time. This leads us in to the next section. For Windows XP systems, restore points will keep copies of LNK files that existed previously on the system.

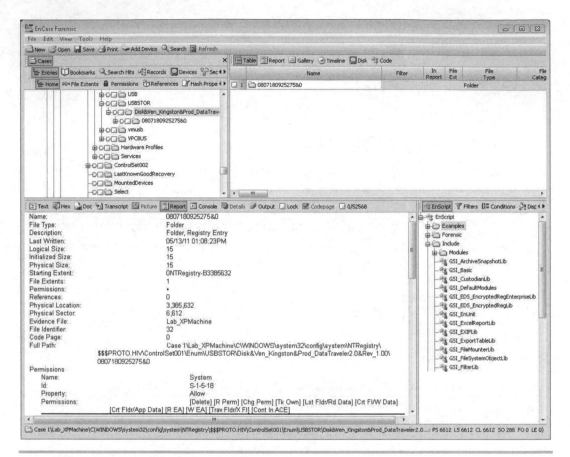

Figure 14-5   Viewing USBStor in EnCase

Identifying LNK Files

A LNK file is created when a file is first accessed. Looking through LNK files can be an exhaustive and painstaking process. For this example, I made it less of a grind by using a clean install of Windows XP in a virtual machine. In actual practice, you'll often come across a computer that has been in use for years and may have been reinstalled, been upgraded, had multiple users, and have bad blocks. This further complicates your search.

Tip

In many cases, you will need to data carve a case to recover LNK files that have been deleted.

Figure 14-6 Viewing USBStor in FLAG for SIFT

In Figure 14-7, I have found the LNKs for stuff472.txt and the external device.

Scrolling down in the EnCase view, you can see more, as shown in Figure 14-8. Unfortunately, the volume name, serial, and base path are all the way at the bottom of the EnCase rendered report.

Forensic Toolkit keeps it simple and easy to view (Figure 14-9).

We open the second LNK file that we see, called KINGSTON (E).lnk (Figure 14-10).

Once again, Forensic Toolkit is easier to review, as shown in Figure 14-11. However, notice the dates. Forensic Toolkit shows a date of 1/1/1980, but EnCase shows 5/13/11. That's because a LNK file actually has two sets of dates. The first set that reflects 5/13/11

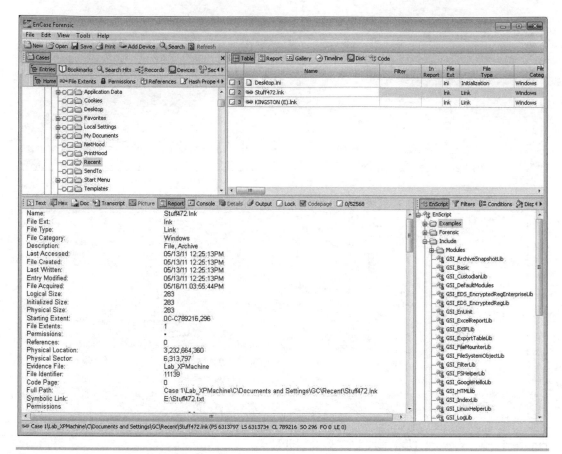

Figure 14-7 Viewing LNK files in EnCase

Volume Name:	KINGSTON
Serial Number:	36DE-3350
Drive Type:	2
Base Name:	E:\Stuff472.txt
Working directory:	E:\

Figure 14-8 Viewing LNK details in EnCase

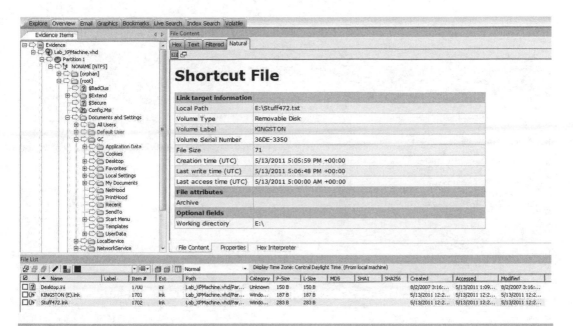

Figure 14-9   Viewing LNK files in Forensic Toolkit

is the time the LNK file itself was created. The second set that reflects 1/1/1980 is the time the thumb drive was formatted. This is the default date in DOS when no date is set that you'll see in many FAT file systems. The same applies to any file that a LNK file points at. This means you can determine when a file was copied onto a device by looking at the creation time of the file the LNK file is pointing to, and you can determine the first time the file was accessed on your suspect's machine by looking at the creation time of the LNK file itself!

With Forensic Toolkit, in this example, you'd have to look at the files listed in the File List tab in the bottom of the screen to see create date and modified date, because the renderer is displaying only the actual contents of the LNK file. EnCase, on the other hand, adds file system meta-data to the report to show created/written/acquired in a consolidated view. It is important that you keep the distinction in mind so you don't get confused.

In Figure 14-11, you can see that I have found the LNK file in the \Documents and Settings\<user>\Recent\ directory as it is highlighted in the file tree in the left frame.

In both Forensic Toolkit and EnCase, you can see the smoking gun. The LNK file shows the file was saved to drive E:\.

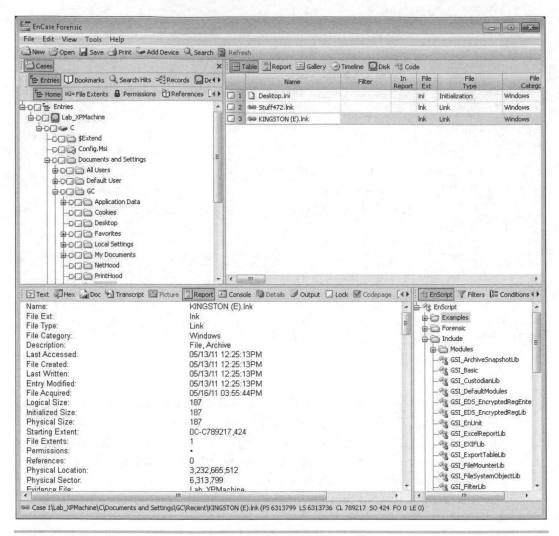

Figure 14-10 Viewing the second LNK file in EnCase

Tip

Always keep in mind the way each tool handles date-time. Notice that Forensic Toolkit specifies the timestamps in UTC (Coordinated Universal Time) and EnCase does not use UTC. However, the Forensic Toolkit date-time in File List frame at the bottom of the interface is adjusted for the time zone you specified for the evidence. It's easy to get tripped up when you're making a case based on timestamps—and many examiners do!

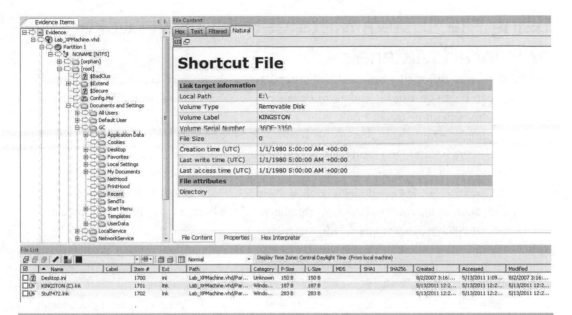

Figure 14-11   Viewing the E:\ drive shortcut in Forensic Toolkit

Note

I regret that I was unable to create examples for LNK files in SIFT that I felt provided quality comparable to the other two products. The tools in SIFT have their strengths and are quickly evolving as a free alternative to expensive tools forensic tools, however.

Wrapping Up the Investigation

We now have what we need to show that Stuff472.txt was saved to an external device. We also know when the file was saved, the Windows serial number associated with the thumbdrive, the volume serial, and the drive letter where it was saved, as well as when it was saved. The next logical step in the investigation would be to request access to the thumbdrive. It's always important to confirm what actually exists on external devices, since our artifacts never tell us everything that exists on a device. Our analysis does not end here, however; there are still more artifacts to examine!

Tip

Ensure that you document your findings in a clear and organized fashion so that you can be prepared when you are asked for details pertaining to the case. Stick to the facts you can prove.

Using File System Meta-data to Track Leaked or Printed Materials

Printed or modified files can easily be re-rendered or they can be carried out the door. Although it can be difficult to determine whether a document has been printed, there are some things to know that can help you.

Examples of important documents for many companies are proprietary CAD drawings (.DWG) containing highly technical and proprietary designs. A CAD document, or any other important documents, can also be printed and taken off site with the suspect.

By reviewing the meta-data embedded in a document through full text indexing engines such as dtSearch (which is a component of the Forensic Toolkit), you have a chance of catching these types of file meta-data.

IMHO

I often print files to PDF for a report or when I pay bills. When I print a document to a PDF printer, some information regarding the source file is retained in the rendered file by default. I use an inexpensive software suite called Pdf995.In past cases, I have come across CAD diagrams printed to PDF and then burned to CD or copied to an external device. When opening a PDF file I printed from an Office 2010 Word document using Pdf995, I was able to identify the source file I used, as shown in this illustration.

```
PˉØ_?ŸØÂÔô=;»Ū±pú–=Ý $)91¡fj~Z–»ᵒY»þÛw&:  •†
½┤›¢‡&óôêãⁱ°0!ᵓAñⁱŸ§ç2¬{0b9YÆp}Þ a–çᴸG›ŒâÃöl
ã g ᴸ¶ᴬ€F┤JĔŽ44¥5Ù]À┴e³Z-p3Úb„b┐Qf
endstream
endobj
2 0 obj
<</Producer(GPL Ghostscript 8.64)
/CreationDate(D:20110516221338-05'00')
/ModDate(D:20110516221338-05'00')
/Title(Microsoft Word - Glossary.docx)
/Creator(PScript5.dll Version 5.2.2)
/Author(dave)>>endobj
xref
0 18
```

As you can see, the source document I printed was called Glossary.docx, and my username is dave. The create date and modified date are also embedded. This can, of course, be stripped, but if you are lucky, your suspect is too lazy or uneducated to take care of this. You can see this data within the forensic tool that you use or within the PDF reader itself by looking at the file's properties within the PDF application.

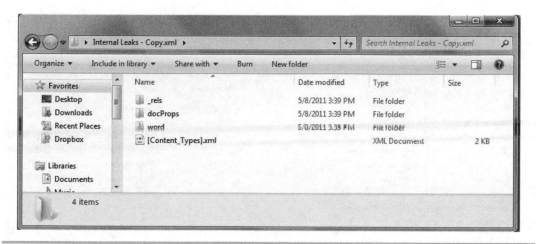

Figure 14-12   Viewing the content of an Office 2010 document

CAD files contain their own internal meta-data that is separate from file system meta-data, and this internal meta-data shows when the innards were last modified and by whom. This is important, because changing one tiny attribute in a CAD (.DWG) file will change the MD5 signature. This even includes the simple act of opening, zooming in or out, and then saving the file since the last saved date is retained within the file! This makes CAD investigations doubly challenging, so they require extra care and deep analysis.

Microsoft Office documents created in Office versions prior to Office 2007 retained Component Object Model/Object Linking and Embedding (COM/OLE) fragments that can contain meta-data, including print history. In Office 2007, the document formats were overhauled and became compressed zip files that contained a series of XML files, as shown in Figures 14-12 and 14-13. However, they still contain the last printed meta-data.

Examples of Office 2010 Word document content is shown in Figures 14-12 and 14-13.

Tip

Other places you can look to recover evidence of print jobs includes carving out printer spools from the unallocated space and examining the network printer's local storage, if it's a model that includes some kind of hard drive.

We've Covered

In this chapter, we expanded on what we saw in Chapter 13 regarding external device access to learn more about the user's activities. Tracking program execution, document metadata,

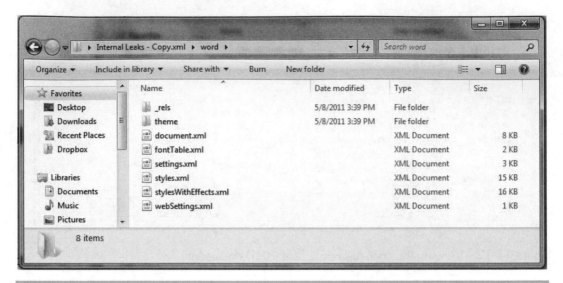

Figure 14-13   Exploring the content of the Word 2010 document archive

and file access helps develop a timeline of events that creates a compelling narrative. Every case you work on will present you with new applications and new artifacts you've never seen before, but building on this base knowledge will help you to know what to expect.

Why internal leaks happen

- Deal with and identify the insider threat.
- Understand the common motivations for insider data leakage.

How to investigate internal leaks

- Access the registry to recover user activity.
  - Review UserAssist and RecentDocs for user activity.
  - Review USBStor for attached devices.
- Understand user file access, on both internal and external storage, with LNK files.

Using file system meta-data to track leaked or printed materials

- Identify meta-data within CAD files to determine their origin.
- Identify meta-data within Office documents to reflect their authorship and usage.
- Work with PDFs and other intermediate document formats to determine source documents.

CHAPTER 15

Keyloggers and Malware

We'll Cover

- Defining keyloggers and malware

- How to detect keyloggers and malware

- Determining how the infection occurred

- Identifying what data was captured

- Finding information about the attacker

This chapter will cover the basics on how to discover the presence of keyloggers and malware on a forensic image. You'll learn where to look for artifacts that can help provide the necessary evidence and information to push an investigation forward.

As a computer forensic examiner, you will eventually work cases that involve the use of keyloggers and malware. This may involve someone such as a past or present employee who has installed these programs in order to spy and steal confidential data from a victim over a period of time. It happens more often than you think, especially when it involves money and theft of intellectual property.

Defining Keyloggers and Malware

A *keylogger* is a malware tool that records a user's keystrokes on a keyboard. Its purpose is to steal password and account information without the user's knowledge. There are several types of keyloggers, but the two most common are hardware- and software-based keyloggers.

A hardware keylogger is a peripheral device that is physically attached between the keyboard and computer so that it can intercept and record all keystrokes. The following illustration shows two types of hardware keyloggers, one for a PS2 (top)—PS2 is an older keyboard/mouse connector not the game console—and the other for a USB keyboard.

Note

A keylogger may be employed within an organization as a tool for purposes that do not involve malicious intent, such as for compliance, security, systems monitoring, and so on. However, this is rare and not the norm. To be clear, keyloggers are malware and should be considered as such.

Software keylogger programs are designed to work on the target computer's operating system. These can be augmented with an array of other features as well. Not only can these tools record keystrokes, but they can record just about every other user activity, such as opening files and folders, opening programs, taking screen shots, capturing web-form text input, and so on, and then upload all this information to a remote location or create backdoors for remote access.

Software-based keyloggers come in a few flavors:

- **API-based**   Relies on a hooking mechanism to capture keystrokes

- **Kernel-based**   Intercepts keystrokes via a modified system driver for the keyboard

- **Form grabbing**   Intercepts or reads web-form data before it is submitted over the Internet

LINGO
Hooking mechanism refers to the ability to use functionality exposed by the operating system for legitimate programs for malicious deeds, in this case, if you attached to the keyboard filter to capture keystrokes instead of providing spell checking.

Note
For more in-depth information on the different types of keyloggers, refer to the following wiki on keystroke logging: http://en.wikipedia.org/wiki/Keystroke_logging.

Finally, *malware*, short for malicious software, is typically used as a catch-all term to refer to any software designed to cause damage to a single computer, server, or computer network, whether it's a virus, spyware, or other type of malicious program.

How to Detect Keyloggers and Malware

Keyloggers and malware are becoming more and more difficult to spot as their designers come up with more elaborate ways to install them and to keep their use hidden from their intended victim and avoid detection. In general, we know that malware can work its way into system startup, running processes, services, install/modify drivers, system files, and more.

Let's begin looking for artifacts in the more common areas of the operating system for their existence, starting with registry files.

Registry Files

We're interested in several registry files (hives). We'll start by looking at the following:

- **HKEY_USERS**   \Documents and Settings\User Profile\NTUSER.DAT
- **HKEY_USERS**   \Users\User Profile\NTUSER.DAT (Vista/Win7)
- **HKEY_LOCAL_MACHINE/SOFTWARE**   \Windows\system32\config\software
- **HKEY_LOCAL_MACHINE/SYSTEM**   \Windows\system32\config\system

After you navigate to the registry file of interest using your forensic tool of choice, right-click the filename and open it using your forensic software's built-in registry viewer (with Forensic Toolkit [FTK]). In EnCase, you'll right-click and select View File Structure; then navigate the registry hive within the tree view in the left panel. If your forensics software does not have a built-in viewer, you can use free registry viewers such as RegRipper, or you can download Registry Viewer from AccessData and run it in demo mode.

Tip

With EnCase and SIFT tools, your time will be better served exporting the registry hives out of the system and using tools such as Registry Viewer or RegRipper to analyze them. You'll find Registry Viewer at http://accessdata.com/support/adownloads and RegRipper at http://regripper.wordpress.com/program-files.

IMHO

I like to start an investigation examining the registry hives, because of the amount of information I can quickly glean as well as the chance of locating an artifact relevant to the case right off the bat. This information can be very handy to have on hand if I'm asked to provide a quick status update.

Registry: User Profiles

Who else has been accessing this computer? This question gets asked all the time, no matter what type of case you are working on. Using Registry Viewer, let's start by examining the ProfileList registry key at HKLM\Microsoft\Windows NT\CurrentVersion\ ProfileList. The ProfileList provides a list of accounts that have accessed this system. We are looking for any accounts that we do not recognize and were active during the timeframe in question. We can determine the last time a user was logged in by looking at the Last Written Time.

An easy way to determine when an account was first created is to navigate to the user's NTUSER.DAT file, as pointed to in the ProfileImagePath shown next, and look at the creation date.

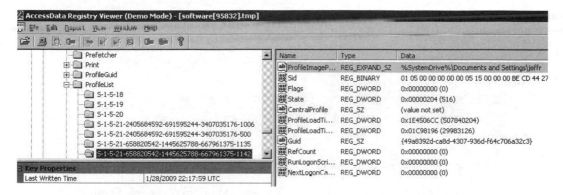

Registry: Run Keys

To begin looking for a malware infection, examine the registry Run keys. The following list contains the latest Windows registry Run keys, where you can look for any rogue startup programs:

- HKLM\Software\Microsoft\Windows\CurrentVersion\Run

- HKCU\Software\Microsoft\Windows\CurrentVersion\Run

- HKLM\Software\Microsoft\Windows\CurrentVersion\RunOnce

- HKCU\Software\Microsoft\Windows\CurrentVersion\RunOnce

- HKLM\Software\Microsoft\Windows\CurrentVersion\Policies\Explorer\Run

- HKCU\Software\Microsoft\Windows\CurrentVersion\Policies\Explorer\Run

Typically, these registry keys will enumerate any programs that are executed at startup and provide the paths to their locations. If you see any programs that you do not recognize, make note; then navigate to the file's location and examine its properties and creation date. Lastly, search online for the filename and see what you can learn. If the file is part of a malware infection, it should become obvious.

The following illustrations show a nasty malware infection; the first shows an infection from the HKLM registry Run key, and the second shows an entry for a keylogger in the ...Policies\Explorer Run key.

Name	Type	Data
MSConfig	REG_SZ	C:\WINDOWS\PCHealth\HelpCtr\Binaries\MSConfig.exe /auto
Xgidadotibuxeru	REG_SZ	rundll32.exe "C:\WINDOWS\afetohap.dll",Startup
HNUGVOXRpcO	REG_SZ	C:\DOCUME~1\GCPART~1\LOCALS~1\Temp\lj1ioi6l.exe
HNUGVOXRme	REG_SZ	C:\DOCUME~1\GCPART~1\LOCALS~1\Temp\avp.exe
HNUGVOXRssc	REG_SZ	C:\DOCUME~1\GCPART~1\LOCALS~1\Temp\winlogon.exe
HNUGVOXRnyc	REG_SZ	C:\DOCUME~1\GCPART~1\LOCALS~1\Temp\csrss.exe
HNUGVOXRpZ	REG_SZ	C:\DOCUME~1\GCPART~1\LOCALS~1\Temp\mdm.exe

Name	Type	Data
SysLogger32	REG_SZ	rundll32.exe "C:\ProgramData\SysLogger\core32_175.dll",z
SysLogger64	REG_SZ	rundll32.exe "C:\ProgramData\SysLogger\core64_175.dll",z

Here are some other registry keys to examine that can kick off programs at startup:

- HKLM\Software\Microsoft\Windows NT\CurrentVersion\Winlogon\Shell

- HKLM\Software\Microsoft\Windows NT\CurrentVersion\Winlogon\Userinit

- HKLM\Software\Microsoft\Windows\CurrentVersion\ShellServiceObjectDelayLoad

- HKLM\System\CurrentControlSet\Control\Session Manager\BootExecute

Note

For more information and to learn about other things to look for in startup programs, refer to the following Microsoft TechNet link: http://technet.microsoft.com/en-us/magazine/ee851671.aspx.

Registry: System Services

It is not uncommon for a malware infection to have services associated with it. We can look to see what services were active at the time at the following registry key: HKLM\System\CurrentControlSet\Services.

Note

Be thorough in your analysis, because it is easy to overlook items and perhaps miss an important clue. Remember that it is getting more difficult to detect rogue services because their creators do not want them to be discovered.

Services will typically point to some sort of driver, *.sys, file located in the Window/System32/drivers directory or an executable file located elsewhere. If you see something that looks suspicious, you will likely have to look up the filename online to see if you can find information such as location, version, size and/or hash values to compare against.

Registry: UserAssist Key

Another place of interest is the UserAssist registry key within the user's NTUSER.DAT. It is possible to find an entry of interest here, which is why it is worth a look. Once you have the User's NTUSER.DAT files open, navigate to HKU\Software\Microsoft\Windows\CurrentVersion\Explorer\UserAssist.

UserAssist entries are encrypted using ROT13 when viewed through Regedit in Windows, as shown in the next illustration. Lucky for us, AccessData's Registry Viewer decrypts these for us automatically. Otherwise, if you are using EnCase, you will need to hunt down an enScript program to do it. Here is an example of what a ROT13 entry looks like before it's deciphered:

HRZR_EHACNGU:P:\QBPHzragf naq Frggvatf\HfreN\Qrfxgbc\sha.rkr

Key Properties	
Last Written Time	12/14/2010 0:25:37 UTC
Value Properties	
Value Name ROT13	UEMF_RUNPATH:C:\Documents and Settings\UserA\Desktop\fun.exe
Time	12/13/2010 23:02:55 UTC
Session ID	137
Times Executed	1

Using RegRipper, you can run rr.exe and select ntuser for the plug-in, as shown here:

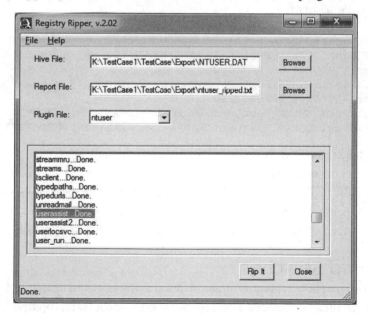

Then do a quick search in the report file for the word "userassist" and you'll locate the entries shown here:

```
Software\Microsoft\Windows\Currentversion\Explorer\UserAssist
Mon Dec 13 23:02:55 2010 (UTC)
UEME_RUNPATH:C:\Documents and Settings\UserA\Desktop\fun.exe (1)
```

Prefetch Files

The prefetch is another area you will want to examine at the beginning of your investigation to detect a malware infection. Windows prefetch (.pf) files contain trace log information for files such as executables (.exe) and dynamic link libraries (DLLs) that an application depends on when it is executed. You can find prefetch files within the following directory: \Windows\Prefetch.

When first examining prefetch files, it's helpful to sort them by their creation date to assist you in going through them. You'll notice that the prefetch files contain the filename and extension for applications being executed as part of the filename. When you come across an application filename that looks suspicious, examine the file's contents. Fortunately, prefetch files capture filenames and locations for not only the application being run, but also for the files it depends on, as shown in the following example (ZIP .EXE-61C23F93.pf):

```
\DEVICE\Disk1\PROGRAMDATA\SYSLOGGER\ZIP.EXE
\DEVICE\Disk1\USERS\PUBLIC\DOCUMENTS\SYSLOGGER\SCREENS\
TestUser1\12052011181907.JPG
\DEVICE\Disk1\USERS\PUBLIC\DOCUMENTS\SYSLOGGER\SCREENS\
TestUser1\12052011181819.JPG
\DEVICE\Disk1\USERS\TestUser1\APPDATA\LOCAL\TEMP\REPORT_TestUser1.ZIP
\DEVICE\Disk1\USERS\TestUser1\APPDATA\LOCAL\TEMP\REPORT_TestUser1.HTML
```

Prefetch files contain a wealth of forensic information. With this information, you may be able to reconstruct a timeline of events as they happened on the system. When you're examining the prefetch, look for the following information: the time of initial infection, how the infection spread, and, possibly, additional pieces of malware. Some malware will download other malware to the system shortly after the initial infection.

Keyword Searches

One of the most powerful tools at our disposal is the keyword search. It is especially helpful in finding commercial keyloggers. If you suspect that a forensic image contains a keylogger, begin with a search for the word "keylogger" and see how many hits you get. Commercial keyloggers market themselves as being stealthy and undetectable, right?

> **Tip**
> You can create a keyword list that contains names of popular keyloggers and other words that you think will generate hits and import them into your search directly if your forensic tool supports it.

Another great thing about keyword searching is that as you go through the search results, you will find other words to search for. It will take a bit of time to go through the results, but you will eventually hit paydirt. Even the expensive, highly rated commercial keyloggers such as WebWatcher leave plenty of artifacts.

It didn't take too long to find this little Micro Keylogger gem—just one of many:

```
Micro Keylogger
Created on 18:19:18 12/05/2011
The Data below has been collected from : 18:19:18 12/05/2011 to 18:19:18 12/05/2011
Monitoring and Blocking Report for Administrator
Report DetailsActivity
```

> **Tip**
> Once you know the name of the keylogger, do some research to see if you can locate and download it. Then you can set up a virtual machine and install the keylogger on it to study its behavior. You can use a tool like the open source RegShot to perform before-and-after file/registry comparisons. This can really aid you in an investigation; it is sort of like having your very own cheat sheet to use as a reference. You can find RegShot at http://sourceforge.net/projects/regshot.

Handling Suspicious Files

So what are your options if you should come across files that look suspicious? I would recommend exporting any suspicious files found in the registry keys or other places to a directory and then uploading the files via the Web to jotti.org (http://virusscan.jotti.org/en), ThreatExpert (threatexpert.com), or a similar automatic analysis site.

Jotti.org will run multiple antivirus packages against submitted binaries and report how they are identified. This can greatly help in your research, since some vendors use a generic name for certain malware, while others will give each variant a specific name. Some vendors do a better job of explaining how a piece of malware works and what files/directories it touches, including MD5 signatures of associated files.

Determining How an Infection Occurred

After you have detected the presence of malware and/or a keylogger on the user's system, you can begin figuring out whether this is just an unfortunate random infection or whether something a bit more sinister has occurred.

Start by asking the following questions:

- What was the user doing at the time of infection?

- Was the user at work, checking e-mail, surfing the Web?

- Was the user away, perhaps home asleep during this time?

Once you know some of the files that are associated with the malware/keylogger, you can use their creation dates to identify the period of time the infection likely took place. This is where timestamps come into play. Sorting actual files based on creation, modified, and last accessed dates will help you determine what kind of activity was taking place around the time of infection. You will also want to check the application, system, and security event logs located in the Windows/System32/Config directory to see if you can find additional info. Make sure to look for remote logins! (Sometimes, event logs are not recoverable or logging was disabled. It is truly amazing how many company laptops and workstations have security logging disabled by default.)

Note
You will need to export the event logs out to view them within Windows Event Viewer. If the logs appear to be corrupted, try viewing them within Event Viewer on the same operating system as the user's. Other third-party tools are also available, such as FixEvt by Rich Murphey (www.murphey.org/fixevt.html).

In the earlier example involving Run keys, one of the filenames of interest that was discovered from the HKLM registry Run key was lj1ioi6l.exe. Keyword searching that filename yields interesting results. Figures 15-1 to 15-4 show search results in EnCase and FTK.

Viewing the contents of the deleted file, 2491_appcompat.txt, shows us a XML table. This file was located in the user's Local Settings\Temp directory. Figure 15-5 shows a snippet of the contents of the infected file.

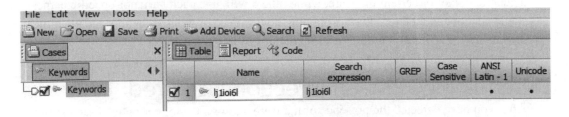

Figure 15-1 EnCase keyword search

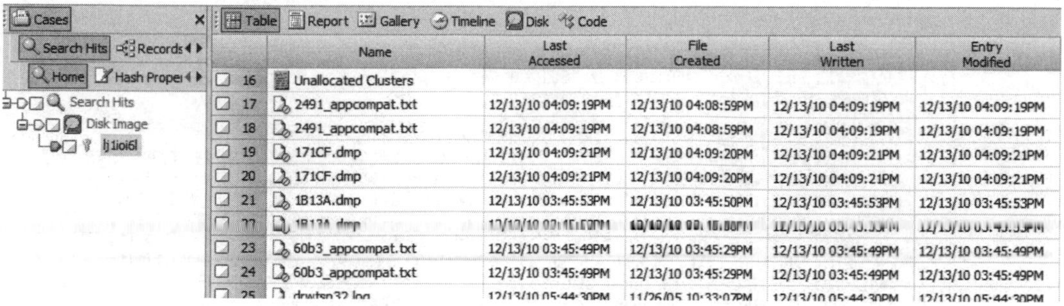

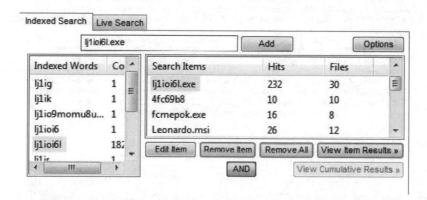

		Name	Last Accessed	File Created	Last Written	Entry Modified
☐	16	Unallocated Clusters				
☐	17	2491_appcompat.txt	12/13/10 04:09:19PM	12/13/10 04:08:59PM	12/13/10 04:09:19PM	12/13/10 04:09:19PM
☐	18	2491_appcompat.txt	12/13/10 04:09:19PM	12/13/10 04:08:59PM	12/13/10 04:09:19PM	12/13/10 04:09:19PM
☐	19	171CF.dmp	12/13/10 04:09:21PM	12/13/10 04:09:20PM	12/13/10 04:09:21PM	12/13/10 04:09:21PM
☐	20	171CF.dmp	12/13/10 04:09:21PM	12/13/10 04:09:20PM	12/13/10 04:09:21PM	12/13/10 04:09:21PM
☐	21	1B13A.dmp	12/13/10 03:45:53PM	12/13/10 03:45:50PM	12/13/10 03:45:53PM	12/13/10 03:45:53PM
☐	22	1B13A.dmp	12/13/10 03:45:53PM	12/13/10 03:45:50PM	12/13/10 03:45:53PM	12/13/10 03:45:53PM
☐	23	60b3_appcompat.txt	12/13/10 03:45:49PM	12/13/10 03:45:29PM	12/13/10 03:45:49PM	12/13/10 03:45:49PM
☐	24	60b3_appcompat.txt	12/13/10 03:45:49PM	12/13/10 03:45:29PM	12/13/10 03:45:49PM	12/13/10 03:45:49PM
☐	25	dwtsn32.log	12/13/10 05:44:30PM	11/26/05 10:33:07PM	12/13/10 05:44:30PM	12/13/10 05:44:30PM

Figure 15-2   EnCase search results

Figure 15-3   FTK indexed search

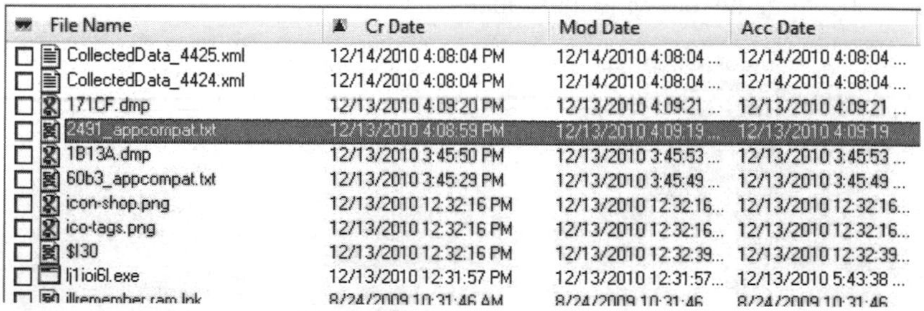

Figure 15-4   FTK search results

```
<?xml version="1.0" encoding="UTF-16"?>
<DATABASE>
<EXE NAME="lj1ioi6l.exe" FILTER="GRABMI_FILTER_PRIVACY">
    <MATCHING_FILE NAME="1450436038.exe" SIZE="0" />
    <MATCHING_FILE NAME="1932122084.exe" SIZE="0" />
    <MATCHING_FILE NAME="247056676.exe" SIZE="0" />
    <MATCHING_FILE NAME="4fc69b8.msi" SIZE="3253760" CHECKSUM="0x7DA177CD" />
    <MATCHING_FILE NAME="88986168.exe" SIZE="21264" CHECKSUM="0x1F6E677E" MODULE_TYPE="V
    <MATCHING_FILE NAME="avp.exe" SIZE="60004" CHECKSUM="0x1F6E677E" MODULE_TYPE="WIN32"
    <MATCHING_FILE NAME="csrss.exe" SIZE="21268" CHECKSUM="0x1F6E677E" MODULE_TYPE="WIN3
    <MATCHING_FILE NAME="fcmepok.exe" SIZE="90112" CHECKSUM="0x3DCA378B" BIN_FILE_VERSION
FILE_VERSION="1, 0, 0, 4" ORIGINAL_FILENAME="checkactivate.dll" INTERNAL_NAME="checkactivate" LE
LINKER_VERSION="0x0" UPTO_BIN_FILE_VERSION="1.0.0.4" UPTO_BIN_PRODUCT_VERSION="1.0.0.4" L
    <MATCHING_FILE NAME="iexplorer.exe" SIZE="2112" CHECKSUM="0x1CE36CAC" MODULE_TYPE="WI
    <MATCHING_FILE NAME="Leonardo.msi" SIZE="1946624" CHECKSUM="0xF5E96D83" />
    <MATCHING_FILE NAME="lj1ioi6l.exe" SIZE="30001" CHECKSUM="0x951CDE70" MODULE_TYPE="WIN
    <MATCHING_FILE NAME="mdm.exe" SIZE="21268" CHECKSUM="0x1F6E677E" MODULE_TYPE="WIN3
    <MATCHING_FILE NAME="mh34mq.exe" SIZE="30000" CHECKSUM="0x951CDE70" MODULE_TYPE="W
    <MATCHING_FILE NAME="nfx4hcvkcycy4h.exe" SIZE="60000" CHECKSUM="0x1F6E677E" MODULE_TY
    <MATCHING_FILE NAME="nsisdt.dll" SIZE="5632" CHECKSUM="0x24C12051" MODULE_TYPE="WIN32"
    <MATCHING_FILE NAME="setup_wm.exe" SIZE="819200" CHECKSUM="0x6ECB5BF6" BIN_FILE_VERSI
Corporation" PRODUCT_NAME="Microsoft(R) Windows Media Player" FILE_VERSION="10.00.00.3646" ORIGI
VERFILETYPE="0x1" MODULE_TYPE="WIN32" PE_CHECKSUM="0xD1C95" LINKER_VERSION="0x50002
States) [0x409]" />
    <MATCHING_FILE NAME="Skype.msi" SIZE="18827264" CHECKSUM="0x61B0050D" />
    <MATCHING_FILE NAME="SkypeToolbars.msi" SIZE="2418176" CHECKSUM="0xD4F21BF2" />
    <MATCHING_FILE NAME="wgfedg.exe" SIZE="279431" CHECKSUM="0x4DD93EAD" MODULE_TYPE="W
    <MATCHING_FILE NAME="winlogon.exe" SIZE="21268" CHECKSUM="0x1F6E677E" MODULE_TYPE="W
    <MATCHING_FILE NAME="xgfuvkeq.exe" SIZE="262656" CHECKSUM="0xF5937B84" MODULE_TYPE="V
    <MATCHING_FILE NAME="batvqrryu\yyxxyouaffm.exe" SIZE="262656" CHECKSUM="0xF5937B84" MODU
    <MATCHING_FILE NAME="bye2.tmp\Disk1\islook.dll" SIZE="40960" CHECKSUM="0x68C5FC04" MODULE
    <MATCHING_FILE NAME="bye2.tmp\Disk1\setup.exe" SIZE="121064" CHECKSUM="0xE00EDBA5" BIN_F
```

Figure 15-5 A portion of the infected file's contents

After you've spent some time keyword searching the filenames in conjunction with doing a bit of research online, it won't take you too long to realize that the infection is associated with a fake virus scan malware software. The big clue was the file yyxxyyouaffm.exe. Searching the filename within the image turned up an interesting bit of text with timestamps within the index. dat file, as shown in the following illustrations:

```
Last Accessed (UTC)
12/13/2010 10:06:35 PM
Last Accessed (Local)
12/13/2010 4:06:35 PM
Last Checked (UTC)
12/13/2010 10:06:36 PM
Expires (UTC)
1/8/2011 10:06:36 PM
Hits
1
Use Count
0
URL
ofnu://C:\DOCUME~1\GCPART~1\LCALS~1\Temp\batvqrryu\yyxxyouaffm.exe/alrt.htm
```

File Name	File Type	Cr Date	Acc Date	Mod Date
yyxxyouaffm.exe	Executable File	12/13/10 12:31 PM	12/13/10 5:43 PM	12/13/10 12:31 PM

What We Know About This Infection

From the artifacts that we have collected, we can start piecing together what took place. This is what we know:

- We have a XML table containing names of malware files.

- We have entries in index.dat for the virus scan pop-up: yyxxyyouaffm.exe /alrt.htm.

- The user was infected on 12/13/2010 at 12:13 P.M.

- Research on the Internet shows yyxxyyouaffm.exe to be some variant of affm.exe, which is a known virus scan malware.

What We Know About the Keylogger

Let's continue with our analysis of the keylogger. We need to know how the keylogger made it onto the machine. We know that after analyzing keyword search results and also looking at our ...\Policies\Explorer Run key entry, we were able to locate a directory created during the keylogger installation called syslogger. Using the directory's creation date, we sorted all actual files around the timestamp. This yielded more artifacts that were associated with the keylogger installation. However, we have yet to explain how the keylogger made it on to the computer—that is, until we noticed a couple of LNK files.

The first illustration shows the LNK file properties, and the second shows the LNK file contents:

File Name	File Type	Cr Date	Acc Date	Mod Date
Readme.lnk	Shortcut File	5/12/11 8:10 PM	5/12/11 8:19 PM	5/12/11 8:19 PM
myprog.lnk	Shortcut File	5/12/11 8:10 PM	5/12/11 8:19 PM	5/12/11 8:19 PM

Local Path	F:\myprog
Volume Type	Removeable Disk
Volume Label	CENTON USB
Volume Serial Number	D02D-413C
File size	0
Creation time (UTC)	5/12/2011 23:10
Last write time (UTC)	5/12/2011 23:10
Last access time (UTC)	5/12/2011 7:00

Local Path	F:\myprog\Readme.html
Volume Type	Removeable Disk
Volume Label	CENTON USB
Volume Serial Number	D02D-413C
File size	8710
Creation time (UTC)	5/12/2011 23:10
Last write time (UTC)	2/23/2011 8:06
Last access time (UTC)	5/12/2011 7:00

Let's take this a bit further, now that we have some new information. Searching for the keyword "myprog" yields an entry in a Windows Defender log file, shown here:

It seems that the install program for this keylogger could very well have been notepad .exe. Fascinating. Perhaps someone was trying to be clever and hide his tracks by renaming the keylogger as an install file. Take a close look at the following log file entry:

```
Begin Resource Scan
Scan ID:{6A660B01-EB29-4004-9017-DFFB26D2B187}
Scan Source:2
Start Time:Thu May 12 2011 18:11:09
End Time:Thu May 12 2011 18:11:11
Explicit resource to scan
Resource Schema:file
Resource Path:F:\myprog\notepad.exe
Result Count:1
Unknown File
Identifier:13912786696220442622
Number of Resources:1
Resource Schema:file
Resource Path:F:\myprog\notepad.exe
Extended Info:0
End Scan
```

[root] \ProgramData\Microsoft\Windows Defender\Support\MPLog-07132009-221054.log

It turns out that this Windows Defender log provides a wealth of information. This file included many other entries for infected keylogger files being scanned.

Next, let's look at the USBSTOR registry key to look for information on the removable disk mentioned within the LNK file. The USBSTOR registry key is located at HKLM\ System\ControlSet001\Enum. Examining the registry key, we find an entry that matches the time on the LNK file. If the custodian of the machine in question is unaware of this removable disk, then it appears that someone else had access to the machine and attached the following thumb drive:

Friendly Name	c.e.n.t.o.n. .D.a.t.a.S.t.i.c.k. .P.r.o. .U.S.B. .D.e.v.i.c.e...
Last Write Time	5/13/2011 1:10:41 UTC
Unique ID - S/N	6&2e67d28f

Notice that the Last Write Time is shown in UTC; in this case, it is +5 hours. UTC, or Universal Time, which is also known as GMT or Greenwich Mean Time, is a way to normalize time so it can be adjusted with offsets to reflect whatever time zone the user is in. We can see more detail about the device in question here; we've seen this registry key before in Chapter 14:

```
Registry Key: Disk&Ven_centon&Prod_DataStick_Pro&Rev_1100\6&2e67d28f&0
Unique ID: 6&2e67d28f&0
```

In an investigation, it is possible for you to verify that you have acquired the USB device that is believed to be the actual device in question. The serial number from the USB device will match the unique ID found in the USBSTOR. To retrieve the serial number from a USB device, you can do the following:

- Use a USB write blocker that will display the information on its display screen.
- Try using forensic imaging software to pull the serial number.

- Use a registry hack, as detailed in Chapter 8, that will disable USB writes on a test box; then attach the USB device, and then compare USBSTOR entries to see if you have a match.

We have collected a lot of artifacts. So what can we accurately say now about the keylogger?

- We know its name: Micro Keylogger
- We know the creation date of the install syslogger directory: 5/12/2011 at 8:11 P.M.
- We know that notepad.exe was executed off a removable disk: 5/12/2011 8:11 (possible install program?)
- We know that a LNK file was created for a removable disk: 5/12/2011 at 8:10 P.M.
- We know that a Centon DataStick Pro USB was attached, with a last write on 5/12/2011 at 8:10 P.M.

Identifying What Data Was Captured

So how can we tell what data was captured off the user's machine? This question will be asked, so you might as well be prepared to answer it. We know that from an earlier artifact, where we learned the name of the keylogger, that reports are being generated. Perhaps it is taking screenshots, too? Fortunately, we were able to locate the Micro Keylogger web site (http://www.microkeylogger.com/), which advertises that its product performs the following:

- Records passwords typed in browsers and applications
- Records Facebook, Google, Yahoo!, and web site passwords
- Records Skype, AIM, MSN, and game passwords
- Records all keystrokes typed by the computer users
- Records all web sites visited, applications used, and files downloaded
- Monitors stealthily and undetectably
- Monitors multiple user accounts in the system
- Captures desktop screenshots by interval

Using this information, our next step would be to locate the files used to generate reports. Through timeline analysis, we should be able find the files/directories that we are looking for, based on last modified, last accessed, and file creation times. We'll sync up these file MAC times against system events and MAC times for malware files already discovered. Filtering files for "actual files" and file types such as documents, graphics, and so on, would make the task easier.

The next illustration shows how lucky we are in identifying the data that was captured:

File Name	File Type	Cr Date
key.txt	Plain Text Document	5/12/2011 8:11:27 PM
application.txt	Plain Text Document	5/12/2011 8:11:28 PM
block.txt	Plain Text Document	5/12/2011 8:11:28 PM
download.txt	Plain Text Document	5/12/2011 8:11:28 PM
navigate.txt	Plain Text Document	5/12/2011 8:11:28 PM
screen.txt	Plain Text Document	5/12/2011 8:11:28 PM
12052011182021.jpg	JPEG/JFIF File	5/12/2011 8:20:21 PM
12052011182121.jpg	JPEG/JFIF File	5/12/2011 8:21:21 PM
12052011182222.jpg	JPEG/JFIF File	5/12/2011 8:22:22 PM
12052011182618.jpg	JPEG/JFIF File	5/12/2011 8:26:18 PM
12052011182718.jpg	JPEG/JFIF File	5/12/2011 8:27:18 PM
12052011182819.jpg	JPEG/JFIF File	5/12/2011 8:28:19 PM
12052011182920.jpg	JPEG/JFIF File	5/12/2011 8:29:20 PM
12052011183055.jpg	JPEG/JFIF File	5/12/2011 8:30:55 PM

Note

Be sure to document your findings and export the files out for review.

In Actual Practice

There will be times when you'll have much less information to go on. Even more challenging is if the malware is taking extra steps to avoid detection—perhaps utilizing packed binaries—and uses encryption, data wiping, obfuscation, or other methods to hide its tracks. This will make forensic analysis more difficult. A possible next step would be to re-create a safe test environment and boot a copy of the forensic image inside a virtual machine to perform live analysis. This would involve the use of system monitoring and network scanning tools, taking before-and-after snapshots of the system, and performing other types of analysis to study the malware's behavior as it reacts to user interactions on the live system. Performing this kind of analysis is difficult, and your findings may not answer the question of exactly what data was taken. Hopefully, your efforts will be rewarded at least in part by your gaining an understanding of how the malware behaves and what it was designed to do.

Performing a live analysis requires serious time and research, and there is no guarantee that you'll get decent results. Make sure that this information is communicated to the client and let them decide if you should proceed or not before taking on such a large task.

Finding Information About the Attacker

During the forensic analysis, in this case with a keylogger, we know that data is being captured—but where is it being sent to? Another artifact that our "stealthy and undetectable" keylogger left behind was a help.html file. And, yes, it truly was a help file. It has examples and directions on how to connect to various webmail accounts and upload to an FTP server.

Once again, we rely on our wonderful keyword search to see what we can find. Let's see if we can identify any webmail accounts. Having a keyword list for various webmail accounts such as Yahoo!, Gmail, Verizon, Hotmail, and so on, will speed things along.

In this case, our search located a Gmail account as well as a couple of Yahoo! accounts and a Verizon account. It was the Gmail account that panned out. Keyword searching on the Gmail account name located a bit of XML text located within the slack space. Not only were we able to retrieve the e-mail address login, but we also found the password for the account. (By the way, I changed the actual login/password in the following illustration.)

```
<mailing_results>
    <mar_send_all>1</mar_send_all>
    <mar_clear_results>1</mar_clear_results>
    <mar_archived>1</mar_archived>
    <mar_b_period>0</mar_b_period>
    <mar_b_size>1</mar_b_size>
    <mar_to_email>example123@gmail.com</mar_to_email>
    <mar_from_email>example123@gmail.com</mar_from_email>
    <mar_mes_subj>MK Report for COMPUTERNAME</mar_mes_subj>
    <mar_hour>0</mar_hour>
    <mar_min>8</mar_min>
    <mar_mb>2</mar_mb>
    <mar_smtp_server>smtp.gmail.com</mar_smtp_server>
    <mar_port>465</mar_port>
    <mar_login>example123</mar_login>
    <mar_password>Password1</mar_password>
    <mar_req_auth>1</mar_req_auth>
    <mar_req_ssl>1</mar_req_ssl>
</mailing_results>
```

Suppose the attacker was uploading data to an FTP server or was logging in remotely to download the captured data. What should you examine in those cases? Should you expand your investigation to include Active Directory servers and have a look at the firewall logs? You will probably want to include a look at proxy/web content filtering logs, VPN logs, DHCP server logs, and so on. Sometimes, the smoking gun comes from evidence outside the forensic image you are analyzing.

What We Know About the Attacker

It looks like we got lucky with that webmail address. Here's what we know about the attacker:

- We know that his keylogger data is being transmitted to a Gmail account.
- We know his login to the Gmail account.
- We know his password for the Gmail account.

In Actual Practice

If you find login information, refrain from logging into a webmail account. Accessing a webmail account—or any other type of account for that matter—without expressed authorization is a legal pitfall you will want to avoid. Remember, you are not technically authorized to proceed. You are better off reporting your findings and letting counsel decide what the next step should be.

Where to Find More About the Attacker

Using the timestamps from the artifacts that you will collect during an investigation as reference, what else would you want to examine to see if you can uncover any more information? The answer depends on the type of attack that has occurred, but here are some other areas of focus that you will want to think about:

- Software/hardware firewall logs
- Virtual private network (VPN) logs
- FTP uploads
- Internet Relay Chat (IRC) logins
- Active Directory logs

We've Covered

This chapter covered the basics of how to discover the presence of keyloggers and malware in a forensic image. You learned where and how to look for artifacts that can provide the necessary evidence and information to push an investigation forward. I've given you a good primer here to start your malware analysis career, but you can go much deeper. Start here, and when these techniques can't uncover the answer, it's time to turn to the blogs and resources listed in Chapter 2 to go further.

Defining keyloggers and malware

- Malware is a catch-all term to refer to any software designed to cause damage to a single computer, server, or computer network.
- A keylogger is a malware tool.

How to detect keyloggers and malware

- Know where to look to find malware.
- Find all the places malware can locate itself to run.
- Work with the system services in which malware can hide.

Determining how an infection occurred

- Work with prefetch files.
- Perform a keyword search for malware fragments.
- Identify malware sample using online scanning sites

Identifying what data was captured

- Profile your malware.
- Research your malware to determine capabilities.
- Find logs and files related to your malware.

Finding information about the attacker

- Define what you know about the attacker.
- Determine how to profile the attacker.
- Find command and control or where the data is being sent.

PART IV

Defending Your Work

CHAPTER 16

Documenting Your Findings with Reports

We'll Cover

● Documenting your findings

● Exploring different types of reports

● Explaining your work

Getting the answers to technical questions during an investigation is only half of your job as a computer forensic investigator. The other half has to do with communicating your results to those who requested your services. This chapter focuses on how to document your findings so that someone who is nontechnical can understand them. You learn about reporting standards and how to explain your work and its meaning to others.

Documenting Your Findings

One of the most common mistakes many first-time report writers make is thinking that whatever report option is built into their favorite computer forensic tool is acceptable. Truth is, that's not the case. No matter how expensive your forensic software, those canned reports are not what you should be providing as your deliverable. A report generated by a forensic tool might, however, provide a nice appendix to your actual written report, because it will contain facts about the forensic images, information about who did the examination, and information about sections of the forensic image you may have bookmarked. What that report does not do is explain in layperson's terms what you were asked to find, what you in fact found, and what it all means.

When you create a report, regardless of what format you use, five basic areas must be covered:

● Who asked you to undertake the investigation

● What you were asked to do

● What you reviewed

● What you found

● What your findings mean

Tip

If you don't have a report template, and the examples in this chapter don't work for you, you can use these bullet points as a report outline. Although they do not form a formal report structure, they might help you organize your findings in a way that will allow you to break it down easily for a nontechnical person. Remember that your report is your deliverable, and your work will be judged on it.

Who Asked You to Undertake the Investigation

Your report will often serve as a way to remind yourself of what you did, at some point in the future. This can be important, because some cases can idle for months, to years. If the organization changes and your authority to perform an investigation is questioned, the fact that you documented who asked you to perform the investigation in the first place will be quite important, even if you summarize this in a sentence: "At the request of John Doe in Human Resources, we began our investigation."

Note

Don't underestimate the importance of this simple information. Being able to state who requested your work will prevent many issues that can come up later, if someone within the company tries to bury your investigation. And, yes, this happens. Conversely, if someone is requesting that you perform an investigation but they can't tell you on whose authority the investigation is to occur, you probably shouldn't take on the job.

What You Were Asked to Do

What you were being asked to investigate is also very important information to include in your report. There are times when, either through the human resources reviews or through an improper termination lawsuit, your suspect will challenge whether they were unfairly targeted or discriminated against via your work as the examiner. Including information about not only who asked you to perform your investigation but what you were asked to investigate will prevent confusion in the future. You can simply say, "Jane Doe was made aware of the offensive browsing habits of Jim Smith and asked us to review his work-issued systems to determine whether he was doing so during company time."

LINGO

An **improper termination lawsuit** is the most common type of lawsuit that an internal computer forensic examiner may get involved with. An ex-employee sues her ex-employer for firing her either because she believes the reasons given for her termination were false or because she alleges that she was unfairly discriminated against in some way or because other employees were not terminated for the same alleged offense.

In Actual Practice

People file many types of lawsuits. Truth is, a person can sue for any reason (though the lawsuit may be thrown out of court if it makes no sense). Even if your evidence is rock solid and a suspect knows he is guilty, he may still threaten an improper termination lawsuit to try to get back his position or additional benefits. This is particularly important when you're dealing with union employees whose contracts may have restrictions on how they can be disciplined and/or terminated.

What You Reviewed

When you describe what you reviewed, you shouldn't limit that to "a laptop." You need to include the user who uses the laptop; who the laptop belongs to; the network name; the laptop make, model, and serial number of the laptop; the make, model, and serial number of the laptop hard drive; and what operating system it is running. This specificity is required because you are stating what evidence now in your possession contains information that leads to your conclusions. If your results are challenged, either internally or in a court proceeding, your ability to state which exact system you investigated prevents any confusion. This information may or may not warrant its own paragraph or section in your report, depending on the number of devices you reviewed. Here's an example of a statement regarding what you reviewed: "Jim Smith's company-issued laptop, identified as JSMITHCORP, is an HP EliteBook laptop, serial number 123456, containing a Hitachi hard drive model aa123, serial number 11003, running Windows 7 Professional. It was reviewed in this investigation and all results cited in this report came from this system."

Tip
When you're describing a system, more detail is better than less detail. The amount of detail you provide in your report will change as you get more comfortable generating and defending your reports. Remember that if you decide not to present all the details in the report, inform whomever is reviewing your report that you can provide additional details if necessary.

LINGO
Evidence in your possession may not always refer to the actual computer from which the image came. Instead, it may refer to the forensic images you created. If the chain of custody for a piece of evidence ends with you, then the evidence is still in your possession.

What You Found

Describing what you found in plain English (rather than using technical jargon) is important. Not only will this serve to remind you of what you found if you have to review this case in the future, but those who requested your work in the first place must be able to understand what you found in order to appreciate it. No matter how many days you put into your investigation and how many forensic artifacts you reviewed, your end result will be judged by your report. This means, for example, that you shouldn't just write, "USBSTOR shows external drive"; instead, you should write, "Forensic artifacts located in the Windows registry under the 'USBSTOR' key reveal that an external storage device was attached to the system."

Depending on the formality of your report, you could include a simple list of bullet points or a full narrative of the suspect's activities. Following are some examples of each, starting with a bulleted list:

Findings

- The Internet history records were deleted the day before we forensically imaged the computer.
- The Internet history records were recovered from the deleted space on the disk.
- The Internet history records reveal regular access to adult web sites during work hours.
- The login records show that Jim Smith was the only user logged into this computer during these times.

And here's the example narrative:

In our examination of the forensic image belonging to Jim Smith's work computer, we first reviewed his Internet history records. Our analysis found that he deleted records that should normally be kept for 30 days on his system by company policy the day before we forensically imaged his system. We were able to recover the records he deleted using our forensic tools. These records revealed that Jim Smith has been regularly accessing adult web sites during work hours. To ensure that these were indeed Jim Smith's accesses, we confirmed that no other user was making use of the system during the days in question.

A narrative provides additional nontechnical details such as the timing of an action—for instance, when the suspect decided to delete everything a day after he was put on notice. You don't need to

LINGO
In a **narrative**, you write the facts of your investigation into a story rather than just listing them.

use flowery prose in a narrative, but you do need to tell your story in such a way that a nontechnical person can understand it and reach the same conclusions that you reached. The power of the narrative can be strong. Your ability to tell the story will help lead the reader to your conclusions in a way that can be much more powerful that a list of bullet points.

What Your Findings Mean

The last, but not least, important area of any report is what your findings mean to you. Typically, you'll include this information in a section called "Conclusions," but it can just as easily be included in the last paragraph of your report starting with a sentence: "In Conclusion…" or "My conclusion is…."

IMHO

You might be wondering why you would need to write out your conclusions if you already listed what you found. Some people will try to say that the reader should draw their own conclusion so as not to bias the investigator. In my experience, the people who are requesting your work are not asking you to do so just so they can read about what you found; they also want to know what it means to you and your interpretation of the evidence. It is especially important to be descriptive if you used a bulleted list style of findings; this is where you can add additional depth to the meaning of your findings.

Finishing up our Jim Smith case, this is how I would write the conclusion:

In conclusion, after having reviewed all the evidence, it is my opinion that Jim Smith violated company policy in viewing adult material on his work laptop on a regular basis during work hours. In addition, it appears that Jim Smith attempted to hide this behavior by deleting his Internet history records from the system. Based on our review of the evidence, we do not believe this evidence was created by another user accessing Jim Smith's system or the result of some virus or malware. Instead, this is the result of Jim Smith's accesses to the system as supported by recovered deleted history records showing him logging into adult sites using his own e-mail address.

Tip

In a conclusion, you are generally allowed to state your own personal opinion. Just make sure you can justify it with evidence that supports it.

Types of Reports

One of the first lessons you learn as a writer is that you must always know who your audience is. The same holds true for your investigation reports. How formal your report is and what format it needs to be written in will depend on who requested you work and what the requestor intends to do with it. You should always ask who will be reading the report and what do they intend to do with it. The answer will determine which of the following types of reports you will write:

- If your report is meant for the review of only the person who requested it to make a decision, an informal report may suitable.

- If your report is meant to detail the impact of an incident (such as malware or an intrusion), an incident report may be required.

- If your report is meant for an internal review by human resources and legal, a formal internal report is likely required.

- The declaration and affidavit are the most formal types of reports if an outside law firm is not involved and you are serving as an expert witness. This type of report is most appropriate when the legal department needs to submit your report to the court in a legal proceeding.

Informal Report

An informal report (Figure 16-1) can be as simple as an e-mail containing your conclusions. However, even in an informal report, it's important that you capture the topics detailed in the first part of this chapter. Although you may not need to detail the make, model, and serial number of the devices in question, you should make it clear who requested you to do the work, what was requested of you, and your conclusions. Even an informal report can be used during litigation, so make sure that you write it appropriately.

Incident Report

Incident reports (Figure 16-2) cover the impacts and exposure of data that may have occurred because of an incident. They typically focus on malware and intrusions, because the originators of the incidents are either outside of any legal jurisdiction or contain no assets that could be used to pay for damages they have caused. In these reports, you should ensure that you detail all the areas discussed at the beginning of the chapter; the reports may be passed on to regulators or legal entities in compliance with breach notification laws.

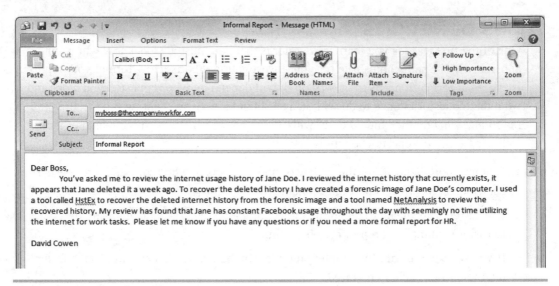

Figure 16-1   An informal report

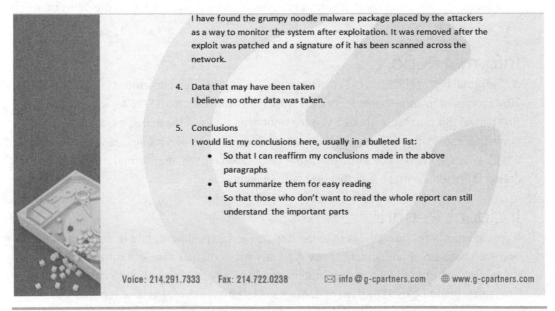

Figure 16-2   An incident report

Internal Report

The internal report (Figure 16-3) is a more traditional investigation report. It contains information on three major areas: Executive Summary, Findings, and Technical Details. The issues described at the beginning of the chapter will fit within these sections, but you will go beyond the level of detail you provide in other reports in the "Technical Details" section, where you place screenshots of artifacts, excerpts from recovered data, and evidence to support your conclusions.

Declaration

A declaration (Figure 16-4) is a legal document—a sworn statement that you are making regarding a legal matter. If you are asked to write a declaration, you should know that it will likely be submitted into materials used in a formal legal matter. If your report is

www.g-cpartners.com

THE POWER
TO PROVE

October 2, 2012

Report of Findings – Example client matter

On August 15, 2012 David Cowen a partner at G-C Partners, LLC was allowed to write a report for a book, the following illustrates what that report would look like. He would summarize his findings here and go into detail in the paragraphs below.

1. A topic of investigation
   These are the detailed results of what I found regarding the first topic, such as USB drive access.

2. Another topic of the investigation
   These are the detailed results of what I found regarding the second topic, such as recovered internet usage.

3. Conclusions
   I would list my conclusions here, usually in a bulleted list:
   - So that I can reaffirm my conclusions made in the above paragraphs
   - But summarize them for easy reading
   - So that those who don't want to read the whole report can still understand the important parts

Figure 16-3   An internal report

<u>DECLARATION OF DAVID COWEN</u>

I, DAVID COWEN, declare as follows:

1.   I am a Partner with G-C Partners LLC ("G-C Partners"), a computer consulting company that focuses on digital litigation support and forensic analysis. G-C Partners has been retained by counsel for Defendant <u>Some</u> guy co ("Some <u>Giy</u>") in connection with confidential investigation to determine the status of Some Guy's computer system after ex-employees attempted to remotely destroy it.

2.   My educational background is technological in nature, featuring more than ten years of experience in the areas of integration, architecture, assessment, programming, forensic analysis and investigation. I currently hold the Certified Information Systems Security Professional certification from (ISC)^2. I have been trained in proper forensics practices by the High Tech Crime Investigators Association, ASR Data and Guidance Software among others. I am an active contributor within the computer security community, including the High Technology Crime Investigators Association, where I frequently present and train on various forensic topics. I have managed, created, and worked with multiple forensics/litigation support <u>teams</u> and associated procedures. My experience spans a variety of environments ranging from high security military installations to large/small private sector companies. I also am the co-author of Hacking Exposed: Computer Forensics, ISBN: 0072256753, published by McGraw-Hill; the Anti-Hacker Toolkit, 3rd Edition ISBN: <u>0072262877,</u> also published by McGraw-Hill and Hacking Exposed: Computer Forensics Second Edition ISBN: 0071626778. I have a Bachelors of Science in Computer Science from the University of Texas at Dallas. I am being paid $250 per hour for my work on this matter.

I declare under penalty of perjury that the foregoing is true and correct.

Dated: November ___, 2012, Dallas, Texas

_____
David Cowen

Figure 16-4   A Declaration

being submitted to other parties, they may retain their own computer forensics experts to critique your work and the truthfulness of your statements. For this reason, it's crucial that you fully consider all the statements you make in a declaration. If someone asks you or convinces you to add in a statement you cannot support or do not agree with, you may face penalties in a court of law for making false statements. Remember that the only person who is liable for the statements made in a declaration is the one who signs it—you.

In Actual Practice

If the document you are submitting is not being sealed under some kind of protective order by the court, it is considered to be a public document. Therefore, in the future, anyone who is trying to challenge your testimony can find that document and question you about it. I bring this up to reinforce how important it is that you are confident and comfortable with all the statements made within any document you sign—you will have to live with what you've written for the rest of your career.

A declaration can comprise any form you want; sometimes your legal counsel will provide a declaration template or a draft of what they want you to attest to. The standard parts of a declaration include all the areas from earlier in the chapter, plus a section on your qualifications. Typically, when you are writing a declaration, you state your education, training, and experience to allow others to understand your expertise when evaluating your statements.

Affidavit

The main difference between an affidavit (Figure 16-5) and a declaration is that an affidavit is signed in the presence of a notary republic. The notary republic will then sign and stamp

FURTHER AFFIANT SAYETH NOT.

_____
DAVID COWEN

GIVEN UNDER MY HAND AND SEAL OF OFFICE this ____ day of October, 2012.

_____
Notary Public, State of Texas

(Notary's Seal/Stamp)

Figure 16-5   An affidavit

the document to attest that you appeared before them and signed the document. Other than a notarized signature, other differences would include changing the title of the report to "Affidavit of *Your Name*" and the signature block.

Explaining Your Work

I've talked about what to include in your report and the different ways your report can be written or presented, but I haven't yet covered how to explain what you found to your audience. Throughout this book, you've noticed the "Lingo" sections that offer definitions of some terms used in this book; in much the same way, you need to make sure you explain any technical terms or acronyms you include in your reports. You also need to ensure that, when you provide an example to explain a concept, you do this in layperson's terms, because the majority of people reading your reports will not be technically savvy. Lastly, make sure that you can explain the meaning and relevance of all the forensic artifacts you discover.

Define Technical Terms

Any time your report makes reference to a computer forensic term, such as *forensic image*, *unallocated space*, *carved file*, *slack space*, or *file fragment*, you need to define it. Some people will notate each technical term and define it separately in a footnote; I prefer to define a word after I use it in the sentence. Defining your technical terms will not only make your report easier to understand, but it prevents confusion with other experts if your report is sent out for review.

Provide Examples in Layperson Terms

When you are explaining a computer forensic concept or artifact, you'll often need to offer an example of how something came to exist. When you need to provide an example, either in the form of a metaphor or a scenario, make sure to put it in terms relatable to the report reader. For instance, when I mention "slack space," I typically refer to other types of linear media, such as cassette tapes or VHS tapes. For example, I might say something like this:

> Slack space works much like an old recording on a VHS tape. Suppose you had a VHS tape that originally had a concert recorded onto it. Sometime later, you used the same tape and recorded your favorite comedy show. If the comedy show was 30 minutes long and the concert was an hour long, you would expect to see the concert on the video about 30 minutes in, after you watch the comedy show. In much the same way, if a file does not completely overwrite a sector, the remains of the file that previously existed there can still be found.

It can be difficult to find examples relevant to your audience—there are so few VHS and cassette tapes in use today, for example—but in using examples, you can make the concepts accessible to the reader.

Explain Artifacts

New investigators sometimes assume that everyone understands the impact of a forensic artifact. After reading this book, for instance, you know a LNK file's meaning if it shows access to files on an external drive. To your report reader, however, if you don't explain the file's significance, this can simply be another confusing fact. When you point out specific artifacts found in your investigation, you need to make sure that you fully explain their meaning, their impact to the investigation, and how they relate to your conclusions.

Here is an example explanation:

> We found three artifacts supporting the conclusion that Mr. Smith placed an external storage device on the system and copied data to it the day of his departure. First, we found an entry in the setupapi.log for the day of his departure. This entry represents the first time that Mr. Smith plugged in a specific storage device to the system. Second, we have the LNK files, showing specific files identified as confidential that were created and accessed on the external drive the same day Mr. Smith plugged in the storage device. Last, we found shellbags that provide the names of additional directories accessed that existed on the external storage device. Although we cannot see the contents of those directories, they match the same directory structure that we found on Mr. Smith's work system and include files accessed via the LNK files. These three artifacts show that on his last day at work, it appears that Mr. Smith attached a new external storage device and then copied confidential data onto it.

We've Covered

In this chapter, we've walked through how to write a report on your forensic investigation. This is where many examiners have the most trouble. Learning and understanding forensic artifacts is fun for technical people who want to prove what someone did, but writing out their findings can be frustrating. I hope the examples provided in this chapter, and available on our web site at www.learndfir.com, make things easier for you. Writing reports is part of the job and the only way the people requesting your work will judge it.

Documenting your findings

- Tool-generated reports are not satisfactory for your written report.
- Know what to include in your report.
- Explain what you found.

Exploring different types of reports

- Know the differences between informal and formal reports.
- Learn how to write an informal report.
- Learn how to write different formal reports.

Explaining your work

- Define technical terms.
- Provide clear examples of technical terms.
- Explain artifacts clearly.

CHAPTER 17

Litigation and Reports for Court and Exhibits

We'll Cover

● What type of witness are you?

● Writing reports for court

● Creating exhibits

Chapter 16 discussed report writing for internal investigations. If your internal investigation makes its way into the legal system, you will have different requirements and duties in both your role and with regard to the report you write. This chapter discusses your involvement as a computer forensic examiner in a legal proceeding.

Note
I am not a lawyer, and the content in this chapter is based on my experience working with lawyers during the last 12 years in support of their lawsuits. This chapter defaults to federal court rules since changes in state courts occur frequently.

Important Legal Terms

Let's start by introducing you to a few important legal terms.

Litigation refers to the judicial process—that is, it's what occurs in courtrooms every day. In civil court, individuals and/or companies are referred to as plaintiffs and/or defendants. The *plaintiff* in a lawsuit is the person and/or company that initiated the lawsuit against the *defendant*. There is usually only one plaintiff, unless the case is a class action lawsuit. The defendant is the person and/or company that is being sued by the plaintiff. Multiple defendants can be involved if the plaintiffs believe that multiple parties have caused harm. In criminal court, the plaintiff is always the government, whether that be the city, county, state, or country. An individual cannot begin criminal action, at least in the United States.

Outside counsel refers to the law firm that a company hires to represent it in a court of law. Lawyers who work in a company legal department typically do not maintain the credentials they need to work in the courts; lawyers must be admitted to practice in the states they go to court in. So outside law firms are retained to represent the people and/or companies or provide them legal advice.

The *discovery* phase occurs in litigation between two parties. During discovery, plaintiffs and defendants are allowed to ask each other for documents they believe to be responsive to their claims or defenses. A *responsive* document is a document that is relevant to the request being made. When plaintiffs and defendants ask for documents from each other, they do so in the form of written requests for production; these identify which types of documents they want. If the document being reviewed matches that criteria and is not excluded for another criteria (such as it is privileged), it is responsive.

Admissibility is the process of determining whether a piece of evidence or a statement should be allowed to be entered into the court record. Information and/or evidence can be determined not to be admissible if it is privileged communication, an attorney-client work product, irrelevant to the proceeding, hearsay, or unable to be authenticated.

Privilege refers to the status of a document or communication with regard to the attorney-client privilege. Any e-mail sent between an attorney and her client is considered privileged by default and is exempt from discovery unless a judge rules otherwise.

Work product or attorney-client work product refers to drafts and materials used in the support of a lawyer's work in a lawsuit. This can include e-mails, documents, and reports that you wrote at the attorney's direction.

In Actual Practice

No matter what you believe to be admissible, responsive, or otherwise, it is ultimately up to a judge to decide what will be produced and admitted into the court and what will not. This is important to remember, because no matter how technically correct your argument is, some IT people like to think of the law like programming logic: a human being will apply his or her rationale thinking and apply past case law with regard to the issue to reach a decision.

What Type of Witness Are You?

As a computer forensic examiner, you can serve multiple roles in a legal proceeding. In a civil court, you can be appointed as a *fact witness*, an *expert consultant*, or an *expert witness*. In a criminal court working for the plaintiffs, you will typically be appointed as a fact witness or expert consultant only. Your role determines your involvement with the lawsuit, the scope of any testimony you provide, and the admissibility of any of your work in the case beyond the forensic images you've created. Remember that you do not decide the role you will be assigned; the outside law firm will work with your company's legal department to decide who will be placed in which role. If you are acting as an outside consultant, you can additionally be appointed as a *special master* or a *neutral*. This section covers the duties of each role and what will be expected of you.

As a witness, you have first-party knowledge of the event—that is, you personally witnessed the event to which you will be testifying. If you heard the information from another party, repeating it would be considered *hearsay* because you did not personally witness it. When acting as a computer forensic examiner, first-party knowledge means that you personally reviewed an image or tested an artifact to prove its meaning. When presenting evidence, you must show that you had first-party knowledge in order to testify to something and have it entered into evidence. As an expert witness, you are allowed to rely on other people's statements, which otherwise would be considered hearsay evidence, but that is the only exception to the first-party knowledge rule.

Fact Witness

A *fact witness* is the most common role for a first-time computer forensic examiner. As a fact witness, your job will be to attest to the facts about how you obtained evidence, plus anything you personally experienced that cannot be re-created from the forensic image.

Your Role

You will bear witness to the facts you personally know. Your first-party knowledge is the basis for the court admissibility of the forensic images you create.

Limits of Testimony

As a fact witness, your testimony will be limited to your qualifications in respect to your role in the case (such as creating a forensic image) and the events that occurred around the facts to which you are testifying. For example, you might be called to testify regarding the creation of the forensic image you made. In your testimony, you would be asked what education you've received, what forensic training you've received, whether you have any certifications, and what experience you have in computer forensics. These questions will explain your qualifications and be used to judge your statements.

Discovery and Admissibility

Your correspondence with attorneys will be considered attorney-client privileged and are therefore not discoverable. You will not have to produce this correspondence, so you can speak candidly in your e-mails with attorneys. Any notes or reports you made involving the investigation will be discoverable, however, if you make reference to them in your testimony. At a minimum, you may be asked to provide the chain-of-custody documents you created.

Expert Consultant

As an expert consultant, you are involved in advising outside law firm attorneys on technical and other details regarding the facts at issue. You act as a consultant to help others understand the technical details of your investigation, but you will not be called on to testify or give a deposition.

Your Role

Your role as an expert consultant is that of an advisor. You will be given access to all materials generated in the lawsuit, even those normally covered under protective orders, so that you can advise the legal team regarding technical issues. How involved you get with the case—from attending hearings to providing questions in depositions—depends on how much assistance your legal team needs.

Limits of Testimony

As an expert consultant, you should not be called on to testify.

Discovery and Admissibility

Expert consultants enjoy full privilege regarding e-mails and documents created while advising the legal team. Those e-mails and documents should be considered work products and are thus inadmissible unless ruled otherwise.

Expert Witness

As an expert witness, you'll review the evidence, testimony, and facts of the case to form an opinion. You then deliver that opinion in the form of a formal written report and through testimony both in a deposition and at trial.

Your Role

As an expert witness, your role is designated by your legal team. They will formally designate you as an expert on

> **LINGO**
> In a **deposition**, you are asked to give testimony and have it recorded by a court reporter. It will be attended by lawyers from both the plaintiff and defendant who will take turns asking you questions. You cannot ask questions at a deposition, but during a break you can advise your legal team of questions you think they should ask you.

a specific topic, such as computer forensics, and the opposing legal team will also know who you are. You will form an opinion based on the evidence in the case, testimony, and facts in your possession and defend that opinion when challenged.

Note
To qualify as an expert, the federal courts and all but six states recognize the Daubert standard, which says that to qualify as an expert, you must show that you have knowledge of the subject based on your experience, education, or training. Having sufficient knowledge in all three of these categories just makes you a great expert witness. During the first part of your testimony, you will be asked questions to determine whether you meet this standard in what is known as *voir dire*.

Limits of Testimony
You can be questioned on your experience, education, training, past opinions, past testimony, current opinions, and anything else a judge deems relevant. You can also be asked questions regarding discussions with attorneys and your client.

Discovery and Admissibility
As of December 2010, experts' e-mails and report drafts are no longer automatically discoverable in federal court. However, they still may be discoverable at a local state court. Ask your legal team about the rules regarding the discovery of your e-mails and report drafts before you send them.

In Actual Practice
Don't rush into being an expert witness. As an expert witness, all your prior testimony as an expert witness is admissible every time you testify, unless it is under seal because of the topics you are discussing. This means that if you go up as an expert witness before you feel ready and find yourself suddenly contradicting yourself and have a jury instructed to ignore your testimony, this will and can follow you for the rest of your career. Although being an expert witness is the end goal for most computer forensic investigators who want to see their investigation to its conclusion in the legal system, being ready for what comes with it will ensure that you can continue to do the work.

Special Master
A special master is a unique role in that it is not something your legal team can appoint. A special master is appointed by a judge in a case to answer a question for the court.

They typically are appointed only when the parties in a lawsuit either can't agree on a fundamental fact of the case or can't answer a judge's question to his or her satisfaction.

Your Role

A special master is an *agent of the court*, which means that the judge gives the special master the authority to request evidence, request people to attend depositions, and conduct onsite inspections to find the truth for the judge. The special master's role ends with a report to the judge detailing his or her findings and an answer to the court's question.

Limits of Testimony

Typically, special masters are not deposed; they deliver their reports directly to the judge.

Discovery and Admissibility

The master's report is available for both parties to review, but his or her work product is typically only for the judge's review.

Neutral

A neutral is a third party who plaintiff and defendant mutually agree to engage to review evidence. The neutral is different from a special master, because the neutral is not selected by the judge, nor does the neutral have any authority to demand the production of any data.

Your Role

Typically, you're engaged as a neutral when there is a contested piece of evidence that one party wants to review but does not trust the opposing party to disclose fully. In such situations, rather than allow a "hostile expert" to have full access to the evidence, the evidence will be given to a neutral expert, who will review the data and then report his or her findings. How the neutral reports and what is reported, searched for, and produced is up to the agreement of both parties.

Limits of Testimony

Neutrals typically do not give testimony unless their work is in question.

Discovery and Admissibility

Neutrals are not retained exclusively by either party, so no e-mails or documents created by the neutral should be considered privileged, unless otherwise agreed to.

Writing Reports for Court

Chapter 16 discussed how to write internal reports, but it did not address report writing for the courts. Different courts have different requirements for the report formatting, but the basic information is always the same. This section covers what you must include in a report to the court.

Declarations in Support of Motions

Declarations and affidavits don't vary much from the descriptions in Chapter 16. Any difference would be based on what your role is and any change in how you start the document. Typically, you will include the name of the lawsuit and what party you are working for. Figure 17-1 shows part of an example declaration. To get a copy of this, go to www.learndfir.com.

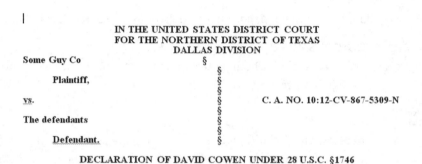

IN THE UNITED STATES DISTRICT COURT
FOR THE NORTHERN DISTRICT OF TEXAS
DALLAS DIVISION

Some Guy Co   §
                               §
        Plaintiff,   §
                               §
vs.   §   C. A. NO. 10:12-CV-867-5309-N
                               §
The defendants   §
                               §
        Defendant.   §

DECLARATION OF DAVID COWEN UNDER 28 U.S.C. §1746

I, DAVID COWEN, declare as follows:

1.   I am a Partner with G-C Partners LLC ("G-C Partners"), a computer consulting company that focuses on digital litigation support and forensic analysis. G-C Partners has been retained by counsel for Defendant Some guy co ("Some Giy") in connection with confidential investigation to determine the status of Some Guy's computer system after ex-employees attempted to remotely destroy it.

2.   My educational background is technological in nature, featuring more than ten years of experience in the areas of integration, architecture, assessment, programming, forensic analysis and investigation. I currently hold the Certified Information Systems Security Professional certification from (ISC)^2. I have been trained in proper forensics practices by the High Tech Crime Investigators Association, ASR Data and Guidance Software among others. I am an active contributor within the computer security community, including the High Technology Crime Investigators Association, where I frequently present and train on various

Figure 17-1   Declaration of David Cowen

Expert Reports

Expert reports are different from other reports, because they have strict requirements regarding what must be included. You must state the following:

- Who retained you
- Your educational background
- Any training you have received
- Any certifications you hold
- What experience you have
- What other cases you've testified in as an expert witness
- What you are paid for your work as an expert witness
- What you have reviewed in forming your opinion

Figure 17-2 shows an example of an expert report.

Creating Exhibits

Rather than try to embed spreadsheets, images, or other artifacts within the report, you may find it easier to refer to them as *exhibits* and attach them separately. Your exhibits don't have to be printed out; they can also be stored on a CD/DVD or other storage device and provided with the report.

> **LINGO**
> An *exhibit* is any supporting document that you include with your report. If including supporting data would make your report unfriendly or unreadable, such as a spreadsheet of copied files, it's better to supply it as an exhibit to your report.

There are two ways to present exhibit documents. If a document renders (prints) well in the PDF or TIFF format, you can place the printed document at the end of your report with full page separators indicating which exhibit follows. If the exhibit will not render well, name it using the exhibit letter or number that you specify in the report and place the document in the same directory as your report on whatever medium you are handing it over on.

Expert Report of

David L. Cowen

Some Guy Co Vs The Defendants

October 12, 2012

I.   OVERVIEW

I have been retained by plaintiffs Some Guy Co in their action against The Defendants in their use of Some Guy Co computer to steal customers data.

II.   QUALIFICATIONS

My educational background is technological in nature, featuring more than ten years of experience in the areas of integration, architecture, assessment, programming, forensic analysis and investigation. I currently hold the Certified Information Systems Security Professional certification from (ISC)^2. I have been trained in proper forensics practices by the High Tech Crime Investigators Association, ASR Data and Guidance Software among others. I am an active contributor within the computer security community, including the High Technology Crime Investigators Association, where I frequently present and train on various forensic topics. I have managed, created, and worked with multiple forensics/litigation support teams and associated procedures. My experience spans a variety of environments ranging from high security military installations to large/small private sector companies. I also am the co-author of *Hacking Exposed: Computer Forensics*, ISBN: 0072256753, published by McGraw-Hill; the *Anti-Hacker Toolkit*, 3rd Edition ISBN: 0072262877, also published by McGraw-Hill and *Hacking Exposed: Computer Forensics Second Edition* ISBN: 0071626778. I have a Bachelors of Science in Computer Science from the University of Texas at Dallas.

III.   PRIOR EXPERT WITNESS TESTIMONY

1. BMC Software Inc, et al v. Crabbhacker.Com, et al (4:03-cv-01300)
2. Inventory Locator v. Partsbase, Inc. (2:02-cv-02695-SHM)
3. Carreker Corporation v. Cannon et al (4:06-cv-00175-RAS-DDB)
4. Super Future Equities Inc v. Wells Fargo Bank NA et al (3:06-cv-00271)
5. SoftWIRE Tech., et al v. National Instruments (1:03-cv-10107-REK)
6. JDI v LMI (State of Texas)
7. Excel Trasporation Services Inc v. Total Transportation Services LLC et al (3:06-cv-00593)
8. Stille Sonesta v Tara Woodruff and David Woodruff (State of Texas)
9. Lockheed Martin v L-3, et al (6:05-cv-1580-Orl-31KRS)
10. State of Nevada v Terrance Watanabe
11. Transfirst Holdings, Inc. et al v Andrew M. Phillips, et al (3:06-CV-2303-P)

IV.   COMPENSATION

I am being paid $XXX an hour for my time. However, I am paid $YYY an hour on weekends and $ZZZ an hour on holidays. I am being paid $AAA an hour for testimony with a four hour minimum. My fees for this engagement our not contingent on the result of this matter.

V.   ITEMS REVIEWED

a.   List here

Figure 17-2   The skeleton of an expert report

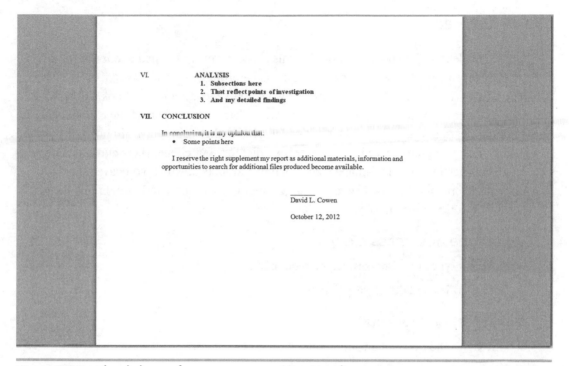

Figure 17-2   The skeleton of an expert report (*Continued*)

Working with Forensic Artifacts

When you are presenting a forensic artifact as an exhibit, make sure that the exhibit is either self explanatory, is explained in your report, or includes a description within the exhibit itself. If you leave the interpretation of an artifact to the reader, your report and exhibit could be misunderstood or used against you.

We've Covered

You've made it to the end of the book. In this chapter, you've learned about the end of your involvement in a forensic investigation—supporting your findings in a court of law. The best advice I can give you as you take what you've learned in this book and apply it to your career is what an attorney told me once: "You are just a part of the overall case, an important part, but just a part." Don't lose perspective that your work, although important, is not on its own going to lead to a favorable verdict for your client. Many equally important legal facts, testimony, and damage claims will be introduced, which you have nothing to do with. Keep your reports clean and your testimony to the facts, and I might just see you across the courtroom someday.

What type of witness are you?

- Different types of witnesses can be required.
- Witness rules and duties vary depending on type.

Writing reports for court

- Affidavits and declarations are required for court.
- An expert report must meet certain requirements.

Creating exhibits

- You can present exhibits with your report.
- Exhibits should be clearly explained.
- You also may need to present artifacts for review.

InfoSec Pro SERIES

GLOSSARY

acceptable use of computers   Defines what activities are acceptable on computer systems owned by the organization.

access attack   An attempt to gain information that the intruder is not authorized to see.

access control   A mechanism used to restrict access to files, folders, or systems based on the identification and authentication of the user.

accountability   The process administration uses to account for an individual's activities and to assign responsibility for actions that have taken place on an information system.

address resolution protocol (ARP) spoofing   A tactic used to forge the MAC address of a system to get packets directed to the attacking computer.

administrative practices   Practices that fall under the areas of policy, procedure, resources, responsibility, education, and contingency plans.

advanced persistent threat (APT)   Generally considered to be a hacker or group of hackers with significant resources, who are targeting specific enterprises. The APT uses exploits that may never have been seen before and compromises systems with the intent of keeping control of them and making use of them for some time.

agents   The people or organization originating a security threat.

anomaly   Something that is out of the ordinary or unexpected.

anti-malware system   A system designed to detect and remove malicious software.

application layer firewall   A firewall that enforces policy rules through the use of application proxies.

audit   1) A formal check to determine policy compliance, typically performed either by internal auditors at a company or organization or by an independent third party. 2) A function in an operating system that provides administrators with a historic record of events and activities that occurred on an information system for future reference.

availability   The degree to which information is available when it is needed by authorized parties. Availability may be measured as the percentage of time information is available for use by authorized web sites. For example, a business web site may strive for availability above 99 percent.

backup   Copies of critical information that are archived in the event of a system crash or a disaster.

backup policy   The policy an organization has in place that documents how backup operations will be conducted.

Balanced Scorecard (BSC)   A performance measurement framework that is intended to enrich traditional financial performance measures with strategic nonfinancial performance measures, thereby providing a more balanced view of organizational performance. Developed in the 1990s by Drs. Robert Kaplan (Harvard Business School) and David Norton. (For additional information, see www.balancedscorecard.org.)

best practices   A set of recommendations that generally provides an appropriate level of security. A combination of those practices proved to be most effective at various organizations.

biometrics   The use of something related to the human body—for example, fingerprints, retina/iris prints, palm prints, hand geometry, facial geometry, or voice recognition—to authenticate an individual's identity for access.

black bag job   A nighttime operation that leaves no evidence of your forensic imaging.

black swan event   An event that is highly improbable and therefore likely to end up at the bottom of the list of priorities to address. See *The Black Swan: The Impact of the Highly Improbable*, by Nassim Taleb (Random House, 2010) for further reading on the Theory of Black Swan Events.

botnet   A malicious botnet is a network of compromised computers that is used to transmit information, send spam, or launch denial-of-service (DoS) attacks. Essentially, a malicious botnet is a supercomputer created by and managed by a hacker, fraudster, or cybercriminal.

brute-force attack   An attempt by a hacker to gain access to a system by trying to log on to one or many accounts using different combinations of characters to guess or crack a password.

buffer overflow   The process of overwriting memory in such a way as to cause an attacker's code to be executed instead of the legitimate program, with the intent of causing the system to be compromised or allowing the attacker to have elevated privileges to the system.

certificate authority (CA)   A central management entity that issues or verifies security credentials.

chain of custody   A document listing in whose possession and control an item was and when.

change control procedure   The process used by an organization to verify the current system configuration and provide for the testing and approval of a new configuration before it is implemented.

charter   A document that describes the specific rights and privileges granted from the organization to the information security team.

ciphertext   Information after it has been obfuscated by an encryption algorithm.

cloud computing   As defined by the National Institute of Standards and Technology (NIST), a model for enabling ubiquitous, convenient, on-demand network access to a shared pool of configurable computing resources (such as networks, servers, storage, applications, and services) that can be rapidly provisioned and released with minimal management effort or service provider interaction.

communications security   The measures employed to secure information while it is in transit.

compliance   A process that ensures that an organization adheres to a set of policies and standards, or adherence to such standards. Two broad categories of compliance are compliance with internal policies (specific to a particular organization) and compliance with external or regulatory policies, standards, or frameworks.

computer security   The means used to protect information on computer systems.

computer use policy   Specifies who can use the organization's computer systems and how those systems can be used.

confidentiality   The prevention of disclosure of information to unauthorized parties.

consultant   A subject matter expert who is contracted to perform a specific set of activities. Typically, a statement of work outlines the deliverables to be completed by the consultant and the deadlines for each deliverable.

core competencies   The fundamental strengths of a program that add value. They are the primary functions of a program and cannot or should not be done by outside groups or partners.

countermeasures   The measures undertaken by an organization to address the identified vulnerabilities of the organization.

cryptanalysis   The art of analyzing cryptographic algorithms with the intent of identifying weaknesses.

cryptographer   An individual who practices cryptography.

cryptographic checksum   A binary string created by running the binary value of the software through a cryptographic algorithm to create a result that will change if any portion of the original binary is modified.

cryptography   The art of concealing information using encryption.

data cleansing   The actions performed on a set of data to improve the data quality and achieve better accuracy, completion, or consistency.

data encryption standard (DES)   A private key encryption algorithm developed by IBM in the early 1970s that operates on 64-bit blocks of text and uses a 56-bit key.

data leakage prevention (DLP)   A mechanism for examining network traffic and detecting sensitive information.

data loss prevention   DLP systems are typically network appliances that review all network traffic on your external network, looking for signs of improper data being sent outside the company.

dd image   Also called a "raw image," a computer forensic image of a system in which the data from the storage device is stored as a single file or multiple files, but without any type of container that stores checksums or hashes.

decryption   The process used by encryption systems to convert ciphertext into plaintext.

default allow   A policy in which any traffic is allowed except that which is specifically denied.

default deny   A policy in which any traffic is denied except that which is specifically allowed.

defendant   In a lawsuit, the person and/or company who is being sued by the plaintiff or who is being tried for a criminal act.

defense in depth   An architecture in which multiple controls are deployed in such a way that weaknesses in one control are covered by another.

denial of access to applications   The tactic of denying the user access to the application that displays the information.

denial of access to information   The tactic of making information the user wants to see unavailable.

denial of access to systems   The tactic used by an attacker to make a computer system completely inaccessible by anyone.

denial-of-service attack   The process of flooding a server (e-mail, web, or resource) with packets to use up bandwidth that would otherwise be allocated to normal traffic and thus deny access to legitimate users.

deperimeterization   The current state of most perimeters—full of holes that reduce or eliminate the effectiveness of the perimeter.

Diffie-Hellman key exchange   A public key encryption algorithm developed in 1976 to solve the problem of key distribution for private key encryption systems. Diffie-Hellman cannot be used to encrypt or decrypt information, but it is used to exchange secret keys.

digital signature   A method of authenticating electronic information by using encryption.

digital signature algorithm   An algorithm developed by the US government as a standard for digital signatures.

dirty data   Data that has unacknowledged correlation or undocumented origins or that is biased, nonindependent, internally inconsistent, inaccurate, incomplete, unsuitable for integration with data from other important sources, unsuitable for consumption by tools that automate computation and visualization, or lacking integrity in some other respect.

disaster recovery   The processes and procedures to protect systems, information, and capabilities from extensive disasters such as fire, flood, or extreme weather events.

disaster recovery plan   The procedure an organization uses to reconstitute a networked system after a disaster.

discovery   A phase in litigation between two parties. During discovery, plaintiffs and defendants are allowed to ask each other for documents they believe responsive to their claims or defenses.

Distributed File System (DFS)   Microsoft uses the term to describe its implementation of this technology within Windows Servers. Multiple systems appear to have local storage, which is actually mapped across multiple systems in the network.

DMZ (demilitarized zone)   A network segment containing systems that can be directly accessed by external users.

DNS (Domain Name Service) spoofing   A tactic that allows an attacker to intercept information from a target computer by exploiting the DNS by which networks map textual domain names onto the IP numbers by which they actually route data packets.

dumpster diving   The act of physically sifting through a company's trash to find useful or sensitive information.

dynamic network address translation   The process used to map multiple internal IP addresses to a single external IP address.

eavesdropping   The process of obtaining information by being positioned in a location at which information is likely to pass.

egress filtering   Filtering traffic that exits through a perimeter.

Elgamal   A variant of the Diffie-Hellman system enhanced to provide encryption, with one algorithm for encryption and another for authentication.

elliptic curve encryption   A public key encryption system based on a mathematical problem related to elliptic curves.

e-mail policy   Governs employee activity and use of the e-mail systems.

emissions security   The measures used to limit the release of electronic emissions.

encryption   The process of changing ciphertext into plaintext.

encryption algorithm   The procedures used for encrypting information.

event   In the context of security risk, this is the type of action that poses a threat.

evidence drive   Also called the "original evidence," this is the hard drive being imaged, versus the storage drive to which we are writing the evidence.

fail-over   Provisions for the reconstitution of information or capability. Fail-over systems are employed to detect failures and then to reestablish capability by the use of redundant hardware.

false negative   A result that indicates no problem exists where one actually exists, such as occurs when a vulnerability scanner incorrectly reports no vulnerability exists on a system that actually has a vulnerability.

false positive A result that indicates a problem exists where none actually exists, such as occurs when a vulnerability scanner incorrectly identifies a vulnerability that does not exist on a system.

Faraday cage A device that blocks electrical fields, including radio waves used for cell phones and tablet devices to communicate.

file carving Techniques used to recover full or partial remnants of files from the unallocated space of the disk or within large files; involves removing pieces of data from a large set and putting it aside, much as you would carve a turkey, taking the meat but leaving the bones.

findings The results of your investigation, or what your review of the evidence revealed.

firewall A network access control device (either hardware or software) designed to allow appropriate traffic to flow while protecting access to an organization's network or computer system.

first-party knowledge You personally witnessed and have knowledge of the event to which you will be testifying. If you heard the information from another party, then repeating it in court would be considered hearsay because you did not personally witness it.

forensic artifact A reproducible file, setting, or system change that occurs every time an application or the operating system performs a specific action.

forensic image A bit-for-bit copy of the data from the entire contents of a piece of digital storage—that is, areas of the storage medium in use and not in use. Typically a forensic image is accompanied by a hash that allows the analyst to verify that the contents have not changed.

forensically sound method A method that does not alter the original evidence; some kind of write protection exists to prevent or intercept possible changes to the disk.

GOST A Russian private-key encryption algorithm that uses a 256-bit key, developed in response to DES.

hacker An individual who breaks into computer systems.

hacktivism Process of hacking a computer system or network for "the common good."

hash A mathematical algorithm that converts data of any length to a fixed set of hexadecimal characters that represent that data.

hierarchical trust model   A model for trust in a public key environment that is based on a chain of authority. You trust someone if someone higher up the chain verifies that you should.

honey pots   Used in research and intrusion prevention systems, honey pots are usually virtual machines that are configured insecurely to lure an attacker in. The attacker's actions are recorded outside of the honey pot and their methods are analyzed.

hot site   An alternative location for operations that has all the necessary equipment configured and ready to go in case of emergency.

identification and authentication   The process that serves a dual role of identifying the person requesting access to information and authenticating that the person requesting the access is the actual person they say they are.

incident response procedures (IRP)   The procedures an organization employs to define how the organization will react to a computer security incident.

information classification standards   Standards that specify treatment of data (requirements for storage, transfer, access, encryption, and so on) according to the data's classification (public, private, confidential, sensitive, and so on).

information control   The processes an organization uses to control the release of information concerning an incident.

information policy   The policy used by an organization that defines what information in an organization is important and how it should be protected.

information security   1) The measures adopted to prevent the unauthorized use, misuse, modification, or denial of use of knowledge, facts, data, or capabilities. 2) The protection of information and information systems from unauthorized access, use, disclosure, modification, or destruction. Also commonly referred to as data security or IT security.

ingress filtering   Filtering traffic that enters through a perimeter.

in-house counsel   A lawyer or lawyers who work in your company. Most large companies have legal departments, and the head of the department is called the general counsel.

integrity   The prevention of data modification by unauthorized parties.

intercept of a line   Identifies the point at which the line crosses the vertical y axis. An intercept is typically expressed as a single value b but can also be expressed as the point $(0, b)$.

interception   An active attack against information by which the intruder puts himself in the path of the information transmission and captures the information before it reaches its destination.

IP spoofing   A tactic used by an attacker to forge the IP address of a computer system.

IPsec (Internet Protocol Security)   A protocol developed by the Internet Engineering Task Force (IETF) to provide the secure exchange of packets at the networking layer.

ISO 27002   The document published by the International Organization for Standardization (ISO) to serve as a guideline for organizations to use in developing information security programs.

JSON   JavaScript Object Notation is a mix of XML and JavaScript used to transfer data between a web browser and a web server without having to reload a web page; Ajax uses JSON in web sites we've come to know as Web 2.0.

key   The data input into an algorithm to transform plaintext into ciphertext or ciphertext into plaintext.

litigation   A lawsuit; a legal proceeding in court that occurs when a plaintiff sues a defendant.

live forensics   The act of performing a forensic examination or acquisition on original evidence, particularly a computer hard drive, that is powered on and running.

MAC duplicating   The process used by an attacker of duplicating the Media Access Control (MAC) address of a target system to receive the information being sent to the target computer.

malicious code   Programming code used to destroy or interfere with computer operations. Generally, malicious code falls into three categories: viruses, Trojan horse programs, and worms.

malware   Malicious software written to cause harm to the victim's computer system by theft of personal information, proliferation of itself, providing remote access to the user's system, or destruction of data, among other things.

man-in-the-middle attack   Also known as interception, this type of attack occurs when the intruder puts himself in the middle of a communication stream by convincing the sender that he is the receiver and the receiver that he is the sender.

masquerading   The act of impersonating someone else or some other system.

MD5   Message Digest Algorithm 5 is a 128-bit hash value that uniquely represents a data set of any size that was computed using it. Every time a piece of data is computed with the MD5 algorithm, it will have the same value unless the data has been changed. Commonly used to check data integrity.

metrics project distance   The amount of a change you want to achieve in your target measurement by the end of the metrics project.

metrics project timeline   How long you want to spend to achieve the metrics project distance.

mission statement   A statement that outlines an information security program's overall goals and provides guidelines for its strategic direction.

modification attack   An attempt by an attacker to modify information that he or she is not authorized to modify.

narrative   A method of organizing the facts of your investigation into a story rather than just listing details. A narrative provides nontechnical details such as the timing of an action—for instance, when the suspect deleted his data after he was put on notice.

network address translation   The process of translating private IP addresses to public IP addresses.

network behavior analysis   An anomaly detection mechanism that watches the flow of traffic on the network. Flow information is acquired from routers and switches or from a device directly connected to the network.

network credentials   Such things as the username and password required to log into a company computer as the administrator, or the password to network routers and security appliances, for example.

network forensics   A monitoring mechanism that collects all traffic that flows across the network in front of the collection point.

network intrusion detection system (NIDS)   A monitoring system that sits out-of-band and watches network traffic looking for indications of an attack.

network intrusion prevention system (NIPS)   A layer 2 network control that sits inline with traffic and watches for indications of an attack. When an attack is identified, the traffic can be blocked.

network-level risk assessment   The assessment of the entire computer network and the information infrastructure of an organization.

network security   The measures used to protect information used on networked systems.

objective desired direction   The direction in which you want the metrics project measurement to go to achieve the benefits of an information security metrics program, especially the benefit of improvement.

offshoring   Contracting work to resources in a different country (either third-party or in-house).

one-time pad (OTP)   The only theoretically unbreakable encryption system, this private key encryption method uses a random list of numbers to encode a message. OTPs can be used only once and are generally used for only short messages in high-security environments.

online analytical processing (OLAP)   A specific type of data storage and retrieval mechanism that is optimized for swift queries that involve summarization of data along multiple factors or dimensions.

orange book   Also known as the Trusted Computer System Evaluation Criteria (TCSEC), this book was developed by the National Computer Security Center for the certification of computer systems for security.

orchestration   The administrative oversight that ensures the workflow is executed as specified. It includes functions such as signing off on a metric definition, deployment of its implementation, scheduling its calculation at regular intervals, and executing and delivering updates. *See also* workflow.

organization-wide risk assessment   An analysis to identify risks to an organization's information assets.

original evidence   The source of a case's evidence.

outside counsel   A law firm retained by a company that desires a third-party opinion regarding a decision, also typically retained to represent the company in litigation.

outsourcing   Contracting work to a third-party vendor.

packet-filtering firewall   A firewall that enforces policy rules through the use of packet inspection filters.

penetration test   A test of the capability of an organization to respond to a simulated intrusion of its information systems.

perimeter   The boundary of a network or network zone.

physical security   The protection of physical assets by the use of security guards and physical barriers.

ping of death   An ICMP echo-request packet sent to the target system with added data with the intent of causing a buffer overflow or system crash.

plaintext   Information in its original form. Also known as cleartext.

plaintiff   The person and/or company who has initiated the lawsuit against the defendant. There is usually only one plaintiff except in a class action lawsuit.

policy decision point   A control that determines a policy violation has occurred.

policy enforcement point   A control that performs an enforcement action.

policy reviews   The process used by an organization to review its current policies and, as necessary, adjust policies to meet current conditions.

prioritization   An exercise in determining relative importance of tasks, projects, and initiatives.

private class addresses   Non-Internet routable IP addresses defined by RFC 1918.

private key encryption   An encryption process requiring that all parties who need to read the information have the same key.

privilege   The status of a document or communication between the attorney and the client (attorney-client privilege). Any e-mails, documents, or other communication between an attorney and a client is considered privileged by default and is exempt from discovery unless a judge rules otherwise.

project management   Defining an end goal and identifying the activities, milestones, and resources necessary to reach that end goal.

project scope   Indicates project coverage, typically by identifying the different regions, different networks, and/or different groups of people the project encompasses.

proxy   A security device used to apply policy to web traffic.

public classification   The least sensitive level of information classification; information that is already known by or can be provided to the public.

public key encryption   An encryption process that requires two keys: one key to encrypt the information and a different key to decrypt the information.

quartiles   Division of all of the observations into four equal groups, which hold the lowest one-fourth of all observed values (first quartile), the highest one-fourth of all observed values (fourth quartile), and the two middle fourths, one-fourth above and one-fourth below the median value (or the value that divides the set of observations into two equal halves).

RASCI   A project management methodology for assigning roles in projects that involve many people and teams. Each letter in RASCI stands for a different type of role, Responsible, Approver, Supporter, Consultant, and Informed, each with corresponding responsibilities.

raw image   Also called a "dd image" (for the dataset definition command, dd). A computer forensic image of a system in which the data from the storage device is stored as a single file or multiple files, but without any type of container that stores checksums or hashes.

red book   Also known as the Trusted Network Interpretation of the TCSEC, this document provided guidelines for system security certifications in a networked environment.

regular expression   A mechanism to match patterns within text.

remote login (rlogin)   Enables a user or administrator to log in remotely to a computer system and to interact as if they were logging in on the actual computer. The computer system trusts the user's machine to provide the user's identity.

repudiation attack   An attack in which attacker targets the accountability of the information.

Request for Proposal (RFP)   A document that an organization uses to solicit proposals for a project that has specific requirements. The organization can then use the responses to the RFP to evaluate and compare the proposals of multiple vendors.

Rijndael   The algorithm used for the advanced encryption standard. This private key cipher uses blocks and keys of 128, 192, and 256 bits.

risk   The potential for loss.

rootkit   A collection of tools used by hackers to cover their intrusion into a computer system or a network and to gain administrator-level access to the computer or network system. Typically, a back door is left for the intruder to reenter the computer or network at a later time.

router   A device used to route IP traffic between networks. Although a router can be used to block or filter certain types of traffic, its primary purpose is to route traffic as quickly as possible.

RSA   Rivest, Shamir, and Adleman developed this public key algorithm that can be used for both encryption and decryption. RSA is based on the difficulty of factoring large numbers.

sacred cow   An idiom for a practice that is implemented simply because it is "how it's always been done," without regard for its usefulness or whether it can help achieve a target goal or outcome.

scan   An attempt to identify systems on a network. A scan may include actions that attempt to identify the operating system version and the services running on the computer system.

script kiddies   Individuals who find scripts on the Internet and use those scripts to launch attacks on whatever computer system they can find (considered a derogatory term).

security appliances   Any type of dedicated system that is made to secure the company's network, such as firewalls, content filters, data leakage prevention systems, and so on.

security information and event monitoring (SIEM)   A system that gathers security logs from many sources and correlates the events to be able to focus on events of importance.

security policy   Defines the technical controls and security configurations that users and administrators are required to implement on all computer systems.

separation of duties   The partition of activities of configuring a policy enforcement function from the activity of verifying the compliance of the function.

SHA1   Secure Hashing Algorithm 1 is a 160-bit value; unlike MD5, it has no known current weaknesses. The SHA1 hash and the MD5 hash provide additional validation that the data has not been altered. If even a single byte of data is changed, the resulting hash will change.

single-factor authentication   The process administration might use with a single authentication method to identify the person requesting access to information. Using a password is a single-factor authentication.

site event   A disastrous event that destroys an entire facility.

slope of a line   A value that represents how fast the y values are rising or falling as the x values of the line increase.

Slope of line = $(y_2 - y_1) / (x_2 - x_1)$, where (x_1, y_1) and (x_2, y_2) are any two points on the line.

smurf attack   This type of attack sends a ping packet to the broadcast address of a large network and spoofs the source address to point the returning information at the target computer. The intent is to disable the target computer.

sniffer   A computer that is configured with software to collect data packets off the network for analysis.

snooping   The process of looking through files and papers in hopes of finding valuable information.

social engineering   The use of nontechnical means (usually person-to-person contact) to gain access to information systems.

SQL injection   An attack that targets applications that take input and use the input in an SQL query.

stack   Controls switching between programs that tell the OS what code to execute when the current code has completed execution.

stakeholders   Leaders responsible for critical decision-making and key supporters who will drive change throughout the organization.

static network address translation   The process used to map internal IP addresses to external IP addresses on a one-to-one basis.

steganography   The science of hiding data in plain sight; the most popular method is hiding data within pictures.

substitution cipher   One of the oldest encryption systems, this method operates on plaintext, one letter at a time, replacing each letter for another letter or character. Analysis of the frequency of the letters can break a substitution cipher.

suspect   The person whose activities we are examining; does not imply that we believe the person is guilty, but merely that he or she is the focus of our examination.

SYN flood   A denial-of-service attack in which the attacker sends a large number of TCP SYN packets to the target computer to render the computer inaccessible.

target   The aspect of an organization's information system that an attacker might attack

technical practices   Practices that implement technical security controls within an organization.

threat   An individual (or group of individuals) who could violate the security of an organization.

threat analysis   A method of identifying and categorizing threats to an organization. This type of analysis identifies individuals and groups who have the motivation and capabilities to cause negative consequences to an organization.

traffic and pattern analysis   The process by an attacker of studying the communications patterns and activities of a target to discover certain types of activities and information.

Triple DES (TDES)   An enhanced version of the data encryption standard (DES) that uses DES multiple times to increase the strength of the encryption.

Trojan horse   Malicious code that appears to be a useful program but, instead, destroys the computer system or collects information such as identification and passwords for its owner.

two-factor authentication   The process implemented by administration that employs two of the three authentication methods for identifying a person requesting access to information. An example of two-factor authentication would be using a smart card with a password.

Twofish   A private key encryption algorithm that uses 128-bit blocks and can use 128-, 192-, or 256-bit keys.

uninterruptible power supply (UPS)   A battery-powered device that serves two purposes: it provides battery power in case the circuit loses power, and prevents your workstation from powering off while you are doing something important, such as capturing a forensic image.

use policy   The policy an organization develops to define the appropriate use of information systems.

virtual private network (VPN)   A communication method that uses encryption to separate traffic flowing over an untrusted network.

virus   Malicious code that piggybacks on legitimate code and, when executed, interferes with computer operations or destroys information. Traditional viruses are executed through executable or command files, but they can also propagate through data files.

VPN Server   A server that serves as an endpoint for a VPN connection.

vulnerability   A potential avenue of attack.

vulnerability scan   A procedure that uses a software tool to identify vulnerabilities in computer systems.

vulnerability scanning   The process of looking for and identifying vulnerabilities intruders may use as a point of attack.

wardialing   An attempt to identify phone lines that connect to computers by dialing a large amount of phone numbers to see which ones return a modem tone.

web application firewall   A security device that operates on the content directed at a web application.

web root   The first folder in the hierarchy from which the web server will return data.

web server   The server that provides web pages to web clients. The amount of systems and processing involved in generating a web page depends on the developers and the underlying code that exists in the page.

web of trust model   A model for trust in a public key environment based on the concept that each user certifies the certificates of people known to him or her.

Windows Explorer   The graphical user interface with which you access your PC desktop when using the Windows operating system. If you are viewing files and folders through My Documents, My Computer, or other Windows areas, you are using Windows Explorer.

Wired Equivalent Privacy (WEP)   A protocol designed to protect information as it passes over wireless local area networks (WLAN). WEP has a design flaw that allows an attacker to determine the key by capturing packets.

witness   A person called upon to testify in a court of law or in a deposition. Anyone can be a witness if they have information relevant to the case and have first-party knowledge of the information.

work product   A legal term that refers to documents, spreadsheets, databases, forensic files, notes, and so on that you produce during your investigation. If your investigation is under the direction of an attorney, your work product may be excluded from being produced during litigation.

workflow   A collection of rules that govern the relationship of steps required to complete a process. Relationships might include sequence order, branching conditions, looping, and number of repetitions.

worms   Programs that crawl from system to system without the assistance of the victim. They make changes to the target system and propagate themselves to attack other systems on the network.

zombies   Computers on the Internet that have been compromised and the programs that have been placed on them to launch a denial-of-service attack either at a specific time or on demand.

Index

Stop Hackers in Their Tracks